Fodor's
Baja &
Mexico's
Pacific Coast
Resorts

Maribeth Mellin

Parts of this book appear in *Fodor's Mexico '92*

Fodor's Travel Publications, Inc.
New York and London

Fodor's Baja & Mexico's Pacific Coast Resorts

Editor: Carolyn Price
Area Editors: Wendy Luft, Maribeth Mellin
Art Director: Fabrizio La Rocca
Map Editor: Suzanne Brown
Cartographer: David Lindroth
Illustrator: Karl Tanner
Cover Photograph: Pat Harrison/Photobank

Design: Vignelli Associates

Contents

Maps

Foreword

Soaring mountains, sweltering deserts, isolated stretches of beach, and quaint fishing villages are just a few of the elements that contribute to making the Baja area a unique and memorable destination for travelers. Baja and the Pacific Coast resorts possess a multitude of charms, whether your interest lies in championship game-fishing, whale-watching, exploring tiny coastal towns, or simply soaking up the Mexican sunshine.

We wish to express our gratitude to those who helped prepare this guide: Gary Grimaud, Jane Onstott, Luis Camalich, Cynthia Cazares, William Yu, Hector Lutteroth, Juan Tintos, Armando Figaredo, Lourdes Berho, Gina Cord, Ruth Shari, Stephanie Sperber, Jorge Escudero, Ernesto and Sandy Alvarez, Enrique Bedoya, and Christian Paris.

While every care has been taken to ensure the accuracy of the information in this guide, the passage of time will always bring change, and consequently, the publisher cannot accept responsibility for errors that may occur.

All prices and opening times quoted here are based on information supplied to us at press time. Hours and admission fees may change, however, and the prudent traveler will avoid inconvenience by calling ahead.

Fodor's wants to hear about your travel experiences, both pleasant and unpleasant. When a hotel or restaurant fails to live up to its billing, let us know and we will investigate the complaint and revise our entries where the facts warrant it.

Send your letters to the editors of Fodor's Travel Publications, 201 East 50th Street, New York, NY 10022.

Highlights and Fodor's Choice

Highlights

Tourism to Mexico continues to climb—at the rate of about 8% in 1990, for a total of 6.5 million foreign visitors. At the same time, the country is nobly striving to bring its tourist services up to par, while not overlooking the increasingly urgent environmental concerns posed by a burgeoning population of 81 million.

Pacific Coast Resorts

Puerto Vallarta leads the other beach destinations of Mexico's west coast in terms of new hotel development, most of it concentrated in the areas known as **Marina Vallarta** and **Nuevo Vallarta**. The **Marriott CasaMagna** (433 rooms), a multi-resort complex in the north part of town, opened in summer 1990 at Marina Vallarta. It will be joined in early 1992 by a 280-room **Conrad**. **Sierra, Radisson,** and **Stouffer** have plans for Marina Vallarta, about 12 miles north of Puerto Vallarta.

Four hours south of Puerto Vallarta, in Manzanillo, the 351-room **Sierra Manzanillo** was unveiled in late 1990, on the same peninsula as Las Hadas. The **Karmina Palace**, a 380-suite property—and, like the Sierra, a *gran turismo* hotel—was expected to open in 1991.

Baja California and Mazatlán

Another of the Mexican government's megaprojects is planned between Tijuana and Ensenada, in the state of Baja California Norte. To be called **Real del Mar,** it will comprise hotels, vacation homes, a shopping center, two marinas, and a cruise-ship pier catering to the San Diego market.

The area known as **Loreto,** in the southern half of the peninsula, is being beefed up with the construction of two five-star hotels. Loreto is adjacent to Puerto Escondido and Nopolo Bay and caters to sportfishing, golf, and tennis enthusiasts.

In the twin resorts of Cabo San Lucas and San José del Cabo, two major new properties should be open by late 1992: the 241-room **Conrad Los Cabos** and the 300-room **Marriott CasaMagna**.

The mainland beach resort of Mazatlán, just across the Sea of Cortés from the southern tip of the Baja peninsula, boasted the highest hotel-occupancy rates of the entire Mexican Riviera in 1990.

Air Transportation

At press time the following new service was available: Air service from the west coast of the United States was boosted by Alaska Airlines' service to Los Cabos and other Pacific Coast destinations; by Aeromexico's expanded schedule between Los Angeles and Puerto Vallarta and Mazatlán; and by Aerocalifornia's addition of service between Los Angeles and Los Cabos.

Ground Transportation Independent travelers who like to explore Mexico in their own automobiles will find this mode of travel considerably simplified by the new availability of **unleaded gas.** Pemex, the state-owned oil company, announced in 1990 that its "Magna Sin" would be sold at stations on 11 major tourist highways.

And for those who enjoy touring by **motorcoach**, the likelihood of a bilateral free-trade agreement has encouraged the U. S. and Mexican governments to sign a memorandum of understanding that will facilitate border crossings by bus tours and charters.

Tour Programs As more North Americans visit Mexico, the country's tour operators are coming up with increasingly creative and adventurous options to cater to the sophisticated, upscale end of the market. Among them is the **Foundation for Field Research** (Box 2010, Alpine, CA 92001, tel. 619/445–9264), which seeks volunteers for a series of scientific expeditions. Current Mexico projects include saving the caguama sea turtles in Baja. Nature and birding are the focus of **Clipper Cruise Line's** (tel. 314/727–2929) two-week cruises to Western Mexico and the Sea of Cortés. **Maya-Caribe Travel** (87 Wolfs La., Pelham, NY 10803, tel. 914/738–8254 or 800/223–4084) offers a "hands-on Mexico" series of regional arts, crafts, and folklore classes for small groups. The courses, which last seven to 10 days, are taught by locals and include black-clay ceramics, glassblowing, archaeology, weaving, folkloric dance, and Mexican cuisine.

Risks of Mopeds, Scuba Diving If you have never driven a moped, you need to understand certain mechanical basics, such as continued throttling of the engine, correct use of the brakes, and how to maneuver turns and hills. Ask for instruction, and stay off highly trafficked streets. Experts also recommend wearing a helmet, long sleeves, long pants, gloves, goggles, and high-top athletic shoes.

Neophyte scuba divers should have a complete physical exam before undertaking a dive, as many diving deaths are caused by cardiovascular problems, asthma, seizure disorders, and diabetes. Drinking before diving is one of the major culprits behind scuba accidents. Finally, if you have travel insurance that covers evacuation, make sure the policy applies to scuba-related injuries, as not all companies provide this coverage.

Fodor's Choice

No two people will agree on what makes a perfect vacation, but it's fun and helpful to know what others think. We hope you'll have a chance to experience some of Fodor's Choices yourself while visiting Baja and the Pacific Coast resorts. For detailed information about each entry, refer to the appropriate chapters within this guidebook.

Major Sights

Acuario Mazatlán, Mazatlán
Cultural Center, Tijuana
The Gray Whales, Guerrero Negro
La Bufadora, Ensenada
Los Arcos and Playa de Amor, Cabo San Lucas
Mexitlan, Tijuana
Museum of Anthropology, La Paz
Riviera del Pacifico, Ensenada
Rosarito Beach Hotel, Rosarito Beach

Shopping

Avenida Revolución, Tijuana
Mercado Municipal, Puerto Vallarta
Sergio Bustamante, Puerto Vallarta

Sports

Jai alai in the Palacio Fronton, Tijuana
Snorkeling off Cabo Pulmo, between La Paz and Los Cabos
Sportfishing out of Loreto, Los Cabos, La Paz, and Mazatlán
Windsurfing at the East Cape, Los Cabos
Surfing the Pacific, Tijuana to Los Cabos

Beaches

Playa de los Muertos, Puerto Vallarta
Playa Isla de los Venados, Mazatlán
Playa Medano, Cabo San Lucas
Playa de Amor, Cabo San Lucas

Hotels

Fiesta Americana, Puerto Vallarta *(Very Expensive)*
Fiesta Americana, Tijuana *(Very Expensive)*
Las Hadas, Manzanillo *(Very Expensive)*
Stouffer Presidente, Loreto *(Very Expensive)*
Las Rosas, Ensenada *(Expensive)*
Palmilla, San José del Cabo *(Expensive)*

Conchas Chinas, Puerto Vallarta *(Moderate)*
La Posada, Manzanillo *(Moderate)*
Los Cuatro Vientos, Puerto Vallarta *(Inexpensive)*

Restaurants

Alfonso's, Cabo San Lucas *(Expensive)*
La Cueva de los Tigres, Ensenada *(Expensive)*
L'Récif, Manzanillo *(Expensive)*
Chico's Paradise, Puerto Vallarta *(Moderate)*
La Paloma, San Jose del Cabo *(Moderate)*
Le Gourmet, Puerto Vallarta *(Moderate)*
La Fogata, San José del Cabo *(Moderate)*
Puerto Nuevo, Rosarito Beach *(Moderate)*
Tres Islas, Mazatlán *(Moderate)*
Willy's, Manzanillo *(Moderate)*
Carnitas Uruapan, Tijuana *(Inexpensive)*
Fish Market, Ensenada *(Inexpensive)*

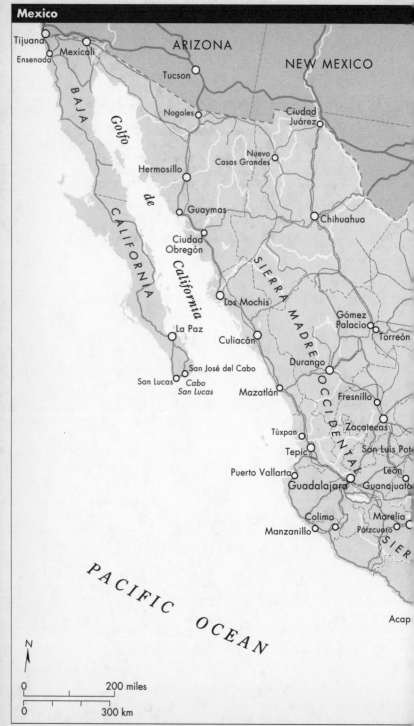

Mexico

ARIZONA

NEW MEXICO

Tijuana

Mexicali

Ensenada

Tucson

BAJA

Golfo

Nogales

Ciudad
Juárez

de

Nuevo
Casas Grandes

Hermosillo

CALIFORNIA

Guaymas

Chihuahua

Ciudad
Obregón

California

S
I
E
R
R
A

Los Mochis

Gómez
Palacio

La Paz

Culiacán

Torreón

San José del Cabo

Durango

M
A
D
R
E

San Lucas

*Cabo
San Lucas*

Mazatlán

Fresnillo

Túxpan

Zacatecas

O
C
C
I
D
E
N
T
A
L

Tepic

San Luis Pot

Puerto Vallarta

León

Guadalajara

Guanajuato

Colima

Morelia

Manzanillo

Pátzcuaro

S
I
E
R

P A C I F I C   O C E A N

Acap

N

0 ⊢——⊣——⊣ 200 miles

0 ⊢——⊣——⊣ 300 km

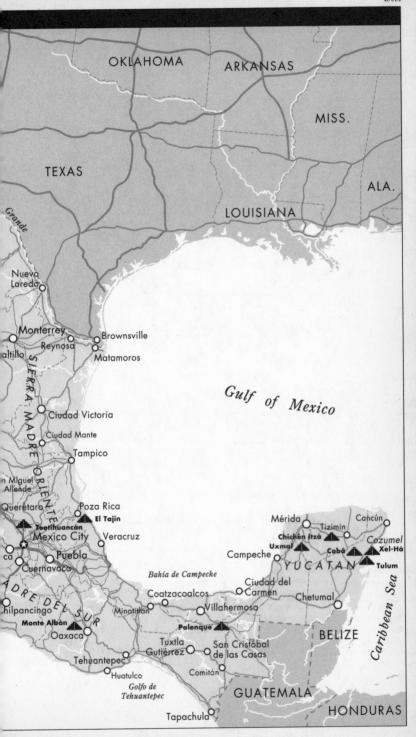

World Time Zones

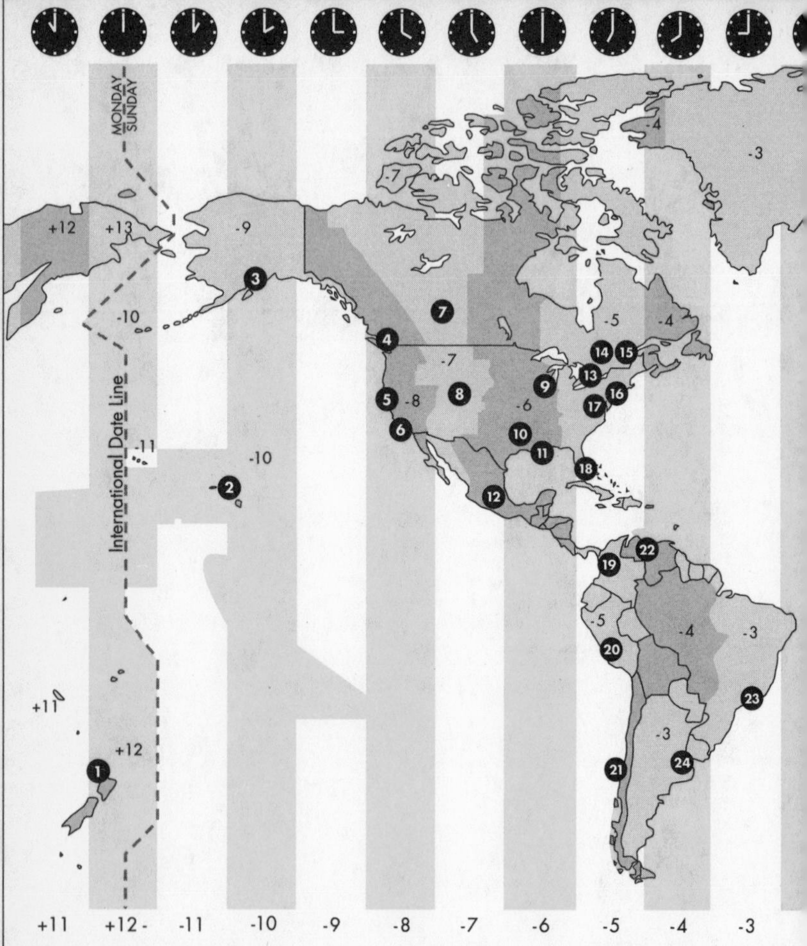

MONDAY
SUNDAY

International Date Line

+12 +13 -9 -7 -4 -3

-10

-11 -10 -8 -7 -5 -4

-7 -6 13 14 15

-9 17 16

5 -8 8 18

6 10

11

12

+11 22

+12 19

1 -5 -4 -3

20

-4

23

-3

21 24

+11 +12 - -11 -10 -9 -8 -7 -6 -5 -4 -3

Numbers below vertical bands relate each zone to Greenwich Mean Time (0 hrs.).
Local times frequently differ from these general indications,
as indicated by light-face numbers on map.

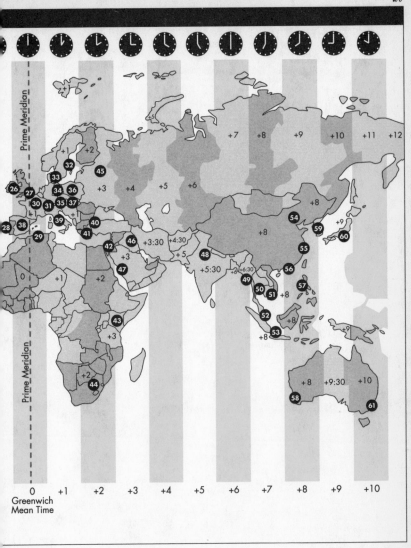

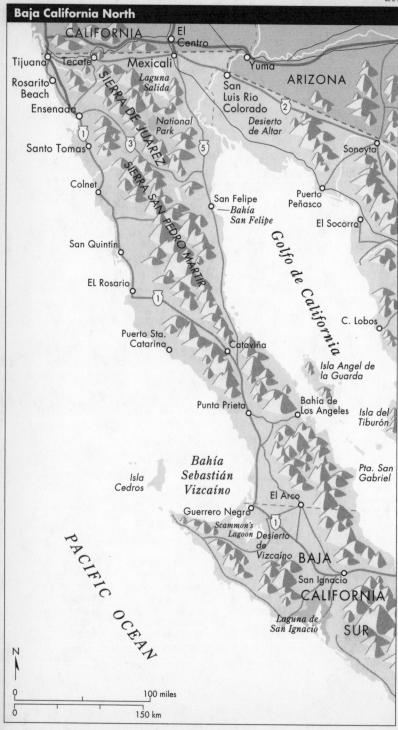

Baja California North

CALIFORNIA

El Centro

Tijuana

Tecate

Mexicali

Yuma

ARIZONA

Rosarito Beach

Ensenada

Laguna Salida

San Luis Rio Colorado

2

Santo Tomas

1

3

National Park

5

Desierto de Altar

Sonoyta

SIERRA DE JUAREZ

Colnet

San Felipe

Bahía San Felipe

Puerto Peñasco

El Socorro

San Quintín

SIERRA SAN PEDRO MARTIR

EL Rosario

1

Golfo de California

C. Lobos

Puerto Sta. Catarina

Cataviña

Isla Angel de la Guarda

Punta Prieta

Bahía de Los Angeles

Isla del Tiburón

Bahía Sebastián Vizcaíno

Isla Cedros

Pta. San Gabriel

El Arco

Guerrero Negro

Scammon's Lagoon

1

Desierto de Vizcaíno

BAJA

PACIFIC OCEAN

San Ignacio

CALIFORNIA

Laguna de San Ignacio

SUR

N

0 — 100 miles

0 — 150 km

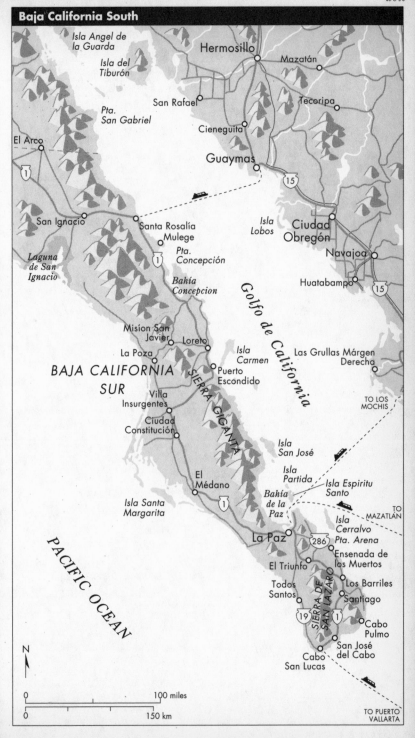

Baja California South

Isla Angel de la Guarda

Isla del Tiburón

Hermosillo

Mazatán

Pta. San Gabriel

San Rafael

Tecoripa

El Arco

Cieneguita

Guaymas

15

San Ignacio

Santa Rosalía
Mulege

Isla Lobos

Ciudad Obregón

Laguna de San Ignacio

1

Pta. Concepción

Navajoa

Bahía Concepcion

Huatabampo

15

Golfo de California

Misíon San Javier

Loreto

Isla Carmen

Las Grullas Márgen Derecha

La Poza

BAJA CALIFORNIA SUR

SIERRA GIGANTA

Puerto Escondido

TO LOS MOCHIS

Villa Insurgentes

Ciudad Constitución

Isla San José

Isla Santa Margarita

El Médano

Isla Partida

Isla Espiritu Santo

1

Bahía de la Paz

TO MAZATLÁN

Isla Cerralvo

La Paz

286

Pta. Arena

PACIFIC OCEAN

El Triunfo

Ensenada de los Muertos

Todos Santos

SIERRA DE SAN LAZARO

Los Barriles

Santiago

19

1

Cabo Pulmo

N

San José del Cabo

Cabo San Lucas

TO PUERTO VALLARTA

0   100 miles

0   150 km

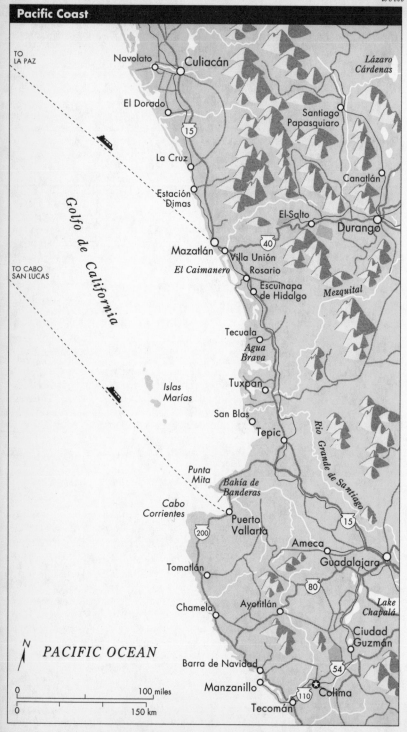

TO
LA PAZ

Navolato

Culiacán

*Lázaro
Cárdenas*

El Dorado

Santiago
Papasquiaro

15

La Cruz

Canatlán

Estación
Dimas

El-Salto

Durango

Golfo de California

Mazatlán

40

Villa Unión

El Caimanero

Rosario

TO CABO
SAN LUCAS

Escuinapa
de Hidalgo

Mezquital

Tecuala

*Agua
Brava*

Tuxpan

*Islas
Marías*

San Blas

Tepic

Río Grande de Santiago

Punta
Mita

*Bahía de
Banderas*

*Cabo
Corrientes*

Puerto
Vallarta

15

Ameca

200

Guadalajara

Tomatlán

80

Chamela

Ayotitlán

*Lake
Chapala*

Ciudad
Guzmán

N

PACIFIC OCEAN

Barra de Navidad

54

0   100 miles

Manzanillo

110

Colima

0   150 km

Tecomán

Introduction

Baja California

Baja (lower) California is a moonscaped finger of land dipping southward from the international boundary that divides California and Mexico. Separated from the Mexican mainland by the 240-kilometer- (150-mile-) wide Sea of Cortés (also called the Gulf of California), Baja extends about 1,300 kilometers (800 miles) into the Pacific. Despite their names, both Baja California and the Gulf of California are part of Mexico.

Although only 21 kilometers (13 miles) across at one point and 193 kilometers (120 miles) at its widest, Baja features one of the most varied and beautiful terrains on the planet. The peninsula's two coasts are separated by soaring mountain ranges, with one peak more than 10,000 feet high. Countless bays and coves with pristine beaches indent both shores, and islands big and small—many inhabited only by sea lions—grace the 3,364 kilometers (2,000 miles) of coastline. There are stretches of desert as empty as the Sahara where only cacti thrive and, in contrast, there are cultivated farmlands and vineyards.

Varied, too, is the demographic makeup of Baja. The border strip of northern Baja is densely populated. Tijuana, Mexico's fourth-largest city, is home to 1.5 million people, making it more populous than the rest of the entire peninsula. La Paz, with about 150,000 residents, is the only city of any size south of Ensenada. The two settlements at Los Cabos (The Capes) are little more than villages.

Baja is divided politically into two states—Baja California Norte (North) and Baja California Sur (South)—at the 25th parallel, about 710 kilometers (440 miles) south of the border. Near the tip of the peninsula, a monument marks the spot where the Tropic of Cancer crosses the Transpeninsular Highway (Mexico Highway 1).

Native Baja Californians will tell you in no uncertain terms that they live in the first California, discovered by pirates, missionaries, and explorers long before the California of the United States. To this day, most of Baja's visitors have that same sense of adventure and the unquenchable desire to discover nature's holdouts. As there are cult films and cult books, perhaps there are cult travel destinations. If so, Baja heads the list. Long before the rich and famous stumbled upon the resorts of mainland Mexico, they found Baja. Back in the days of Prohibition, when Hollywood was new, the movie crowd learned the joy of having an international border so near. John Steinbeck brought attention to La Paz when he made it a setting for his novella *The Pearl*. Erle Stanley Gardner put aside his typewriter in Baja to battle marlin off Los Cabos. Bing Crosby put up some of the money for the first resort hotel in San José del Cabo, when the only way to get there was aboard a yacht or private plane.

Tijuana and Mexicali, the peninsula's border entries, are U.S. suburbs in a sense. Spanish and English are spoken interchangeably, and rock music blares in high-tech discos while mariachi bands blast their horns in corner bars. Manufacturers from throughout the world are setting up *maquiladoras* (factories) to make, among other things, computer chips and televisions.

Tijuana is one of the busiest international borders in the world. In the 1870s the United States put up the first customs station along the border, and a few shacks were erected on what, legend has it, was called El Rancho de Tía Juana (Aunt Jane's Ranch). Americans periodically sought to create an independent republic on the Mexican side of the border, with little success. When Prohibition was enacted in the United States in the 1920s, Tijuana boomed, and its reputation as "Sin City" took hold. During World War II, sailors flocked to San Diego, then headed to Mexico for bawdier pleasures than they could find in the States.

Today, Tijuana is far more than a bawdy border town. Upscale shopping centers and gourmet restaurants line the Zona Río. It has an international airport; a fine cultural center that presents professional music, dance, and theater groups from throughout the world; deluxe high-rise hotels; and a burgeoning population. Although its government would love Tijuana to become a major tourist destination and have visitors stay for days and even weeks, the city is still best known as a place for an intense, somewhat exotic, day-long adventure.

Mexicali, 185 kilometers (115 miles) east of Tijuana, is the capital of Baja California Norte. Mexicali is not considered to be a tourist destination, but it is the departure point for the Sonora–Baja California Railroad, which travels southeast into mainland Mexico. **Tecate,** located between Tijuana and Mexicali, is a typical village whose main claim to fame is the Tecate brewery, where one of Mexico's most popular beers originates. **San Felipe,** about 200 kilometers (120 miles) south of Mexicali, is the northernmost town on the Sea of Cortés. San Felipe has long been a popular getaway for fishermen, campers, and dune buggy riders, but plans to turn this small fishing village into a major resort have never materialized. There is an international airport with an impressively long runway, but no commercial airlines fly here. Such are the travails of tourism in Baja.

On Baja's Pacific Coast, travelers stream down the Transpeninsular Highway to **Rosarito Beach** and **Ensenada.** Both coastal towns were popular with the anti-Prohibition set, and competitive investors created the area's three pleasure palaces: Agua Caliente in Tijuana, the Rosarito Beach Hotel in Rosarito, and the Riviera Pacífico in Ensenada. As long as gambling was legal in Mexico and alcohol illegal in the United States, these three ornate gambling halls attracted a glamorous Hollywood crowd. Then Prohibition ended, and gambling was outlawed. Agua Caliente and Riviera Pacífico closed, but the Rosarito Beach Hotel held on, and to this day it is a required stop on the way down the coast. Rosarito is in the midst of a building boom, and the hotel has more competition now. On weekends the town is packed with young, bar-hopping revelers, and traffic is bumper-to-bumper along the dusty main drag.

Ensenada, on the Bahía Todos Santos 104 kilometers (65 miles) south of Tijuana, is the Pacific Coast's main port and sportfishing center and a popular weekend getaway for southern Californians. The big attractions are the beaches, the seafood restaurants, the handicrafts shops, and the bars. On weekends Ensenada looks and sounds like Palm Springs or Fort Lauderdale during spring break.

Before the 1,708-kilometer-long (1,059-mile) Transpeninsular Highway (Mexico Highway 1) was completed in 1973, traveling south of Ensenada was a rough, lonely, and somewhat dangerous adventure. After the paved, four-lane highway was built, thousands of people found their way south, and in 1974 Baja California Sur became Mexico's 30th state. Still, Highway 1 could hardly be called a freeway. It travels through some of the most desolate land imaginable.

From Ensenada, Highway 1 bypasses the Sierra de Juárez Mountains, where alpine meadows blossom in the Parque Nacional Constitución de 1857 east of Ensenada, as well as the Sierra San Pedro Martir range and Picacho del Diablo (Devil's Peak), which, at 10,126 feet, is Baja's highest point. Dirt roads, where even cars with four-wheel drive have trouble much of the year, lead from the highway to secluded ranches and campgrounds in these mountain ranges.

Scattered through these mountains and the Sierra del Gigante in Baja Sur are scores of monumental cave paintings, larger-than-life figures drawn with remarkable skill in red, blue, yellow, and black. They date back some 2,000 years, and no one can say who did them. The caves are difficult to reach and, sadly, tours are discouraged (to keep vandals away), but there are some excellent reproductions of the paintings on the walls of the Twin Dolphin Resort in Los Cabos.

Every January through April thousands of great gray whales migrate 8,000 kilometers (6,000 miles) from the Bering Strait to **Guerrero Negro,** at the border between Baja Norte and Baja Sur. On the edge of the Vizcaíno Desert, Guerrero Negro is not a hospitable place. If it weren't for the whales' breeding ground at Scammon's Lagoon and the salt flats between the desert and the sea, no one would be here. The highway has brought more traffic through, and there are a few modest hotels and cafés, but you wouldn't call this a tourist area. Just below Guerrero Negro, the Transpeninsular Highway crosses the Vizcaíno Desert, passes through forests of Joshua trees and barrel cactus, ciros, and cardóns to San Ignacio, an oasis of palms with a 70-foot-high, white-dome mission church constructed in 1728. Santa Rosalia, the first town on the Sea of Cortés south of Guerrero Negro, has a bizarre, prefabricated iron church designed by A. G. Eiffel, creator of the Eiffel Tower in Paris. Mulegé, another 64 kilometers (40 miles) south, has the only navigable river in Baja.

Loreto is the site of the first mission in the Californias, established by Padre Eusebio Kino in 1683. Four Indian tribes—the Kikiwa, Cochimi, Cucapa, and Kumyaii—inhabited the barren lands of Baja at that time. It didn't take long for civilization's wars and diseases to nearly obliterate them. The first mission church, still in use, was built in Loreto by Padre Juan Salvatierra in 1697, and it was from here that Fray Junípero Serra began a chain of missions throughout Baja and what was then Alta California (now California, United States). Loreto was also the first capital of California, but a violent hurricane in 1829 and a severe earthquake in 1877 destroyed the settlement, and the capital was moved south to La Paz.

In the late 1970s Fonatur, the government's tourism developers, aimed to make Loreto, a quiet haven for fishermen, into a Cancún-style resort. An international airport was built, and the infrastructure for tourist zones was begun in Loreto, Nopoló, and Puerto Escondido. Fonatur owns over 25,000 acres in this region, and projects that Loreto's population will increase from its current 8,000 to 38,000 in the next decade. For now, there is only one resort hotel—the 250-room Stouffer Presidente—and precious few planes at the airport.

La Paz, 354 kilometers (220 miles) south of Loreto, was the first settlement established by the Spaniards in Baja. Hernán Cortés and his followers were drawn to La Paz by stories of the magnificent pearls and beautiful women to be found here. The Jesuits arrived in 1720, and a permanent settlement was established in 1811. Pirates and explorers of all sorts stopped by for their share of black pearls from the oyster beds until disease destroyed the oysters in the 1940s. Today, La Paz is a busy governmental center and sportfishing city, with plans for resorts, marinas, and increased tourism.

The southernmost tip of the peninsula is a natural rock archway where the Pacific Ocean and the Sea of Cortés merge. Marlin and sailfish leap high above the warm sea waters, glistening in the sun that shines 300 days a year, bringing fishermen and sun worshippers to Cabo San Lucas and San José del Cabo, called **Los Cabos** (The Capes). Los Cabos, also a Fonatur development, has a dozen or so deluxe resorts, a nine-hole golf course, a marina, and scores of condominium complexes. The resorts are spread far apart along the 37 kilometers (23 miles) of Highway 1 between San José del Cabo and Cabo San Lucas, with stretches of incredibly stark and dramatic coastline and clear turquoise coves in between. Despite all the development, and the steep prices, Los Cabos remains a mysteriously natural hideaway.

Pacific Coast Resorts

Across the Sea of Cortés from the Baja peninsula lies **Mazatlán,** the beginning of what cruise-ship operators now call the Mexican Riviera. The Sea of Cortés (or Gulf of California) ends just below the Tropic of Cancer, leaving the Pacific coastline open to fresh sea breezes. The Mexican Riviera resorts of Mazatlán, Puerto Vallarta, and Manzanillo are less muggy than gulf towns to the north. The water, however, is colder, and waves can get very rough. Deserted palm-fringed bays and tropical jungles border high-rise hotels and luxury resorts, and the emphasis is on enjoying the tropical climate and broad beaches.

The Pacific Coast doesn't have the rich cultural heritage of Mexico's inland colonial villages and cities, and the history is sketchy at best. This is not an area for touring ruins, museums, and cathedrals, but rather a gathering spot for sun worshippers, sportfishermen, surfers, and swimmers. Sightseeing involves touring the resorts and shopping areas rather than combing ancient Aztec shrines. Not far from the resort regions are jungles and coves that seem remote and undiscovered. The majority of visitors never venture to these isolated sites, preferring instead to immerse themselves in the simultaneously bustling and restful resort lifestyle, where great dining, shopping, and sunbathing are the major draws.

Mazatlán is Mexico's largest Pacific port and the closest major Mexican resort to the United States, some 1,200 kilometers (750 miles) south of the Arizona border. It is first and foremost a busy commercial center, thanks both to its port and the fertility of the surrounding countryside. More than 600,000 acres of farmland near Mazatlán produce tomatoes, melons, cantaloupe, wheat, and cotton, much of which is shipped to the United States. Nearly all the 150,000 tons of shrimp that are hauled in annually are processed and frozen for the American and Japanese markets.

Sportfishing accounts for Mazatlán's popularity as a resort area. The port sits at the juncture of the Pacific and the Sea of Cortés, forming what has been called the world's greatest natural fish trap. Mazatlán has Mexico's largest sportfishing fleet, and fishermen here routinely haul in the biggest catches in size and number on the coast. But fishing is not the only attraction. Hunters are drawn to the quail, duck, and dove that thrive in the hills, and surfers find great waves on nearby beaches. Another draw is the relatively low price of accommodations. El Cid, the largest resort in Mexico, is in the city's Zona Dorada (Golden Zone), as are dozens of high-rise hotels and small *posadas* (inns) with rates at about half those of Cancún resorts. Between Mazatlán and Puerto Vallarta is Tepic, capital of the state of Nayarit. Tepic is the closest station to the coast for trains from inland Mexico and the United States border; travelers headed for Puerto Vallarta or Mazatlán take public buses from here to the coast, some three hours west. For those driving to the coast, Mexico Highway 15 ends here, becoming Highway 200. The closest coastal town to Tepic is San Blas, some 37 kilometers (23 miles) northwest through the jungle. San Blas is a small seaside village favored by budget travelers and escapists who eschew the megaresorts.

Some 323 kilometers (200 miles) south of Mazatlán is Puerto Vallarta, by far the best-known resort on the upper Pacific coast. The late Hollywood director (and onetime resident) John Huston put the town on the map when he filmed Tennessee Williams's *Night of the Iguana* on the outskirts of the village. Richard Burton, one of the movie's stars, brought Elizabeth Taylor with him—scandalous behavior in 1964, as Burton and Taylor were married but not to each other. Gossip columnists and the Hollywood press flocked to cover the goings-on. In between titterings, stories were filed about the Eden that Huston had discovered—this quaint Mexican fishing village, with its cobblestoned lanes and whitewashed, tile-roofed houses. Before long, travel agents were deluged with queries about Puerto Vallarta, a place many had never heard of.

Actually, Huston did not discover Puerto Vallarta. A handful of Americans—some fabulously rich, others in the same tax bracket as church mice—had happened upon it some years before. The settlement already had a street called Gringo Gulch and a cluster of cozy inns to which the traveling cognoscenti repaired as an escape from the rigors of civilization. Three times a week a Méxicana DC-3 dropped out of the skies to bounce along a grassy joke of a landing strip. No roads worth the name linked the village with the outside world, and the town's two or three taxis had been brought in by sea. There was electricity, but lights flickered out every evening at 10. When Westin Hotels opened the Camino Real hotel in 1970, every room had a telephone but there were no outside lines.

More than 150,000 people live in Puerto Vallarta today, and upward of 1.5 million tourists arrive each year. The fabled cobblestone streets are clogged with bumper-to-bumper traffic during the holiday season, and the sounds of construction often drown out the pounding surf. Despite its resort status, parts of Puerto Vallarta are still picturesque. For a sense of the Eden that once was, travel out of town to the lush green mountains and Río Tomatlán, which tumbles over boulders into the sea.

Manzanillo, at the south end of the central Pacific Coast, had more of a storybook start than Puerto Vallarta. Conquistador Hernán Cortés envisioned the area as a gateway to the Orient: From these shores, Spanish galleons would bring in the riches of Cathay to be transported across the continent to Veracruz, where they would be off-loaded to vessels headed for Spain. But Acapulco, not Manzanillo, became the port of call for the Manila galleons that arrived each year with riches from beyond the seas. Pirates are said to have staked out Manzanillo during the colonial era, and chests of loot are rumored to be buried beneath the sands.

With the coming of the railroads, Manzanillo became a major port of entry, albeit not a pretty one. Forty or 50 years ago, a few seaside hotels opened up on the outskirts of town, which vacationers reached by train. The jet age, however, seemed to doom the port as a sunny vacation spot. Then came Anteñor Patiño.

Patiño made millions mining tin in Bolivia. A healthy chunk of that fortune went into building Las Hadas (The Fairies), which, as its name implies, is sort of a fairyland. Inspired by Moorish villages along the Mediterranean, the complex took 10 years to build. The inaugural party in 1974, the "Gala in White," was the social event of the year. Patiño even gave funds to the government to build a new airport, one that could accommodate his friends' jets. For a while Las Hadas was better known than Manzanillo itself. The film *10* made a star of the resort as well as of Bo Derek.

For many visitors, Manzanillo is not so much a city as an airport, the last stop before a holiday begins. Older hotels have been spruced up and condos and all-inclusive resorts built. The Jalisco state line is just a few miles up the coast from the airport. North of the line are the villages of Barra de Navidad, Melaque, Tenacatita, and Costa de Careyes. In these towns and on the isolated beaches between them are self-contained resorts. Manzanillo's tourist industry is working hard to turn the whole coast into a tourist zone. Plans are under way to build a pedestrian walkway along the shore from Santiago to Las Hadas road, forming a *malecón* (waterside promenade) where visitors will stroll by the sea, shop in designer boutiques, and dine in luxury.

The 967-kilometer (600-mile) coastline on the Sea of Cortés north of the Mexican Riviera doesn't yet sport a catchy moniker, and the resorts are few and far between. But this corner of northwest Mexico has a character and ambience similar to that of the Baja peninsula. The state of Sonora begins at the Arizona border at Nogales. Americans regularly cross the border in search of bargains and treasures; from Nogales many travelers begin the drive south on Mexico Highway 15 toward the Gulf Coast.

This stretch of the northwest is reminiscent of the old Wild West in the United States. Cowboys ride the range, and ranchero ballads not unlike country-western songs are played in saloons. Irrigated ranchlands feed Mexico's finest beef cattle, rivers flowing from the Sierra Madre to the east are diverted by giant dams to the once-barren land that now produces cotton, sugarcane, and vegetables. Hermosillo, Sonora's capital, bustles with commerce in the midst of the fertile lands, which turn barren again toward the coast. Kino Bay, 104 kilometers (65 miles) west of Hermosillo, is a quiet beach resort, long favored by travelers in recreational vehicles. Visitors from Arizona with a need for more luxurious accommodations have begun building condominiums and private homes along Kino Bay.

The Sierra Madre meets the Sea of Cortés 645 kilometers (400 miles) south of the border at Guaymas, the northwest coast's major resort area. An active city and seaport, Guaymas once drew only the hardy, adventuresome traveler, but hotels and restaurants now abound, along with plans for future developments. The northwest's farmlands extend south into the state of Sinaloa and the city of Los Mochis. Centered in a fertile valley fed by the Río Fuerte, El Fuerte is a picturesque colonial town. Some 78 kilometers (48 miles) southwest is Los Mochis, the starting point for the Copper Canyon railroad trip into the Sierra Madre. From here, Highway 15 cuts inland from the coast and few roads branch off to the sea until you reach the entrance to the Mexican Riviera at Mazatlán.

1 Essential Information

Before You Go

Government Tourist Offices

For a current calendar of events, train schedules and fares, and other general information about travel in Mexico, contact the nearest **Mexican Government Tourism Office.**

In the U.S. 405 Park Avenue, Suite 1002, New York, NY 10022, tel. 212/755–07261; 1616 L Street NW, Suite 430, Washington, DC 20036, tel. 202/659–8730; 70 East Lake Street, Suite 1413, Chicago, IL 60601, tel. 312/565–2786; 2707 North Loop West, Suite 450, Houston, TX 77008, tel. 713/880–5153; 10100 Santa Monica Boulevard, Suite 224, Los Angeles, CA 90067, tel. 213/203–9335.

In Canada 1 Place Ville Marie, Suite 2409, Montreal, Quebec H3B 3M9, tel. 514/871–1052; 181 University Avenue, Suite 1112, Toronto, Ontario M5H 3M7, tel. 416/364–2455.

In the U.K. 7 Cork Street, London W1X 1PB, tel. 441/734–1058.

Tour Groups

Mexico is a genuine travel bargain. The combination of a weak peso and the buying power of tour operators creates some attractively priced packages. In the resort areas, independent packages are a good choice: The beach and other attractions are nearby and usually easy to reach. Group tours are more common for exploring Mexico's interior or pursuing special interests like archaeology and Maya or Aztec culture. Below is a sampling of available packages.

When considering a tour, find out: exactly what expenses are included—particularly tips, taxes, side trips, additional meals, and entertainment; government ratings of all hotels on the itinerary and the facilities they offer; cancellation policies for both you and the tour operator; the number of travelers in your group; and if you are traveling alone, the cost of the single supplement. Most tour operators request that bookings be made through a travel agent—in most cases there is no additional charge for doing so.

General-interest Tours **American Express Vacations** (P.O. Box 5014, Atlanta, GA 30302, tel. 800/241–1700 or 800/282–0800 in Georgia) has a vast array of tours; if you don't see a package you like, they can design one for you. **GoGo Tours** (69 Spring St., Ramsey, NJ 07446, tel. 800/821–3731 or 201/934–3500) offers a wide selection of tours at an equally wide range of prices. **Mexico Travel Advisors** (1717 N. Highland Ave., Suite 1100, Los Angeles, CA 90028, tel. 213/462–5345) has been leading tours to Mexico for 59 years. Other leading Mexican tour operators include **American Leisure** (9800 Center Pkwy., Suite 800, Houston, TX 77036, tel. 713/988–6098 or 800/777–1980), **Gadabout Tours** (700 E. Tahquitz Way, Palm Springs, CA 92262, tel. 619/325–5556); and **Friendly Holidays** (1983 Marcus Ave., Lake Success, NY 11042, tel. 800/221–9748 or 516/358–1200).

Special-interest Tours
Adventure Nobody knows Baja like **Baja Expeditions** (2625 Garnet Ave., San Diego, CA 92109, tel. 619/581–3311 or 800/843–6967 outside CA) which has specialized in Baja travel for over 15 years, with bicycle, kayak, ship, scuba, and hiking trips throughout

Baja, the Pacific, and the Sea of Cortés. **Sobek Expeditions** (Box 1089, Angels Camp, CA 95222, tel. 209/736–4524 or 800/777–7939) sponsors outings that include a strenuous trek through Copper Canyon (Barrenca del Cobre) and Baja by bicycle.

Copper Canyon Fishing **Sanborn Tours** (Box 761, Bastrop, TX 78602, tel. 512/321–1131) offers deep-sea fishing packages using Cabo San Lucas or Mazatlán as a base.

Whale-watching/ Conservation **Baja Expeditions** (*see* Special-interest Tours, above) is tops in whale-watching trips with the grays at Magdalena Bay in the Pacific, and the blue and humpback whales in the Sea of Cortés. **Baja Discovery** (Box 152527, San Diego, CA 92115, tel. 619/262–0700 or 800/829–BAJA) operates a whale-watching camp at Laguna San Ignacio south of Guerrero Negro, with tent camping on an island in the lagoon, and boat trips among the whales. **Oceanic Society Expeditions** (Fort Mason Center, Bldg. E, San Francisco, CA 94123, tel. 415/441–1106) sails for Baja in ships that accommodate 20 to 30 passengers for whale-watching, encounters with other sea life, and snorkeling. **The Sierra Club** (730 Polk St., San Francisco, CA 94109, tel. 415/776–2211) offers two kayaking tours of Baja, with opportunities to encounter whales and sea lions.

Fishing The many operators offering deep-sea fishing trips in the Pacific and the Sea of Cortés include **Squideo** (tel. 800/227–4387), **Tony Reyes Tours** (tel. 714/538–8010), and **Baja Fishing Tours** (tel. 800/832–BAJA).

Package Deals for Independent Travelers

All the general-interest tour operators above also offer air/hotel packages, some including options like half-day sightseeing tours and discounted car rental. Many airlines also feature packages: **American Fly AAway Vacations** (tel. 800/443–7300), **Continental Grand Destinations** (tel. 800/634–5555), **Delta Airlines** (tel. 800/872–7786), and **United Vacations** (tel. 800/328–6877).

Tips for British Travelers

Tourist Information Contact the **Mexican National Tourism Office** (60–61 Trafalgar Square, London WC2N 5DS, tel. 01/734–1058 or 01/734–1059) for brochures and tourist information.

Passports and Visas You will need a valid, 10-year passport (cost £15) and a tourist card to enter Mexico. No vaccinations are required, but immunization for malaria, polio, and typhoid is recommended. Passport applications in the United Kingdom are available through travel agencies or a main post office. Send the completed form to a regional Passport Office. The application must be countersigned by your bank manager or by a solicitor, barrister, doctor, clergyman, or justice of the peace who knows you personally. In addition, you'll need two photographs and the £15 fee.

Customs Upon returning to the United Kingdom, if you are 17 years or older you may bring in (1) 200 cigarettes, or 100 cigarillos, or 50 cigars, or 250 grams of tobacco; (2) two liters of table wine and one of the following in addition, (a) one liter of alcohol over 22% by volume (most spirits), or (b) two liters of alcohol under 22% by volume (fortified or sparkling wine), or (c) two more liters of table wine; (3) 60 cc of perfume and 250ml of toilet water; and (4) other goods of a value of up to £32, but not more than 50 liters of beer or 25 mechanical lighters.

Insurance We recommend that you insure yourself against sickness and motoring mishaps with **Europ Assistance** (252 High St., Croydon, Surrey CR0 1NF, tel. 081/680–1234). It is also wise to take out insurance to cover the loss of luggage (although check that such loss isn't already covered in any existing homeowner's policies you may have). Trip-cancellation insurance is another wise buy. **The Association of British Insurers** (Aldermary House, 10–15 Queen St., London, EC4N 1TT, tel. 071/248–4477) gives comprehensive advice on all aspects of vacation insurance.

Tour Operators Here is a selection of the companies offering packages to Pacific Coast resorts in Mexico. Also contact your travel agent for the latest information.

Cosmosair (Ground Floor, Dale House, Tiviot Dale, Stockport, Cheshire SK1 1TB, tel. 061/480–5799) offers 7 and 14-night packages to Acapulco, and a "Magic of Mexico" 4-day tour combined with 11 nights in Acapulco. Kuoni Travel (Kuoni House, Dorking, Surrey RH5 4AZ, tel. 0306/740500) offers a 14-night "Mexican Panorama" tour to Mexico City, Mérida, Oaxaca, and Acapulco; a 2-week tour of the colonial cities, and holiday packages to Acapulco.
Mexican Holidays (23 Eccleston St., London SW1, tel. 01/730–8640) will custom design a holiday in any part of Mexico.

Airlines and Airfares British Airways has a direct flight to Mexico City. Other airlines flying to Mexico, with brief stops en route, include Continental (via Houston), American (via Dallas), KLM (via Amsterdam), Pan Am (via Miami), TWA, Avianca, and Iberia. Mexican Airlines, which operates domestic routes within the country, also offers flights to Mexico from Miami and New York City. A standard return APEX fare to Mexico City from London at press time ranged from £603 in low season to £688 in high season. Check *Time Out* and the Sunday papers for charters and cut-price flights.

When to Go

Make no mistake—Baja California is a desert, and it can become unbearably hot on summer days and downright brisk at night in the winter. It's dry 90% of the time, and rain is rarely a problem except along the border.

While the Pacific Coast is comfortable year-round, reaching the mid-80s in the summer, the Gulf Coast often has temperatures over 100° in July and August, and the desert is sizzling from June to September. The same goes for Mexicali, which has the smog and pollution of a big city combined with temperatures over 100°. The temperatures in the Los Cabos area also reach above 100° in the summer, and since the tip of the peninsula is below the Tropic of Cancer, the climate is more tropical, with humidity, occasional thunderstorms, and *chubascos* (violent hurricanes). During the summer, only the most dedicated Bajaphiles venture far along the Transpeninsular Highway and only the most determined fishermen camp out along the coast.

Baja is at its best between September and December. Though Los Cabos is billed as having 360 days of sunshine a year, the sun often has to fight cloud cover in midwinter. The peak season for tourism is from Thanksgiving to New Year's, but it is usually not difficult to find a room on the peninsula even during these times. Room rates usually rise by 25% in mid-November and stay high until April.

The holidays bring throngs of people to the Pacific Coast, and if you're headed for Puerto Vallarta, Mazatlán, or Manzanillo you'd best have reservations before you arrive. Puerto Vallarta swells with visitors in December. The best time to visit the coast is in the fall, when the summer rains have ended, the air and water are still warm, and the crowds have yet to arrive. June, July, and August are rainy, and the mosquitoes thrive in the rivers and lagoons. Some swear this is their favorite time on the coast, and if you're a fan of humidity and heat, you may agree. High season on the Pacific Coast runs from November to April, with room rates rising by 25%.

Mexicans travel during traditional holiday periods: Christmas/ New Year's, Semana Santa (Holy Week, the week before Easter), and school vacations in the summertime, as well as over extended national holiday weekends, and during festivals (*see* Festivals and Seasonal Events, below). If your trip coincides with these times, reserve both lodging and transportation well in advance. For flights within Mexico, remember to get to the airport early: Airlines in Mexico have a practice, especially during heavy travel periods, of bouncing ticket holders who haven't checked in at least one hour before flight time.

Climate What follows are the average daily maximum and minimum temperatures for some Baja and Pacific Coast towns.

Ensenada	Jan.	64F	18C	**May**	70F	21C	**Sept.**	77F	25C
		45	7		54	12		61	16
	Feb.	66F	19C	**June**	72F	22C	**Oct.**	73F	23C
		46	8		57	14		55	
	Mar.	66F	19C	**July**	75F	24C	**Nov.**	72F	22C
		46	8		61	16		48	9
	Apr.	68F	20C	**Aug.**	75F	24C	**Dec.**	66F	19C
		52	11		63	17		46	8

La Paz	Jan.	72F	22C	**May**	88F	31C	**Sept.**	92F	33C
		57	14		64	18		76	24
	Feb.	74F	23C	**June**	92F	33C	**Oct.**	89F	32C
		56			69	21		71	22
	Mar.	80F	27C	**July**	95F	35C	**Nov.**	81F	27C
		56			75	24		66	19
	Apr.	83F	28C	**Aug.**	93F	34C	**Dec.**	74F	23C
		60	16		76	24		59	15

Mazatlán	Jan.	71F	22C	**May**	80F	27C	**Sept.**	85F	29C
		61	16		70	21		77	25
	Feb.	71F	22C	**June**	84F	29C	**Oct.**	85F	29C
		61	16		76	24		77	25
	Mar.	73F	23C	**July**	86F	30C	**Nov.**	80F	27C
		63	17		77	25		71	22
	Apr.	76F	24C	**Aug.**	95F	35C	**Dec.**	86F	30C
		64	18		73	23		64	18

Puerto Vallarta

Jan.	84F	29C	**May**	91F	33C	**Sept.**	93F	34C
	63	17		68	20		73	23
Feb.	86F	30C	**June**	93F	34C	**Oct.**	93F	34C
	61	16		73	23		73	23
Mar.	86F	30C	**July**	95F	35C	**Nov.**	91F	33C
	63	17		73	23		68	20
Apr.	88F	31C	**Aug.**	95F	35C	**Dec.**	86F	30C
	64	18		73	23		64	18

Current weather information for more than 750 cities around the world may be obtained by calling **WeatherTrak** information service, at 900/370–8728 (cost: 95¢ per minute). A taped message will tell you to dial the three-digit access code for the destination in which you're interested. The code is either the area code (in the United States) or the first three letters of the foreign city. For a list of all access codes, send a stamped, self-addressed envelope to Cities, 9B Terrace Way, Greensboro, NC 27403. For more information call 800/247–3282.

Festivals and Seasonal Events

Mexico has a full calendar of national holidays, saints' days, and special events; below are some of the most important or unusual ones. For further information and exact dates, contact the Mexican Government Tourism Office (*see* Government Tourist Offices, above).

Jan. 1: New Year's Day is celebrated throughout the country. Agricultural and livestock fairs are held in the provinces.
Jan. 6: Feast of Epiphany is the day the Three Kings bring gifts to Mexican children.
Jan. 17: Feast of San Antonio Abad is the day when animals all over Mexico—household pets and livestock alike—are decked out with flowers and ribbons and taken to a nearby church for a blessing.
Feb.: Día de la Candelaria (Candlemas Day) means fiestas, parades, bullfights, and lantern-decorated streets.
Feb.–March: Carnival is celebrated throughout the region, but most enthusiastically in Mazatlán.
Mar.–Apr.: Semana Santa (Holy Week) is observed throughout the country with special passion plays during this week leading up to Easter Sunday.
May 1: Labor Day is a day for workers to parade through the streets.
May 5: Cinco de Mayo marks the anniversary of the French defeat by Mexican troops in Puebla in 1862.
May 15: Feast of San Isidro Labrador is celebrated nationwide with the blessing of new seeds and animals.
June 1: Navy Day is commemorated in all Mexican seaports.
June 24: Saint John the Baptist Day is a popular national holiday, with many Mexicans observing a tradition of tossing a "blessing" of water on most anyone within reach.
July 16: Feast of the Virgin del Carmen is a celebration, with fairs, bullfights, fireworks, sporting competitions, even a major fishing tournament.
Late July: Feast of Santiago is a national holiday that features *charreadas*, Mexican-style rodeos.
Aug. 15: Feast of the Assumption of the Blessed Virgin Mary is celebrated nationwide with religious processions.
Sept. 15–16: Independence Day is when all of Mexico celebrates

independence with fireworks and parties that outshine New Year's Eve.

Oct. 4: Feast of St. Francis of Assisi is a day for processions dedicated to St. Francis in various parts of the country.

Oct. 12: Columbus Day is a national holiday in Mexico.

Nov. 2: All Soul's Day or **Day of the Dead** is when Mexicans remember the departed in an oddly merry way, with candy skulls sold on street corners and picnickers spreading blankets in cemeteries.

Nov. 20: Anniversary of the Mexican Revolution is a national holiday.

Dec. 12: Feast Day of the Virgin of Guadalupe is the day that Mexico's patron saint is feted with processions and native folk dances, particularly at her shrine in Mexico City.

Dec. 12-Jan. 31: The Feast of the Immaculate Conception is an ongoing religious feast celebrated with lights and flowers.

Dec. 25: Christmas is the day for *posadas* (processions) that lead to Christmas parties and piñatas (decorated, suspended, hollow balls) that are broken open to yield gifts.

What to Pack

Pack light: Baggage carts are scarce at airports, and luggage restrictions on international flights are tight. Also, you'll want to save space for purchases. Mexico is filled with bargains on clothing, leather goods, arts and crafts, and silver jewelry.

Clothing What you bring depends on your destination. For the resorts, bring lightweight sports clothes, bathing suits, and coverups for the beach. Bathing suits and immodest clothing are inappropriate for shopping and sightseeing, both in cities and beach resorts. Jeans are acceptable for shopping and sightseeing, but shorts are frowned upon for men or women. You'll need a lightweight topcoat for winter and an all-weather coat and umbrella for sudden summer rainstorms.

Resorts are both casual and elegant; you'll see high-style designer sportswear, tie-dyed T-shirts, cotton slacks and walking shorts, and plenty of colorful sundresses. The sun can be fierce; bring a sun hat (or buy one locally) and sunblock lotion for the beach and for sightseeing. You'll need a sweater or jacket to cope with hotel and restaurant air-conditioning, which can be glacial. Few restaurants require jacket and tie.

Miscellaneous Bring a spare pair of eyeglasses and sunglasses and an adequate supply of prescription drugs. You can probably find what you need in the pharmacies, but you may need a local doctor's prescription. You are allowed to bring one regular and one movie camera, with eight rolls of film for each; bring the limit because film is expensive in Mexico. Also bring insect repellent, especially for the beach resorts, and a small flashlight for electric power outages, which are frequent.

Carry-on Luggage Passengers on U.S. airlines are limited to two carry-on bags. For a bag you wish to store under the seat, the maximum dimensions are $9 \times 14 \times 22$ inches. For bags that can be hung in a closet or on a luggage rack, the maximum dimensions are $4 \times 23 \times 45$ inches. For bags you wish to store in an overhead bin, the maximum dimensions are $10 \times 14 \times 36$ inches. Any item that exceeds the specified dimensions may be rejected as a carryon and checked. Keep in mind that an airline can adapt the rules to the circumstances, so on an especially crowded flight don't be surprised if you are only allowed one carry-on bag.

In addition to the two carryons, you may bring aboard a handbag (pocketbook or purse), an overcoat or wrap, an umbrella, a camera, a reasonable amount of reading material, an infant bag, and crutches, a cane, braces, or other prosthetic devices, upon which the passenger is dependent. Infant/child safety seats can also be brought aboard if parents have purchased a ticket for the child or if there is space in the cabin.

Foreign airlines have different policies. In tourist class they generally allow only one piece of carry-on luggage in addition to handbags and bags filled with duty-free goods. Passengers in first and business class are allowed one garment bag as well. It is best to call your airline to find out its current policy.

Checked Luggage U.S. airlines allow passengers to check two suitcases whose total dimensions (length × width × height) do not exceed 62 inches and whose weight does not exceed 70 pounds per bag.

Rules governing foreign airlines can vary, so before you go check with your travel agent or the airline itself. All airlines allow passengers to check in two bags. In general, expect the weight restriction on the two bags to be not more than 70 pounds each, and not more than 62 inches total dimensions per bag.

Taking Money Abroad

Traveler's checks and all major U.S. credit cards are accepted in most tourist areas of Mexico. The large hotels, restaurants, and department stores accept cards readily. Some of the smaller restaurants and shops, however, operate on a cash-only basis. Credit cards are generally not accepted in small towns and villages, except in tourist-oriented hotels. When shopping, you can usually get much better prices if you bargain with dollars.

Although you won't get as good an exchange rate at home as in Mexico, to avoid long lines at airport currency exchange booths, it's wise to change a small amount of money into pesos before you go. Many U.S. banks will change your money into pesos. If your local bank can't provide this service, you can exchange money through **Thomas Cook Currency Service.** To find the nearest office, contact Thomas Cook, at 630 Fifth Avenue, New York, NY 10011, tel. 212/635–0515.

It's always wise to carry some traveler's checks. The most widely recognized are **American Express, Barclays, Thomas Cook,** and those issued through major commercial banks such as **Citibank** and **Bank of America.** Some banks will issue the checks free to established customers, but most charge a 1% commission. Buy some of the traveler's checks in small denominations to cash toward the end of your trip. This will save you from having to cash a large check and ending your stay with more pesos than you need; generally the peso, a floating currency, is very low against the dollar. Remember to take the addresses of offices in Mexico where you can get refunds for lost or stolen traveler's checks.

The best places to change money are at banks and *casas de cambio* (exchange houses). Banks give the best rate of exchange. Most airports have money exchanges that give the same rate as banks. You can usually get more pesos for your dollars at Mexican airports or banks than at U.S. airports. Hotels will also change money, but they give the poorest rates.

Getting Money from Home

There are at least three ways to get money from home:

1) Have it sent through a large commercial bank with branches in Mexico. The only drawback is that you must have an account with the bank; if not, you will have to go through your own bank, and the process will be slower and more expensive.

2) Have money sent through **American Express.** If you are a cardholder, you can cash a personal check or a counter check at an American Express Office; the amount varies with the type of card you have. If you have a personal (green) card, you can cash a check for up to $1,000; $200 will be in cash and $800 in traveler's checks. Generally there is a 1% commission on the traveler's checks. You can also get money through **American Express MoneyGram.** Through this service, you can receive up to $5,000 cash. You call home and ask someone to go to an American Express office or an American Express MoneyGram agent located in a retail outlet and fill out an American Express MoneyGram. It can be paid for with cash or any major credit card. The person making the payment is given a reference number and telephones you with that number. The American Express MoneyGram agent calls an 800 number and authorizes the transfer of funds to an American Express office or participating agency in Mexico. In most cases, the money is available immediately on a 24-hour basis. You pick it up by showing identification and giving the reference number. Fees vary according to the amount of money sent. For sending $300, the fee is $24; for $5,000, $160. For the American Express MoneyGram location nearest your home and the location of offices in Mexico, call 800/543–4080. You do not have to be a cardholder to use this service.

3) Have money sent through **Western Union.** The U.S. number is 800/325–6000. If you have a MasterCard or Visa, you can have money sent for amounts up to your credit limit. If you do not have those credit cards, have someone take cash or a certified check to a Western Union office. The money will be delivered within one business day to a bank in Mexico. Fees vary with the amount of money sent. For $500, the fee is $30; for $1,000, $34. There is an additional $4 fee for using a credit card.

Mexican Currency

The unit of currency in Mexico is the peso, subdivided into 100 centavos. Mexicans use the dollar sign, often accompanied by the initials M.N. (for *moneda nacional,* or national currency), although banks and international financiers favor the prefix "P$." Because of inflation, centavos are rarely used; bills are issued in denominations of 500, 1,000, 2,000, 10,000, 20,000, and 50,000 pesos. Coins come in 1-, 5-, 10-, 20-, 50-, 100-, 200-, 500, and 1,000-peso denominations. The peso is devalued daily to keep pace with inflation. At press time (1989), the official exchange rate was about 2,980 pesos to the U.S. dollar, 2,574 pesos to the Canadian dollar, and 5,242 pesos to the pound sterling.

Dollars are widely accepted in many parts of Mexico, particularly near the border and in Cozumel, a free port. Many tourist shops and market vendors take them as well.

What It Will Cost

Prices in Baja and along the Pacific Coast are now competitive with those in other Mexican resorts. Budget travelers will only find bargains in Baja if they plan to camp during their stay; a double room for under $15 is rare. Even the towns of Tijuana and Mexicali are far more expensive than they once were, with rooms and meals costing what they would in the United States. Dollars are accepted as readily as pesos on the Pacific Coast and in much of Baja, except in the most remote regions.

Mexico has a value-added tax called I.V.A. *(impuesto de valor agregado)* of 15%, which is occasionally (and illegally) waived for cash purchases. In addition, many hotels add a 10% or 15% service charge to your bill. Be sure to check the service charge policy when you check in, and tip accordingly. An airport departure tax of U.S. $10 or the peso equivalent must be paid at the airport for international flights from Mexico.

Sample Costs Mazatlán is the least expensive destination on the Pacific Coast, with rooms ranging from $15 to $70. The best shrimp or lobster supper won't cost more than $15, not including the many *cervezas* (beers) that typically accompany such feasts. In Puerto Vallarta and Manzanillo expensive rooms can easily cost over $100 per night, and finding one for under $30 can be a chore. Dinners are more likely to cost $20 or more.

Baja's prices have risen dramatically, and during high season in Los Cabos an expensive room can easily cost $150 or more, while a moderate room can cost $80 or more. A taxi from Cabo San Lucas to San José del Cabo will run about $10 each way, which adds considerably to your bill if you're going to town for dinner. If you're looking for bargains, Los Cabos is not the place to start. Rather, try La Paz, Loreto, or the border areas for a selection of moderately priced rooms and inexpensive restaurants.

Passports and Visas

Americans U.S. citizens can enter Mexico with a tourist card and proof of citizenship. The only acceptable proof of citizenship is either a valid passport or an original birth certificate plus a photo ID. Tourist cards can be obtained from a travel agent, an airline agent at the airport, or from local Mexican consulates. A tourist card is valid for a single entry of up to three months. For stays of up to 180 days, get permission at the border or at your local Mexican consulate. To obtain a new passport, apply in person; renewals can be obtained in person or by mail. First-time applicants should apply at least five weeks in advance of their departure date to one of the U.S. Passport Agency offices. In addition, local county courthouses, many state and probate courts, and some post offices accept passport applications. Necessary documents include (1) a completed passport application (Form DSP–11); (2) proof of citizenship (birth certificate with raised seal or naturalization papers); (3) proof of identity (unexpired driver's license, employee ID card, or any other document with your photograph and signature); (4) two recent, identical, two-inch square photographs (black and white or color); and (5) a $42 application fee for a 10-year passport (those under 18 pay $27 for a five-year passport). If you pay in cash, you must have exact change. No change is given. Passports are mailed to you in about 10 working days. To renew your passport by mail, you'll need to send a completed Form DSP–82, two recent, identical passport photographs, and a check or money order for $35. For further information, contact the Embassy of Mexico, 1019 19th. St., Suite 810, N.W., Washington, D.C. 20036, tel. 202/293–1710.

Canadians Canadian citizens can enter Mexico with a tourist card and proof of citizenship. The only acceptable proof is a valid passport or your original birth certificate plus a photo ID. The tourist card can be obtained from travel agents, airlines, or local Mexican consulates. To acquire a passport, send a completed application (available at any post office or passport office) to the Bureau of Passports, Suite 215, West Tower, Guy Favreau Complex, 200 René Lévesque Blvd. West, Montreal, Quebec H2Z 1X4. Include $25, two photographs, a guarantor, and proof of Canadian citizenship. Applications can be made in person at regional passport offices in 12 locations, including Edmonton, Halifax, Montreal, Toronto, Vancouver, and Winnipeg. Passports are valid for five years and are nonrenewable.

Britons *See* Tips for British Travelers, above.

Customs and Duties

On Arrival Upon entering Mexico, you may be given a baggage declaration form and asked to itemize what you're bringing into the country. You are allowed to bring in three liters of spirits or wine for personal use, 400 cigarettes, two boxes of cigars, a reasonable amount of perfume for personal use, one movie camera and one regular camera, eight rolls of film for each, and gift items not to exceed a total of $120.

There are no restrictions or limitations on the amount of cash, foreign currencies, checks, or drafts that can be imported or exported by visitors.

On Departure If you are bringing any foreign-made equipment into Mexico, such as cameras, it's wise to carry the original receipt with you or register the equipment with U.S. Customs before you leave (Form 4457). Otherwise you may end up paying duty on your return.

U.S. Residents You may bring home duty-free up to $400 of foreign goods, as long as you have been out of the country for at least 48 hours. Each member of the family is entitled to the same exemption, regardless of age, and exemptions may be pooled. For the next $1,000 worth of goods, a flat 10% rate is assessed; above $1,400, duties vary with the merchandise. Included in the allowances for travelers 21 or older are one liter of alcohol, 100 cigars (non-Cuban), and 200 cigarettes. Only one bottle of perfume trademarked in the United States may be imported. There is no duty on antiques or works of art over 100 years old. Anything exceeding these limits will be taxed at the port of entry and may be taxed additionally in the traveler's home state. Gifts valued at under $50 may be mailed duty-free to friends or relatives at home, but you may not send more than one package per day to any one addressee and packages may not include perfumes costing more than $5, tobacco, or liquor.

Canadian Residents Exemptions for returning Canadians range from $20 to $300, depending on length of stay out of the country. For the $300 exemption, you must have been out of the country for one week. In any given year, you are only allowed one $300 exemption. You may bring in duty-free up to 50 cigars, 200 cigarettes, two pounds of tobacco, and 40 ounces of liquor, provided these are declared in writing to customs on arrival and accompany you in hand or checked-through baggage. Personal gifts should be mailed labeled "Unsolicited Gift—Value under $40." Obtain a copy of the Canadian Customs brochure *I Declare* for further details.

British Residents *See* Tips for British Travelers, above.

Traveling with Film

If your camera is new, shoot and develop a few rolls of film before leaving home. Pack some lens tissue and an extra battery for your built-in light meter. Invest about $10 in a UV or skylight filter and screw it onto the front of your lens. It will protect the lens and also reduce haze.

Film doesn't like hot weather. If you're driving in summer, don't store film in the glove compartment or on the shelf under the rear window. Put it behind the front seat on the floor, on the side opposite the exhaust pipe.

On a plane trip, never pack film in checked luggage; if your bags are X-rayed, say goodbye to your pictures. Always carry undeveloped film with you through security, and ask to have it inspected by hand. (It helps to isolate your film in a plastic bag, ready for quick inspection.) Inspectors at American airports are required by law to honor requests for hand inspection; abroad, you'll have to depend on the kindness of strangers.

The old airport scanning machines—still in use in some countries—use heavy doses of radiation that can turn a family portrait into an early morning fog. The newer models—used in all U.S. airports—are safe for anything from 5 to 500 scans, depending on the speed of your film (fast film is more easily damaged). The effects are cumulative: You can put the same roll of film through several scans without worry. After five scans, though, you're asking for trouble.

If your film is fogged and you want an explanation, send it to the **National Association of Photographic Manufacturers** (550 Mamaroneck Ave., Harrison, NY 10528). They will try to determine what went wrong. The service is free.

Language

Spanish is the official language of Mexico, although Indian languages are spoken by approximately 20% of the population, many of whom speak no Spanish at all. Basic English is widely understood by most people employed in tourism; less so in the less developed areas. At the very least, shopkeepers will know the numbers for bargaining purposes.

As in most foreign countries, knowing some words and phrases in the mother tongue has a way of opening doors. Unlike some other nationalities, Mexicans are not scornful of visitors' mispronunciations and grammatical errors; on the contrary, they welcome even the most halting attempts to use their language.

Staying Healthy

There are no serious health risks associated with travel to Mexico. Many travelers are eventually hit with an intestinal ailment known facetiously as Montezuma's Revenge or the Aztec Two-Step. Generally, it lasts only a day or two. A good antidiarrheal agent is paregoric, which dulls or eliminates abdominal cramps. You will need a doctor's prescription to get it in Mexico. The National Institute of Health recommends Pepto-Bismol, diphenoxylate (Lomotil), and loperamide (Imodium) for mild cases of diarrhea. If you come down with it, rest as much as possible, drink lots of fluids (such as tea without milk) or, in severe cases, rehydrate yourself with a salt-sugar mixture added to water.

If you are going off the beaten path, check with your physician or call the **U.S. Public Health Quarantine Station** nearest you for information on vaccination requirements and recommendations. For travel in some areas, you might want to take precautions against malaria. In Mexico you can purchase malaria-preventive Aralen tablets without a prescription. To be effective, the tablets must be taken before entering a malarial region.

If you have a health problem that might require purchasing prescription drugs while in Mexico, have your doctor write a prescription using the drug's generic name (brand names vary widely from country to country).

The **International Association for Medical Assistance to Travelers (IAMAT)** is a worldwide organization offering a list of English-speaking doctors whose training meets British and American standards. For a list of physicians in Mexico who are part of this network, contact IAMAT (417 Center St., Lewiston, NY 14092, tel. 716/754–4883; in Canada: 40 Regal Rd., Guelph, Ontario N1K 1B5; in Europe: 57 Voirets, 1212 Grand-Lancy, Geneva, Switzerland). Membership is free.

Insurance

Travelers may seek insurance coverage for areas such as health and accident, lost luggage, and trip cancellation. Your first step should be to review your existing health and homeowner's policies; some health insurance plans cover medical expenses incurred while traveling, some major medical plans cover emergency transportation, and some homeowner's policies cover luggage theft.

Health and Accident Several companies offer coverage designed to supplement existing health insurance for travelers:

Carefree Travel Insurance (Box 310, 120 Mineola Blvd., Mineola, NY 11501, tel. 516/294–0220 or 800/323–3149) provides coverage for emergency medical evacuation and accidental death and dismemberment. It also offers 24-hour medical phone advice.

International SOS Assistance (Box 11568, Philadelphia, PA 19116, tel. 215/244–1500 or 800/523–8930), a medical assistance company, provides emergency evacuation services, worldwide medical referrals, and optional medical insurance.

Travel Guard International, underwritten by Transamerica Occidental Life Companies (1145 Clark St., Stevens Point, WI 54481, tel. 715/345–0505 or 800/782–5151), offers reimbursement for medical expenses with no deductibles or daily limits and emergency evacuation services.

Wallach and Company, Inc. (243 Church St. NW, Vienna, VA 22180, tel. 703/281–9500 or 800/237–6615) offers comprehensive medical coverage, including emergency evacuation services worldwide.

Lost Luggage Luggage loss is usually covered as part of a comprehensive travel insurance package that includes personal accident, trip cancellation, and, sometimes, default and bankruptcy insurance. Companies that offer comprehensive policies include:

Access America, Inc., a subsidiary of Blue Cross–Blue Shield (Box 11188, Richmond, VA 23230, tel. 800/334–7525 or 800/284–8300); **Carefree Travel Insurance** (*see* Health and Accident Insurance, above); **Near Services** (450 Prairie Ave., Suite 101, Calumet City, IL 60409, tel. 708/868–6700 or 800/654–6700); **Travel Guard International** (*see* Health and Accident Insurance, above).

Luggage Insurance On international flights, airlines are responsible for lost or damaged property only up to $9.07 per pound (or $20 per kilo) for checked baggage and up to $400 per passenger for carry-on baggage. If you're carrying valuables, either take them with you on the airplane or purchase additional insurance. Some airlines will issue additional insurance when you check in, but many do not. One that does is American Airlines. Rates are $2 for every $100 valuation, with a maximum valuation of $5,000 per passenger. Hand luggage is not included. Insurance for lost, damaged, or stolen luggage is available through travel agents or directly through various insurance companies.

Two companies that issue luggage insurance are **Tele-Trip** (P.O. Box 31685, 3201 Farnam St., Omaha, NE 68131, tel. 800/228–9792), a subsidiary of Mutual of Omaha, and **The Travelers Corporation.** (Ticket and Travel Dept., 1 Tower Sq., Hartford, CT 06183, tel. 203/277–0111 or 800/243–3174). Tele-Trip operates sales booths at airports and also issues insurance through travel agents. Rates vary according to the length of the trip. The Travelers will insure checked or hand luggage for a $500–$2,000 valuation per person, for a maximum of 180 days. Rates for up to five days for a $500 valuation are $10, for 180 days, $85.

Before you go, itemize the contents of each bag in case you need to file an insurance claim. Be certain to put your home address on and in each piece of luggage, including carry-on bags. If your luggage is stolen and later recovered, the airline will deliver the luggage to your home or hotel free of charge.

Trip Cancellation Flight insurance is often included in the price of a ticket purchased with an American Express, Visa, or other major credit or charge card. It is usually included in combination travel insurance packages available from most tour operators, travel agents, and insurance agents.

Student and Youth Travel

The **International Student Identity Card (ISIC)** entitles students to rail passes, special fares on local transportation, and discounts at museums, theaters, sports events, and many other attractions. If purchased in the United States, the $14 cost of the ISIC also includes $3,000 in emergency medical insurance, plus hospital coverage of $100 a day for up to 60 days. Apply to the **Council on International Educational Exchange** (CIEE) (205 E. 42nd St., New York, NY 10017, tel. 212/661–1414). In Canada, the ISIC is available for $7 from **Travel Cuts** (187 College St., Toronto, Ont. M5T 1P7, tel. 416/979–2406) for CN$12.

Council Travel, a CIEE subsidiary, is the foremost U.S. student travel agency, specializing in low-cost charters and serving as the exclusive U.S. agent for many student airfare bargains and student tours. CIEE's 80-page *Student Travel Catalog* and "Council Charter" brochure are available free from any Council Travel office in the U.S. (enclose $1 postage if ordering by mail). In addition to the CIEE headquarters at 205 East 42nd Street (tel. 212/661–1450) and a branch office at 35 West 8th Street (tel. 212/254–2525) in New York City, there are Council Travel offices in Amherst, Austin, Berkeley, Boston, Cambridge, Chicago, Dallas, La Jolla, Long Beach, Los Angeles, Portland (OR), Providence, San Diego, San Francisco, and Seattle to name a few.

The **Educational Travel Center** (438 N. Frances St., Madison, WI 55703, tel. 608/256–5551) is another student travel specialist worth contacting for information on student tours, bargain fares, and bookings.

Students who would like to work abroad should contact **CIEE's Work Abroad Department** (205 E. 42nd St., New York, NY 10017, tel. 212/661–1414). The council arranges paid and voluntary work experiences overseas for up to six months. CIEE also sponsors study programs in Latin America and Asia and publishes many books of interest to the student traveler. These include *Work, Study, Travel Abroad: The Whole World Handbook* ($10.95 plus $1 postage) and *Volunteer!: The Comprehensive Guide to Voluntary Service in the U.S. and Abroad* ($6.95 plus $1 postage).

The Information Center at the **Institute of International Education** (IIE, 809 UN Plaza, New York, NY 10017, tel. 212/984–54) has reference books, foreign-university catalogues, study-abroad brochures, and other materials that may be consulted free of charge by students and nonstudents alike. The Information Center is open weekdays 10–4.

IIE administers grant and study programs offered by U.S. and foreign organizations and publishes a well-known annual series of study-abroad guides. The institute also publishes *Teaching Abroad*, a book of employment and study opportunities overseas for U.S. teachers. For a current list of IIE publications, prices, and ordering information, write to Institute of International Education Books (809 UN Plaza, New York, NY 10017). Books must be purchased by mail or in person; telephone orders are not accepted. General information on IIE programs and services is available from regional offices in Atlanta, Chicago, Denver, Houston, San Francisco, and Washington, DC.

Traveling with Children

Getting There All children, including infants, must have a passport for foreign travel; family passports are no longer issued. (For more information, *see* Passports and Visas, above.)

On international flights, children under age 2 not occupying a seat pay 10% of adult fare. Various discounts apply to children age 2–12. Reserve a seat behind the bulkhead of the plane, which offers more legroom and can usually fit a bassinet (supplied by the airline). At the same time, inquire about special children's meals or snacks, offered by most airlines. (Refer to "TWYCH's Airline Guide" in the February 1988 issue of *Family Travel Times* for a rundown on children's services furnished by 46 airlines.) Ask if you can bring aboard your child's car seat. (For the pamphlet "Child/Infant Safety Seats Acceptable for Use in Aircraft," write the Community and Consumer Liaison Division, APA-200, Federal Aviation Administration, 800 Independence Ave. SW, Washington, DC 20591, tel. 202/267–3479.)

Publications *Family Travel Times* is an 8- to 12-page newsletter published 10 times a year by TWYCH (Travel with Your Children, 80 8th Ave., New York, NY 10011, tel. 212/206–0688). A subscription includes access to back issues and twice-weekly opportunities to call in for specific information. Send $1 for a sample issue.

Great Vacations with Your Kids, by Dorothy Jordan (founder of TWYCH) and Majorie Cohen, offers complete advice on planning a trip with children (toddlers to teens) and reports on special travel accommodations available to families ($11.95 paperback, E. P. Dutton, 2 Park Ave., New York, NY 10016, tel. 212/725–1818).

Hints for Disabled Travelers

The **Information Center for Individuals with Disabilities** (Fort Point Place, 1st fl., 27–43, Wormwood St., Boston, MA 02210, tel. 617/727–5540; TDD 617/727–5236) offers useful problem-solving assistance, including lists of travel agents who specialize in tours for the disabled.

Moss Rehabilitation Hospital Travel Information Service (1200 West Tabor Rd., Philadelphia, PA 19141–3009, tel. 215/456–9600; TDD 215/456–9602) provides information on tourist sights, transportation, and accommodations in destinations around the world. The fee is $5 for up to three destinations. Allow one month for delivery.

Mobility International USA (Box 3551, Eugene, OR 97403, tel. 503/343–1284) has information on accommodations and organized study around the world.

The Society for the Advancement of Travel for the Handicapped (26 Court St., Penthouse Suite, Brooklyn, NY 11242, tel. 718/858–5483) offers access information. Annual membership costs $45, $25 for senior travelers and students. Send $1 and a stamped, self-addressed envelope.

Publications *The Itinerary* (Box 2012, Bayonne, NJ 07002, tel. 201/858–3400) is a bimonthly travel magazine for the disabled. Call for a subscription ($10 for one year, $20 for two); it's not available in stores.

Access to the World: A Travel Guide for the Handicapped, by
Louise Weiss, is useful though out of date. It is available at your
local bookstore or from Henry Holt & Co. for $12.95 plus $2
shipping (tel. 800/247–3912; the order number is 0805 001417).

Hints for Older Travelers

The **American Association of Retired Persons** (AARP, 1909 K
St. NW, Washington, DC 20049, tel. 202/872–4700) administers a Purchase Privilege Program through which independent
travelers can get discounts on hotels, airfare, car rentals, and
sightseeing. American Express Vacations (Box 5014, Atlanta,
GA 30302, tel. 800/241–1700 or 800/637–6200 in GA) arranges
group tours and cruises at reduced rates. AARP members
must be at least 50 years old. Annual dues are $5 per person or
per couple.

If you're planning to use an AARP or other senior-citizen identification card to obtain a reduced hotel rate, mention it at the
time you make your reservation rather than when you check
out. At participating restaurants, show your card to the maître
d' before you're seated; discounts may be limited to certain set
menus, days, or hours. Your AARP card will identify you as a
retired person but will not ensure a discount in all hotels and
restaurants. For a free list of hotels and restaurants that offer
discounts, call or write the AARP and ask for the "Purchase
Privilege" brochure or call the AARP Travel Service. When
renting a car, be sure to ask about special promotional rates
which might offer greater savings than the available discount.

Travel Industry and Disabled Exchange (TIDE, 5435 Donna
Ave., Tarzana, CA 91356, tel. 818/368–5648) is an industry-
based organization with a $15 per person annual membership
fee. Members receive a quarterly newsletter and information
on travel agencies and tours.

National Council of Senior Citizens (925 15th St. NW, Washington, DC 20005, tel. 202/347–8800) is a nonprofit advocacy group
with some 4,000 local clubs across the country. Annual membership is $12 per person or $12 per couple. Members receive a
monthly newspaper with travel information and an ID for reduced rate hotels and car rentals.

Mature Outlook (6001 N. Clarke St., Chicago, IL 60660, tel.
800/336–6330), a subsidiary of Sears, Roebuck & Co., is a travel
club for people older than 50. It offers discounts at Holiday Inns
and a bimonthly newsletter. Annual membership is $9.95 per
couple. Instant membership is available at participating Holiday Inns.

Travel Tips for Senior Citizens (Dept. of State Publication
8970, revised Sept. 1987) is available for $1 from the Superin-
tendent of Documents (U.S. Government Printing Office,
Washington, DC 20402-9325, tel. 202/783–3238).

The International Health Guide for Senior Citizen Travelers,
by Dr. W. Robert Lang, MD, is available for $4.95 plus $1 for
shipping from Pilot Books (103 Cooper St., Babylon, NY 11702,
tel. 516/422–2225).

The Discount Guide for Travelers Over 55, by Caroline and Wal-
ter Weintz, lists helpful addresses, package tours, reduced-
rate car rentals and other useful information in the United

States and abroad. To order, send $7.95 plus $1.50 shipping and handling to NAL/Cash Sales, Bergenfield Order Department (120 Woodbine St., Bergenfield, NJ 07021, tel. 800/526–0275).

Further Reading

Visitors to Baja might enjoy reading the *Sea of Cortez*, by John Steinbeck and E. F. Ricketts, the story of the research cruise conducted by these two men off the coast of Baja to collect marine animals and explore Baja's shores over 50 years ago. *The Baja Feeling*, by Ben Hunter, is the story of a couple who leave Los Angeles in the 1960s to explore Baja by land.

For a humorous glimpse at life in Baja, read *God and Mr. Gomez*, by Jack Smith, in which the *Los Angeles Times* columnist describes the difficulties of building a home in Baja. *Off the Beaten Track in Baja*, by Erle Stanley Gardner, describes the peninsula where he wrote many of his mystery novels. An Englishman's grueling, adventurous, amusing, and sometimes frightening walk the length of the peninsula is recounted in *Into a Desert Place*, by Graham Macintosh.

Finally, for up-to-the-minute news on the area, dedicated Baja lovers depend on the Mexico West Travel Club (Box 1646, Suite 107, Bonita, CA 92010, tel. 619/585–3033) and its monthly newsletter, with helpful information on road conditions, accommodations, insurance, fishing, and other details, including an extensive listing of books on Baja.

Arriving and Departing

From the U.S. by Plane

Airports and Airlines The number of airlines serving Mexico from the United States is constantly changing as the two nations continue to revise their bilateral agreements. Since 1986, however, Mexico has been opening the way for more charter flights, an increasingly popular option for inexpensive air service. The country's two major international carriers—Aeroméxico and Mexicana—are being supplemented by several smaller airlines serving domestic destinations and a charter company, Latur. For Southern Californians, significantly lower airfares can frequently be had by flying further into Mexico from the Tijuana airport.

As with all air travel, a number of fare types and booking restrictions apply; consult a travel agent. Sometimes it is also worth investigating package tours for flights even if you do not wish to use a tour's other services (hotels, meals, transfers, etc.). Because a packager can book seats by blocks, the price of a flight-plus-lodging package can sometimes be less than the cost of airfare that is booked separately.

Airports with frequent direct (although not always nonstop) service to the United States include Los Cabos, Loreto, Mazatlán and Puerto Vallarta.

Airlines specifically serving Mexico from major U.S. cities include **Aero California** (1960 E. Grand Ave., El Segundo, CA 90245, tel. 800/258–3311); **Aeroméxico** (tel. 800/237–6639); **Alaska Airlines** (Box 8900, Seattle, WA 98168, tel. 800/426–0333); **American** (Dallas/Fort Worth Airport, Dallas, TX 75261, tel. 800/433–7300) from Chicago and Dallas/Fort Worth; **Continental** (Box 4607, Houston, TX 77210, tel. 800/525–0280) from Houston and Newark, NJ; **Delta** (Hartsfield Atlanta International Airport, Atlanta, GA 30320, tel. 800/345–3400) from Los Angeles and Phoenix; **Mexicana** (9841 Airport Blvd., Los Angeles, CA 90045, tel. 800/531–7921) from Baltimore/Washington, Chicago, Dallas, Denver, Los Angeles, Miami, Philadelphia, San Antonio, San Francisco, Seattle, and Tampa; **Northwest** (International Airport, Minneapolis, MN 55111, tel. 800/225–2525) from Memphis; and **Pan Am** (200 Park Ave., New York, NY 10166, tel. 800/221–1111) from Miami and New York.

Flying Time It takes 4¼ hours to reach Mexico from New York; 3½ hours from Chicago; and 2 hours from Los Angeles.

Enjoying the Flight If you're able to sleep on a plane, it makes sense to fly at night. Unless you are flying from Europe, jet lag won't be a problem, as there is little or no time difference between the United States, Canada, and Mexico. Sleepers usually prefer window seats to curl up against; those who like to move about the cabin should request an aisle seat. Bulkhead seats (located in the front row of each cabin) have more legroom, but seat trays are attached rather awkwardly to the arms of your seat.

Discount Flights If you have the flexibility, you can sometimes benefit from last-minute sales that tour operators have to fill a plane or bus. A number of brokers specializing in such discount sales also have sprung up. All charge an annual membership fee, usually about $35–$50. Among these are **Stand-Buys Ltd.** (3033 S. Parker Rd., Aurora, CO 80014, tel. 800/255–1488), **Moment's Notice** (425 Madison Ave., New York, NY 10017, tel. 212/486–0503), **Discount Travel International** (114 Forrest Ave., Suite 205, Narberth, PA 19072, tel. 215/668–7184), and **Worldwide Discount Travel Club** (1674 Meridian Ave., Miami Beach, FL 33139, tel. 305/534–2082). Sometimes tour and charter-flight operators advertise in Sunday travel supplements, as well. Try to find out whether the tour operator is reputable, and specifically, whether you are tied to a precise round-trip or whether you will have to wait until the operator has a spare seat to return.

Smoking If smoking bothers you, ask for a seat far away from the smoking section. If the airline tells you there are no nonsmoking seats, insist on one: Department of Transportation regulations require U.S. airlines to find seats for all nonsmokers on the day of the flight, provided they meet check-in time restrictions.

From the U.S. by Car

There are two absolutely essential things to remember about driving in Mexico. First and foremost is to carry Mexican auto insurance, which can be purchased near border crossings on either the U.S. or Mexican side. If you injure anyone in an accident, you could well be jailed—whether it was your fault or not—unless you have insurance. Guilty until proven innocent is part of the country's *Code Napoléon*.

The second item is that if you enter Mexico with a car, you must leave with it. The fact that you drove in with a car is stamped on your tourist card, which you must give to immigration authorities at departure. If an emergency arises and you must fly home, there are complicated customs procedures to face. The reason is that cars are much cheaper in the United States, and you are not allowed to sell your vehicle in Mexico.

Remember that your foreign car insurance coverage is not good in Mexico. Purchase enough Mexican automobile insurance at the border to cover your estimated trip. It's sold by the day, and if your trip is shorter than your original estimate, a prorated refund for the unused time will be issued to you upon application after you exit the country. **Dan Sanborn's Insurance** and **Seguros Atlantico** (Allstate reps) have offices in most border cities. **Instant Mexico Auto Insurance, in** San Ysidro, California, and **International Gateway Insurance Brokers** in Chula Vista, California, specialize in Baja insurance. All three are experienced and reliable.

There are several major highways into Mexico from the American border. From California, at Tijuana, a good highway (Mexico Highway 1) runs over 1,000 miles down the length of Baja California, with ferries to the mainland at Santa Rosalia and La Paz. From Nogales, Arizona, Highway 15 follows the Gulf of California coast on the mainland for 750 miles to Mazatlán on the Pacific, then turns gradually inland to Guadalajara. The Sierra Madre Occidental's ruggedness prevents any highway from crossing it north of the spectacular Durango–Mazatlán road (Highway 40). The farther south you get, the more east–west links exist, tying together the major north–south arteries.

Renting and Hiring Cars

When considering this option, remember that Mexico is still a developing country. The highway system is very uneven: in some regions, modern, well-paved superhighways prevail; in others, particularly on the Baja peninsula, potholes and dangerous, unrailed curves are the rule.

To rent a car in Mexico you need a valid driver's license from your country of residence. Mexican rental agencies are more familiar with U.S. and Canadian licenses than with the international driver's licenses issued by the American Automobile Association, which must be obtained before you leave home. You will need to leave a deposit—the most acceptable being a blank, signed credit card voucher. Without a credit card, you may not be able to rent a car.

Mexican auto insurance is imperative, if inadequate, as deductibles can be exceedingly high. The largest U.S. rental car agencies are represented in Mexico, which also has its own national and local firms (their rates are frequently less expensive). Although you can book in advance from home, do not count on getting the make and model of your choice upon arrival. Manual transmission cars are more common than automatics.

Rental cars are extremely expensive in both Baja and the Pacific Coast resorts. A Volkswagen Beetle—the most readily available rental car—will cost around $70 per day. With luck, insurance will be included in the price, but the 15% tax will not. Think twice before you rent a car in one location and drop it off at another: Arranging a drop-off is difficult and charges are hefty—about $100.

For day trips and local sightseeing, engaging a car and driver (who often acts as a guide) for a day can be a hassle-free, more economical way to travel. Hotel desks will know which taxi companies to call, and you can negotiate a price with the driver. In Mazatlán, Puerto Vallarta, and Manzanillo, the multitude of travel guides and tour services can be a fun and easy sightseeing option.

The following car rental firms have offices in Baja: **Avis** (tel. 800/331–1212), **Budget,** (tel. 800/527–0700), **Hertz** (tel. 800/654–3131), and **National** (tel. 800/245–4442).

From the U.S. by Train, Bus, and Ship

By Train   Rail service from Nogales or Mexicali is available to the Pacific resorts of Mazatlán and Manzanillo. There is no rail service to the Baja peninsula. Contact the **Mexican National Railroad** (tel. 800/228–3225) or **Amtrak** (tel. 800/872–7245) for further information.

By Bus   Getting to Mexico by bus is for the adventurous or budget-conscious. It involves a transfer at one of the southern Texas or border cities, such as El Paso, Del Rio, Laredo, McAllen, Brownsville, or San Antonio. These gateways are served by several small private bus lines as well as by **Greyhound Lines** (tel. 800/237–8211). Comfortable first-class buses with air-conditioning and rest rooms are sometimes available in Mexico.

By Ship   Many cruise lines include Mexico as part of their cruise itineraries. Most originate from across the Gulf of Mexico, usually at Miami, stopping in Key West, Cancún, and Cozumel. Others sail from Los Angeles and San Diego to Baja and the Pacific Coast. Still others include both coastlines, passing through the Panama Canal. Many large travel agencies, such as **Empress Travel,** organize cruise packages from major U.S. ports, such as Miami, Fort Lauderdale, and San Diego.

Cruise lines with Mexican stops include **Admiral Cruises** (tel. 800/327–2693), **Carnival Cruise Line** (tel. 800/432–5424), **Epirotiki** (tel. 212/599–1750), **Holland America Lines** (tel. 800/426–0327), **Norwegian Cruise Lines** (tel. 800/327–7030), **Princess Cruises** (tel. 800/421–0880 or 800/421–0522), **Royal Caribbean Cruise Line** (tel. 800/327–6700), **Royal Viking Line** (tel. 800/233–8000), and **Society Expeditions** (tel. 800/426–7794). For details on the possibility of freighter travel to or from Mexico, consult *Pearl's Freighter Tips* (Box 188, 16307 Depot Rd., Flushing, NY 11358).

Staying in Baja

Getting Around

By Plane   **Mexicana** and **Aeroméxico,** the principal domestic carriers, provide the bulk of air service within Mexico, with international airlines offering connecting flights between the large beach resorts and Mexico City. Reworking of the country's air system has led to the emergence and expansion of regional carriers and charter operators: **Aero California** serves Guadalajara, Los Mochis, Hermosillo, La Paz, Loreto, Los Cabos, Mazatlán, and Tijuana.

Aeroméxico and Mexicana have air-hotel packages called V.T.P., which stands for *viaje todo pagado* (all-inclusive trip). Certain discounts on these carriers may apply for flights originating in the United States.

By Train Since 1987 the **Ferrocarriles Nacionales de México** (Mexican National Railways, tel. 5/547–1084) has been putting luxury trains into service around the country, with upgraded dining and club cars, first-class service, and several with sleeping cars.

One of the most popular tourist trains coasts alongside the Copper Canyon from Chihuahua to Los Mochis on the Pacific Coast (tel. 14/16–1657). Other railways include the **Chihuahua–Pacific Railway** (tel. 5/54–5325), the **Pacific Railway** (tel. 5/547–2019), and the **Sonora–Baja California Railway** (tel. 65/7–2101).

Primera especial (special first-class) tickets on overnight trains entitle passengers to reserved, spacious seats that turn so traveling companions can face each other. *Primera regular* (regular first-class) service is also available on many trains. Second-class coaches are less comfortable. Sleeping accommodations consist of *camarines* (private rooms with bath and one lower berth), *alcobas* (same as *camarines*, but with an upper and a lower berth), and couchettes.

Train tickets must be purchased at least one day in advance, from Mexico City's Buenavista Station or local stations. Rail passes and discount packages are not available in Mexico.

By Bus Mexican buses run the gamut from comfortable air-conditioned coaches with bathrooms on board (deluxe and first-class) to dilapidated "vintage" buses (second- and third-class) on which pigs and chickens travel and stops are made in the middle of nowhere. Since second-class fares are only about 10% less than first-class, travelers planning a long-distance haul are well-advised to take the latter. Seats can be reserved in advance.

The Mexican bus network is extensive, far more so than the railroads, as buses are the poor man's form of transportation. In deciding between bus and train travel, your choice will often be determined by availability and flexibility: Buses go where trains do not, service is more frequent, and tickets can be purchased on the spot (except during holidays and on long weekends, when advance purchase is crucial). Smoking is permitted on all Mexican buses.

In the large cities, bus stations are located a good distance from the center of town, which can be inconvenient. Some towns have different stations for each bus line, but fortunately there is a trend toward consolidation. **Central de Autobuses** (Plaza del Angel, Londres 161, tel. 5/533–2047), a travel agency in the capital, will make reservations and send bus tickets to your hotel for a small fee. The best first-class lines include **Transportes del Norte,** which goes up to the U.S. border from the Northern Bus Terminal (tel. 5/587–5511).

By Car In rural areas, especially in mountainous regions, roads are
Road and Traffic quite poor: Caution is advised, especially during the rainy sea-
Conditions son, when rock slides are a problem. Generally, driving times are longer than for comparable distances in the United States.

Topes (road cops, or bumps) are also common; it's best to slow down when approaching a village.

Driving at night is not recommended because of poor visibility (few roads are lit at night), the difficulty of getting assistance in remote areas, and the preponderance of cattle and other animals wandering along the roads. Common sense goes a long way in this regard: If you have a long distance to cover, start out early and fill up on gas. Allow extra time for unforeseen occurrences as well as for the trucks that seem to be everywhere. During the day, be alert to animals, especially cattle and dogs.

Always lock your car, and never leave valuable items in the body of the car (the trunk will suffice for daytime outings).

The Mexican Tourism Ministry publishes a good general road map, available free from its offices. PEMEX, the state-owned oil company, has an excellent, highly detailed road atlas *(Atlas de carreteras);* Guía Roji puts out current city, regional, and national road maps. PEMEX and Guía Roji publications are available in bookstores; gas stations generally do not carry maps.

Rules and Safety Regulations Illegally parked cars are not treated lightly. Cars are either towed or have their license plates removed, which requires a trip to the traffic police headquarters for payment of a fine. When in doubt, avoid street parking and look for a parking lot, where your car is likely to be safer.

If an oncoming vehicle flicks its lights at you in daytime, slow down: it could mean trouble ahead. When approaching a narrow bridge, the first vehicle to flash its lights has the right of way. One-way streets are common in many communities. One-way traffic is indicated by an arrow; two-way, by a two-pointed arrow. A circle with a diagonal line through the letter *E* (for *estacionamiento)* means "no parking." Other road signs follow the now widespread system of international symbols, a copy of which will usually be provided when you rent a car in Mexico.

Speed Limits Mileage and speed limits are given in kilometers: 100 kph and 80 kph (62 and 50 mph, respectively) are the most common maximum speeds. A few of the newer toll roads allow 110 kph (68.4 mph). In cities and small towns, observe the posted speed limits, which can be as low as 30 kph (18 mph).

Fuel Availability and Costs PEMEX franchises all the gas stations in Mexico. Stations are located at most road junctions, cities, and towns, but some do not accept credit cards or dollars. Fuel prices, however, are the same at all stations and about the same as in the United States. Unleaded gas is not widely available.

At the gas stations, keep a close eye on the attendants, and if possible, avoid the rest rooms: they're generally filthy.

National Road Emergency Services The Mexican Tourism Ministry operates a fleet of almost 250 pickup trucks (known as the *Angeles Verdes,* or Green Angels) to render assistance to motorists on the major highways. The bilingual drivers provide mechanical help, medical first aid, radio-telephone communication, basic supplies and small parts, towing, tourist information, and protection. Services are free, and spare parts, fuel, or lubricants are provided at cost. Tips are always appreciated.

The Green Angels patrol fixed sections of the major highways twice daily from 8 AM to 8 PM. If you break down, pull off the road as far as possible, lift the hood of your car, hail a passing vehicle, and ask the driver to notify the patrol. Most bus and truck drivers will be quite helpful. The Green Angels' 24-hour hotline is 250–0123 or 250–0151, nationwide.

If you witness an accident, do not stop to help but instead locate the nearest official.

By Taxi Taxis in Mexican cities are the best alternative to public transportation, which, though inexpensive, is slow and prone to pickpockets. The quintessential rule is to establish the fare beforehand. In most of the beach resorts, there are inexpensive fixed-route fares, but if you don't ask, or your Spanish isn't great, you may get taken. In the cities meters do not always run, and if they do, their rates have usually been updated by a chart posted somewhere in the cab. For distances longer than several kilometers, negotiate a rate beforehand; some drivers will start by asking how much you want to pay to get a sense of how street smart you are.

Taxis are available on the street, at taxi stands *(sitios)*, and by phone. Street taxis—usually VW Beetles—are always cheapest; large limousines standing in front of hotels will charge far more. Never leave luggage unattended in a taxi.

In addition to private taxis, many cities operate bargain-priced collective taxi services using VW minibuses, both downtown and at the airports. The vehicle itself is called a *combi;* the service, *colectivo* or *pesero*. Peseros run along fixed routes, and you hail them on the street and tell the driver where you are going. The fare—which you pay before you get out—is based on distance traveled.

Telephones

The Mexican telephone system is antiquated. Lines are frequently tied up, the number of digits varies from city to city, obtaining information from the operator is not always possible, and public phones are often out of order. Collect calls generally cannot be made from pay phones.

Local and long-distance calls can also be made from telephone company offices, specially marked shops (usually with a telephone symbol hanging out front), and from hotels, although the latter place an excessive surcharge on top of the phone tax and value-added tax, which comes to about 58%. For international calls, call collect whenever possible; there is often a charge whether or not the call is completed. Direct-dial to the United States is available from most luxury hotels, but if you must go through an operator, expect a long wait to be connected. International operators speak English. Dial 09 to place international calls; 02 for long-distance calls; 04 for local information; 01 for long-distance information.

Mail

The Mexican postal system is notoriously slow and unreliable; *never* send, or expect to receive, packages, as they may be stolen (for emergencies, use a courier service). There are post offices *(oficinas de correos)* even in the smallest villages, and numerous branches in the larger cities. Always use airmail for overseas correspondence; it will take anywhere from 10 days to two weeks or more, where surface mail might take three weeks to arrive. Service within Mexico can be equally slow. The rates are quite low: P$1,100 for a letter (up to 10 grams) or postcard to the United States, and P$300 to the United Kingdom.

To receive mail in Mexico, you can have it sent to your hotel or use *poste restante* at the post office. In the latter case, include the words "a/c Lista de Correos" ("general delivery") and the zip code. A list of names for whom mail has been received is posted and updated daily by the post office. American Express cardholders can have mail sent to them at the local American Express office. For a copy of the *Traveler's Companion*, which lists the offices worldwide, write to American Express (Traveler's Companion, Box 678, Canal Street Station, New York, NY 100).

Addresses

The Mexican method of naming streets is exasperatingly arbitrary. Streets in the centers of many colonial cities (those built by the Spaniards) are laid out in a grid surrounding the *zócalo* (main plaza) and often change names on different sides of the square; other streets simply aquire a new name after a certain number of blocks. The naming system for numbered streets is identical to the American habit of designating numbered streets as either "north/south" or "east/west" on either side of a central avenue. Streets with proper names, however, can change mysteriously from Avenida Juárez, for example, to Francisco Madero, without any way of knowing where one begins and the other ends. On the other hand, blocks are often labeled numerically, according to distance from a chosen starting point, as in "Calle de Pachuca 1a," "Calle de Pachuca 2a," etc.

Many Mexican addresses have "s/n" for *sin numéro* (no number) after the street name. This is common in small towns where there are fewer buildings on a block. Similarly, many hotels give their address as "Km. 30 a Querétaro," which indicates that the property is on the main highway 30 kilometers from Querétaro.

As in Europe, addresses in Mexico are written with the street name first, followed by the street number. The five-digit zip code *(código postal)* precedes, rather than follows, the name of the city. "Apdo." *(apartado)* means "post office box."

Veteran travelers to Mexico invariably make one observation about asking directions in the country: Rather than say they do not know, Mexicans tend to offer guidance that may or may not be correct. This is not out of malice, but out of a desire to please. Therefore, patience is a virtue when tracking down an address.

Tipping

When tipping in Mexico remember that the minimum wage is the equivalent of $4 a day and that the vast majority of workers in the tourist industry live barely above the poverty line. How-

ever, there are Mexicans who think in dollars and know, for example, that in the United States porters are tipped about $1 a
bag; many of them expect the peso equivalent from foreigners
(P$2,500) but are happy to accept P$500 from Mexicans. They
will complain either verbally or with a facial expression if they
feel they deserve more—you and your conscience must decide.
Overtipping, however, is equally a problem. Following are
some general guidelines, in pesos:

Porters and bellboys at airports and at moderate and inexpen-
sive hotels: P$1,000 per bag
Porters at expensive hotels: P$2,000 per bag
Hotel room service: P$1,000 *(expensive);* P$400 *(moderate* and
inexpensive)
Chambermaids: P$1,000 per night (all hotels)
Waiters: 10–20% of the bill, depending on service (make sure a
10%–15% service charge has not already been added to the bill)
Taxi drivers: no tip unless they have done something extraordi-
nary
Gas station attendants: P$400
Children (windshield-wiping, car-watching, etc.): P$200
Parking attendants and theater ushers: P$400

Opening and Closing Times

Banks are open weekdays 9–1:30. In some larger cities, a few
banks also open weekdays 4–6, Saturday 10–1:30 and 4–6, and
Sunday 10–1:30. Banks will give you cash advances in pesos
(for a fee) if you have a major credit card. Traveler's checks can
always be cashed (for less favorable exchange rates) at hotels,
airports, shops, and restaurants. Stores are generally open
weekdays and Saturdays from 9 or 10 to 7 or 8; in resort areas,
they may also be open on Sundays. Business hours are 9–7,
with a two-hour lunch break from about 2 to 4. Government offices are usually open 8–3. All government offices, banks, and
most private offices are closed on national holidays.

Shopping

Mexico is one of the best countries in the world to purchase
handicrafts *(artesanías).* The work is varied, original, colorful, and inexpensive, and it supports millions of families who
are carrying on ancient traditions. Though cheap, shoddy mer-
chandise—masquerading as "native handicraft"—is on the
rise, careful shoppers who take their time can come away with
real works of art.

At least three varieties of outlets feature Mexican crafts: municipal markets (indoor and outdoor); government-run shops
(known as Fonart); and tourist boutiques in the towns, shopping malls, and hotels. The boutiques are overpriced but convenient, and they usually accept credit cards if not dollars. (You
may be asked to pay up to 10% more on credit-card purchases;
savvy shoppers with cash have greater bargaining clout.) The
15% tax (I.V.A.) is charged on most purchases but will be
waived by eager or desperate vendors.

It is not always true that the closer to the source of an article,
the better the selection and price. As a general rule, prices are
always higher at the beach resorts.

Bargaining is accepted in most tourist areas of Mexico and is most common in the markets. Start by offering no more than half the asking price and then come up very slowly, but do not pay more than 70%. Always shop around. In major shopping areas, shops will wrap and send purchases back to the United States. In some areas you will be able to have items like huaraches, clothing, and blankets tailor-made. Mexican craftspeople in given regions excel in ceramics; weaving and textiles; silver, gold, and semiprecious stone jewelry; leather; woodwork; and lacquerware.

Sports and Outdoor Activities

Hunting, Fishing, and Bird-watching The best area for these activities is Baja California and the Sea of Cortés. For information on hunting and the hunting calendar, contact the Dirección General de Area de Flora y Fauna Silvestres (Dirección General de Conservación Ecológica de los Recursos Naturales, Río Elba 20, Col. Cuauhtémoc, 06500 México, D.F., tel. 905/553–5545). Licenses can be obtained from Mexican consulates in Texas, California, New Mexico, and Arizona, or in Mexico from the Secretaría de Desarrollo Urbano y Ecología. For information on fishing and mandatory permits, contact the Secretaría de Pesca (Alvaro Obregón 269, 06700 México, D.F., tel. 5/211–0063).

Tennis and Golf Most major resorts have lighted tennis courts, and there is an abundance of 18-hole golf courses in Mexico, many of them designed by such noteworthies as Percy Clifford, Larry Hughes, and Robert Trent Jones. Contact the Federación Mexicana de Tenis (Durango 225-301, México, D.F., tel. 5/514–3759) and the Federación Mexicana de Golf (Cincinati 40, 02710 México, D.F., tel. 5/563–9194) for information. At private golf and tennis clubs, you must be accompanied by a member to gain admission. Often hotels that do not have their own facilities will secure you access to ones in the vicinity. Many deluxe international hotel chain properties also feature extensive health-club facilities.

Camping Camping is not a particularly popular pastime among the Mexicans. Though many national parks provide free camping facilities, most camping takes place outside them. Camping is best on the Pacific Coast and in Baja, which is endowed with forests of pine, granite formations, and lagoons.

Spectator Sports

***Charreadas* (Mexican Rodeos)** This Mexican rodeo is a colorful event involving elegant flourishes and maneuvers, handsome costumes, mariachi music, and much fanfare. Charreadas are held most Sunday mornings; inquire at the tourist office or a travel agency.

Soccer As in Europe, this is Mexico's national sport (known as *futbol*). It is played almost year-round in most of the large cities.

Jai alai, horse racing, dog racing, cockfights, boxing, and bullfights are practiced all over Mexico. Again, ask at the tourist office, travel agencies, and hotels, or pick up the local newspaper.

Beaches

Beaches are the reason most tourists visit Mexico. Generally speaking, the Pacific is rougher and the waters less clear than the Caribbean; consequently there is better snorkeling and scuba-diving at the latter. Deep-sea fishing is particularly renowned off the northern Pacific and in the Sea of Cortés, between Baja California and Mazatlán. All beach resorts offer a variety of water sports, including waterskiing, windsurfing, parasailing, and, if the water is clear enough, snorkeling and scuba diving.

Caution is advised when venturing out in the Mexican sun. Sunbathers lulled by a slightly overcast sky or the sea breezes can be burned badly with as little as 20 minutes of exposure. Use strong sunscreens, and avoid the peak sun hours of noon to 2 PM.

Dining

Mexican cooking is developing an international reputation and popularity. It is not subtle. It is spicy, varied, and exotic. The poor subsist on staples of rice, beans, and tortillas, which form the basis for creative variations on sophisticated national dishes.

Seafood is abundant, not just on the coasts but also in the lake regions around Guadalajara and in the state of Michoacán. Ceviche—raw fish and *mariscos* (shellfish) marinated in lime juice and topped with cilantro (coriander), onion, and chilis—is a local favorite, though it originated in Peru. Shrimp, lobster, and oysters can be huge and succulent, but when ordering oysters, bear in mind the folk adage about eating oysters only in months with names that contain the letter *R*. Other popular seafood includes *huachinango* (red snapper), abalone, crab, turtle steak, and abalone.

Mexicans are fond of red meat, and consume lots of beef, pork, and goat, with a variety of sauces. Chicken and other poultry are used in enchiladas, tacos, or burritos, and are delicious when roasted over an open fire. Regional variations are described in the appropriate chapters.

Maize was sacred to the Indians, who invented innumerable ways of preparing cornmeal, from the faithful tortilla to the *tamale* (cornmeal wrapped in banana leaves or corn husks), tostada (lightly fried, open tortilla heaped with meat, lettuce, etc.), and simple taco (a tortilla briefly heated, filled, and wrapped into a slim cylinder; one variation on this is called *flauta*, or flute).

Fresh fruits and vegetables are another Mexican forte. Jicama, papaya, avocado, mango, guayaba, peanuts, squash, and tomatoes are just some of the produce native to Mexico. (All fresh produce should be washed or peeled before eating, however, because of the frequently primitive hygienic conditions.)

Other Mexican specialties less common abroad are *antojitos* or *botanas* (appetizers), *chilaquiles* (a rich breakfast made with chilis, tortilla, tomatoes, onions, cream, and cheese), and *chile nogado* (a large chili pepper stuffed with pork, raisins, onion, olives, and almonds and covered with heavy cream, walnuts, and pomegranates). Soups are rich—particularly the pork-based *pozole, sopa azteca* (avocado and tortilla in a broth), and *sopa de flor de calabaza* (squash-flower soup). But this barely touches on the plenitude and diversity of Mexican cuisine, which also encompasses an astonishing assortment of breads, sweets, beers, wines (which are fast improving), and cactus-based liquors. Freshly squeezed fruit juices and *licuados* (fruit shakes) are safe to drink if made with purified water; coffee varies from standard American-style and Nescafé to espresso and *café de jarra*, which is laced with chocolate and served in a coarse clay mug. Imported liquor is very expensive; middle-class Mexicans stick with the local rum.

A word on hygiene: Most travelers to Mexico are only too familiar with the caveat, "Don't drink the water" (*see* Staying Healthy, in Before You Go, above). Stick to bottled waters and soft drinks, and when ordering cold drinks, skip the ice *(sin hielo)*. Hotels with purified water systems will post signs to that effect in the rooms. *Tacos al pastor*—thin pork slices grilled on a revolving spit and garnished with the usual cilantro, onions, and chilis—are delicious but dangerous. Be wary of Mexican hamburgers because you can never be certain what meat they are made with. And if you're not keen on spiciness, ask that a dish be served *no muy picante*.

Mexican restaurants run the gamut from humble hole-in-the-wall shacks, street stands, and chairs and tables in the markets to *taquerías*, American-style fast-food joints, and internationally acclaimed gourmet restaurants. Prices, naturally, follow suit. One bargain found everywhere in Mexico is the fixed-menu lunch known as *comida corrida*, which is served between 1 and 4.

Lunch is the big meal; Mexicans rarely dine before 8. There is no government rating of restaurants, but you'll know which ones cater to tourists simply by looking at the clientele and the menu (bilingual menus usually mean slightly higher prices than at nontourist restaurants). Credit cards—especially Master Card (Banamex and Carnet) and Visa (Bancomer)—are increasingly accepted.

Lodging

The price and quality of accommodations in Mexico vary about as much as the country's restaurants, from super-luxurious, international-class hotels and all-inclusive resorts to modest budget properties, seedy places with shared bathrooms, *casas de huéspedes* (guest houses), youth hostels, and *cabanas* (beach houses).

More and more of the international hotel chains are moving into Mexico, and some of them are adding budget lines to the existing upscale products. Since many are franchises, service standards vary, but travelers can count on a certain standardization of rooms, English-speaking staff, guaranteed dollar rates, and toll-free reservation numbers in the United States. Companies with several Mexican properties include Club Med (tel. 800/CLUB MED), Holiday Inn *(Hoteles Fiesta Americana, Posadas de Mexico,* and *Fiesta Inns,* tel. 800/HOLIDAY), Hyatt International (tel. 800/228–9000), Inter-Continental (tel. 800/332–4246), Marriott (tel. 800/228–9290), Princess (tel. 800/223–1818 or 800/442–8418 in NY), Quality

Inn *(Hoteles Calinda,* tel 800/228–5151), Sheraton (tel. 800/
325–3535), and Westin *(Hoteles Camino Real,* tel. 800/582–
8100). Good Mexican-owned chains include Stouffer El Presidente (tel. 800/472–2427), Krystal (tel. 800/231–9860), and
Misión (tel. 5/525–0393).

Hotel rates are subject to the 15% value-added tax and service
charges and meals are generally not included. The Mexican
government categorizes hotels, based on qualitative evalua-
tions, into *gran turismo* (super-deluxe hotels, of which there
are only about 20 nationwide); 5-star down to 1-star; and economy class. Keep in mind that many hotels that might otherwise
be rated higher have opted for a lower category to avoid higher
interest rates on loans and financing.

High- versus low-season rates can vary significantly (*see* When
to Go, in Before You Go, above). Hotels in this guide have air-
conditioning and private bathrooms, unless stated otherwise,
but bathtubs are not common in inexpensive hotels and properties in smaller towns.

Mexican hotels—particularly those owned or managed by the
international chains—are always being expanded. In the case
of older properties, travelers may often have to choose between newer annexes with modern amenities and rooms in the
original buildings with possibly fewer amenities and—equally
possible, but not certain—greater charm.

Reservations must be made in advance if you are traveling during high season or holiday periods. Overbooking is a common
practice in some parts of Mexico, such as Cancún, and there is
little you can do to avoid this. Travelers to remote areas will
encounter little difficulty in obtaining rooms on a "walk-in" basis. If you arrive in Mexico City without a reservation, the
Mexican Hotel and Motel Association operates a booth at the
airport that will assist you (tel. 5/286–5455).

Home Exchange See *Home Exchanging,* by James Dearing ($9.95 paperback,
Globe Pequot Press, Box Q, Chester, CT 06412, tel. 800/243–
0495 or 800/962–0973 in CT).

Villa Rentals **At Home Abroad, Inc.** (405 E. 56th St., Suite 6H, New York, NY
10022, tel. 212/421–9165) has properties in Puerto Vallarta.

Hideaway International (Box 1270, Littleton, MA 01460, tel.
508/486–8955) handles rentals in Puerto Vallarta.

Villas and Apartments Abroad (420 Madison Ave., Room 305,
New York, NY 10017, tel. 212/759–1025) can set you up in a villa
in Manzanillo or Puerto Vallarta.

Villas International (71 W. 23rd St., New York, NY 10010, tel.
212/929–7585 or 800/221–2260) can find villa rentals in
Manzanillo and Puerto Vallarta.

Credit Cards

The following credit card abbreviations are used throughout
this guide: AE, American Express; DC, Diners Club; MC,
MasterCard; V, Visa.

Personal Security and Comfort

Many Americans are aware of Mexico's reputation for corruption. The patronage system is a well-entrenched part of Mexican politics and industry, and workers in the public sector—notably policemen and customs officials—are notoriously underpaid. Everyone has heard, at least secondhand, some of the horror stories about Americans (not to mention the Mexicans themselves) languishing away in Mexican jails; highway assaults; pickpocketing; and the preponderance of bribes.

Use common sense, as you would anywhere. Wear a money belt; make use of hotel safes; and carry your own baggage whenever possible. Don't bother going to the police to report a crime unless you speak excellent Spanish and have a great deal of patience.

Women traveling alone in Mexico are likely to be subjected to *piropos* (catcalls). Avoid direct eye contact with men on the street, as it invites further acquaintance. Don't wear tight clothes if you don't want to call attention to yourself. If you speak Spanish, pretend you don't and ignore would-be suitors or say "no" to whatever they say. Don't enter street bars or cantinas unaccompanied.

2 Portrait of Baja

Hunting for Friendlies

by James C.
Simmons

A freelance
writer
specializing in
travel, wildlife,
and history,
James C.
Simmons has
written seven
books and over
200 magazine
articles.

Exploding out of the murky depths of San Ignacio Lagoon like a Polaris missile, a 40-foot whale, tall as a three-story building, breached. Its massive body turned slowly as it hung momentarily in the air before falling back with a tremendous splash that reverberated off the distant hills of sculptured white sand and then was swallowed up in the immense silence of the desert beyond.

For the four of us riding out the show in a 14-foot inflatable Zodiac a few hundred feet away, the breach was a satisfying climax to a day spent in the midst of one of the most spectacular wildlife phenomena in the world, the annual gathering of thousands of gray whales in the shallow warm-water lagoons of the Pacific coast of Mexico's Baja California peninsula.

Jutting out from the underside of the continent like a desiccated appendix, Baja California was until recently the last truly unspoiled desert frontier in North America. That began to change in late 1973 with the completion of the narrow strip of paved road that connects Ensenada in the north to La Paz, 600 miles to the south. An area that had been all but inaccessible suddenly opened up, and thousands of campers, hikers, and fishermen poured in.

San Ignacio has so far escaped the mobile homes, dirt bikes, and dune buggies. Situated midway between Ensenada and La Paz, its isolation has been preserved by a triple barrier of rugged mountain ranges, impassable roads, and inhospitable desert. If there are such things as ends of the world, then surely this corner of Baja, so isolated it appears cut off from time itself, must be one of them.

"Portentious and mysterious." Melville used those words to describe his whales, but they apply equally well to San Ignacio Lagoon. The Vizcaíno Desert reaches southward to embrace the area, but no soaring cardons or majestic *yuccas validas* dominate its horizon. Here the desert is an empty and bleak wilderness, a vast expanse of flat tableland, its surface punctuated by scattered clumps of withered salt bush and small pockets of ocotillo, their branches twisted into grotesque shapes by the hot winds. A handful of families eke out a precarious existence in several tiny fishing settlements. During the whale season small cruiseboats from San Diego occasionally anchor far out in the mouth of the lagoon, launch a few skiffs jammed to the gunwhales with camera-clicking whale watchers, and then

James C. Simmons "Hunting for Friendlies" originally appeared as "Close Encounters in Baja" in Americas magazine in October 1981.

move on up the coast during the night. Otherwise, the out-side world has been kept at bay.

In the spring of 1976 reports filtered back to Southern California of an extraordinary new development in the lagoon. Whales there were openly seeking friendly contacts with human beings. Porpoises, of course, had been doing this for generations. But such friendly behavior from whales was radically new and unexpected and confounded the cetalogists. What follows is an account of an expedition sent to the area the next year to document this new behavior on film.

In February 1977 I was offered the opportunity for some concentrated whale watching in San Ignacio Lagoon from a shore-based camp. Piet Van de Mark has for over a decade set up a base camp there and brought in small groups of whale enthusiasts for the best whale watching on the West Coast. No one else knows the central Baja region as well as Piet, who spends much of his time before and after the whale season in the still virtually unexplored Santa Clara Mountains nearby, looking for the legendary lost Baja mission.

His camp proved as comfortable as one might expect under the circumstances (the nearest source of fresh water was a five-hour drive away). Piet was also providing support for a couple of marine biologists, Steven Swartz and Mary Lou Jones, there for three months on a grant from the Marine Mammal Commission to conduct the first serious study of gray whale behavior in the lagoon. Also in the camp was a crew of seven from the National Geographic Society to gather footage of friendly whales for a television special.

The first evening we gathered in the big mess tent around an ancient potbellied stove for a meal of broiled lobster while the wind outside gusted to 30 knots. The talk was of sea monsters, falls into crevasses, and, of course, friendly whales. Piet recounted an experience with one of his clients the week before. "We had been cruising the lagoon for three days looking for friendlies with no luck. Lots of courting, breaching, and spy-hopping but no friendlies. Finally a bearded seminarian from Colorado pipes up: 'Maybe if we sing a hymn, God will send us a whale.' The next moment he's belting out *Amazing Grace* loud and clear. And then, right in the middle of his song, up pops this 35-foot cow alongside our Zodiac and stays with us for 40 minutes. Of course, we named her Grace."

Steven and Mary Lou, by now old hands at friendly whales, played a tape they made during one such encounter, when the whale rolled alongside their small boat for almost an hour. After playfully bumping against the side of the boat, nudging the motor, allowing Steve and Mary Lou to rub his back, blowhole, and lips, the whale slid his nose under their Zodiac, lifted it up, and slowly, gently spun the boat around. "Hey," someone squealed on the tape, "but this is a tippy boat!" Mary Lou said later, "I put on a mask and stuck my head into the water, and there he was—a giant eye three feet away, looking back at me!"

Everyone had his pet theory as to the reason for the sudden change in the behavior of the grays. But all those with previous experience around the friendlies agreed on one point: their determined gentleness toward the small boats. The irony could not have been sharper, for a century ago those same animals earned themselves a fearful reputation among the men who came to the lagoons from San Francisco to hunt them for their oil and bone. The whalers called them the Devilfish and Hardheads, and no other species of whales wrought such an awful destruction upon the men who pursued them. Eventually, the whalers were triumphant and the grays were brought to the edge of extinction, but only at a terrible cost in lost and maimed lives.

Charles Scammon, the 19th-century whaler-turned-naturalist, left behind a full account of his experience with the grays in Baja California. "In the winter of 1856, we were whaling about . . . Magdalena Bay, where, in attacking 16 whales, 2 boats were entirely destroyed, while the others were staved 15 times; and out of the 18 men who officered and manned them, 6 were badly jarred, one had both legs broken, and another 3 ribs fractured, and still another was so injured internally that he was unable to perform duty during the rest of the voyage. All these serious casualties happened before a single whale was captured."

And so there is a supreme irony to the fact that those whales that so terrorized their 19th-century pursuers should have been the first to seek friendly encounters with human beings. But then our knowledge of grays, as with most other whales, comes almost exclusively from those periods when they have been ruthlessly hunted, frequently to the point of extinction. The observations made when the animals were under considerable stress have all too quickly been accepted as absolute truth.

The friendly whale phenomenon is still too new to draw any hard and fast conclusions as to why it occurred. But the key may well lie in the fact that the gray whale population today is a relatively young one, and very few of the adults have been hunted. Protected by international agreement from commercial hunting since 1937, the population has returned from the brink of extinction. It now numbers close to 13,000. The younger grays, therefore, have not been conditioned in the flight response common to the older adults and to most other cetacean species.

Nor is there any doubt that today those same grays would, if attacked, respond with the same cold ferocity they displayed a century ago. In 1970 Jacques-Yves Costeau's crew attempted to attach a tracking buoy to a gray: When the harpoon to which the buoy was attached struck home, the apparently docile whale suddenly turned and breached full length across their small craft, almost killing the three men in it. And the Eskimos on Point Barrow, Alaska, who can legally hunt the grays for food, regard it as an extremely dangerous animal that will almost always attack the offending boats and hunters.

In San Ignacio Lagoon the grays have not been disturbed, and so it is only natural that over a lengthy period of time they should adapt to and accept the flotilla of small boats in their immediate environment. Gray whales are intelligent and curious animals, and it was only a matter of time before the more aggressive individuals made the first tentative, cautious approaches to the boats and their passengers. And this behavior has been encouraged and rewarded by the constant rubbing they receive from the whalewatchers in the boats. As with most cetaceans, the grays take great pleasure in the touch-stimulus, and they engage in constant bodily contacts with one another.

The next morning we went hunting for the friendlies. To venture out into the middle of San Ignacio Lagoon in February or March when upwards of 1,500 gray whales are in residence is to experience one of the greatest spectacles in the natural world. Scores of whales are about, blowing at every point of the compass and engaged in all kinds of activities— breaching, sleeping, diving, and courting.

Within 15 minutes we encountered our first whales, a cow and her calf, playing together on the surface, quite unmindful of our boat a few yards away. The name of the game, we decided, was Blow and Bounce. The cow would submerge and blow a terrific blast of bubbles underneath her calf, which would spin delightedly in the boiling water. Then the cow would surface and slide her rostrum under the calf and gently bounce and roll it in the surge of the waves.

The experience suggested one of the gray's most unusual qualities—its accessibility. Because the gray whale spends so much of its time in the shallow waters close to the land, it has been more thoroughly studied. And the marine biologists have learned enough to suggest it is a very remarkable animal indeed.

The most significant fact in the life of the gray whale is its annual migration, the longest undertaken by any mammal in the world, from the Arctic seas in the north to the coastal lagoons of Baja California in the south, a round-trip of almost 14,000 miles. Even more unusual is that for the duration of the migration, almost eight months of the year, the whales fast, drawing their nourishment from the thick blankets of blubber encasing their bodies.

By late January most of the whales have arrived in the coastal lagoons of Baja. The pregnant cows push their way into the deepest recesses of the lagoons to the nurseries, shallow, warm, protected areas, perfect for the births of their calves. When the time arrives, a second cow will often be in attendance in the capacity of midwife to aid in the birth and to assist the new-born baby to the surface to draw its first breath.

Almost 17 feet in length, the calf weighs more than a ton at birth and comes into the world with an enormous appetite. To satisfy it, the cow must produce daily more than 50 gallons of extremely rich (40% fat) milk, and the calf gains almost 50 pounds a day during the first two months. By April the calf has matured sufficiently to accompany its mother on the long northward swim to the summer feeding grounds off Siberia.

But it was still February and the cow and calf playing Blow and Bounce a few yards from our boat clearly had several halcyon weeks to go before they undertook the swim northward. After 30 minutes of watching the games, Piet started the motor and took us farther out into the lagoon in search of a friendly.

When it came to wildlife, we soon learned, there was much more to San Ignacio than just the whales. Bottlenose porpoises would suddenly appear from nowhere, ride our bow wave for a while and then just as quickly get bored and disappear. Solitary sea lions floated on their backs, heads and flippers held high, basking in the heat of the sun. Whenever we ran the boat into shallow water, the sandy bottom literally exploded as we flushed dozens of leopard sharks, guitarfish, and stingrays.

Whales, whales everywhere, but the friendlies were not all that easy to come by. When the surf was up, the whales were down (the grays hate rough water—it floods their blowholes). So we contentedly passed long hours exploring the mangrove swamps and streams on the western edge of the lagoon. Cutting the motor and using the oars, we enjoyed some of the best birding in North America. Curlews, willets, royal and elegant terns, godwits, and plovers jammed the sandbars and shoals, hundreds of them together.

White ibises and reddish and showy egrets decorated the tops of mangrove trees, and brown pelicans fished from dead stumps, unmindful of our presence a few yards away. Great blue herons sailed gracefully overhead while ospreys, often with small silver fish clasped in their talons, hung in the air. We ate fresh oysters plucked from the roots of mangroves exposed at low tide while all about us mullets leaped and in the distance small grebes dove into shallow water, feeding on insects and minnows.

And then it was back to the lagoon to look for our friendly. Late in the afternoon of the fourth day she found us. Piet had idled the motor, and we drifted lazily in the swells. Suddenly a mottled gray shape, like some giant torpedo, materialized out of the green depths below us and slowly floated to the surface. A huge head covered with patches of barnacles thrust out of the water. Behind the blowhole we saw three white slashes, scars, possibly from a collision with an outboard motor years before. "It's Grace," breathed Piet. "She's come back."

There she was, all 35 feet of her. She lifted a saucer-size eye out of the water and studied us closely for a moment. Convinced we were safe, she slowly investigated us, swimming over to the side of the boat, rubbing up against the engine mount. Gently and deliberately, she slid her rostrum beneath our boat and lifted us up and revolved us about.

"Hi there, Grace, how are you today, big girl?" Piet was talking to her exactly as though she were a favorite sheepdog. When the whale moved away from the boat, he thumped the rubber tubing, called her by name, and waved her back to us. She came and stretched out alongside the boat. "OK, let's do a massage. Grace wants her reward," Piet said, leaning over the side to rub her vigorously around her blowhole. And then suddenly there we were, the four of us, laughing and falling over one another to give this big, beautiful, barnacle-covered whale her massage. We rubbed her lips and she gaped open a mouth that seemed large enough to swallow a dune buggy, letting us stroke her baleen and tongue.

If whales could purr, Grace would have been purring. Instead she broke away, submerged herself beneath our boat, and blew out a great blast of bubbles. Blow and Bounce. What more could we have asked for?

We left Grace and her crowd at the end of February. Since then the number of friendly contacts between whales and humans has proliferated at an incredible rate. Many of these now involve cows with calves, and sometimes three or more animals simultaneously approach a single boat. Most of the whale-watchers who now visit San Ignacio Lagoon in February and March have an opportunity to pet a whale. Curiously enough, only the whales of this one lagoon have exhibited this friendly, playful behavior.

Although the reasons for this behavior are still obscure, it is quite clear that for such encounters to have occurred in the first place, both the whales and the people needed to have overcome some very natural inhibitions and fears about overreaching biological boundaries to establish physical contacts. The experience of the friendly whales in San Ignacio Lagoon suggests how little man understands of the true nature of these marvelous animals. And it underscores the urgency with which we need to guard them from further exploitation.

As Ronn Storro-Patterson, an environmental scientist at the University of California, has observed: "The needs of whales have come to symbolize the needs of man—to live peaceably and in balance with the resources of the earth."

3 Tijuana

Introduction

Just 29 kilometers (18 miles) south of San Diego lies Mexico's fourth-largest and fastest-growing city, Tijuana. With more than 1.5 million residents, Tijuana can no longer be called a "border town." It is a city, yet so unlike a U.S. city that the traveler feels instantly immersed in a foreign country. The official language is Spanish, but many speak "Spanglish," a mix of Spanish and English. Residents hail from all over Mexico and Central America; visitors come from throughout the world.

The border crossing at Tijuana is the busiest, and often the most troublesome, international border in the United States. Border officials know there is no way to stem the flow north and south. Tijuana attracts hundreds of new residents a week, drawn to border-town wages that far exceed the income in their hometowns. For many of the newcomers, Tijuana is the last stop before their hoped-for homeland, the United States. The border fence that stretches through the canyons and hills between Tijuana and California is filled with man-size holes; helicopters and jeeps patrol these barren landscapes, attempting to deter illegal immigration. But these immigrants are not among the thousands who cross the border legally each day: Tijuana also attracts hordes of visitors, coming to work and play. Tourism in Tijuana and neighboring Rosarito Beach and Ensenada increases dramatically each year, and is easily the area's leading industry. In this sense, Tijuana is most assuredly a border town.

As foreign as Tijuana may seem to the visitor, it is steeped in American influence. The border area has served as a gigantic recreation center for southern Californians since the turn of the century. Before then it was a ranch, populated by a few hundred Mexicans. In 1911 a group of Americans invaded the area and attempted to set up an independent republic; they were quickly driven out by Mexican soldiers. When Prohibition hit the United States in the 1920s, Tijuana boomed. The Agua Caliente Racetrack and Casino opened in 1929, about the same time as the Rosarito Beach Hotel and Ensenada's Pacífico Riviera Casino were built. Americans seeking alcohol, gambling, and more fun than they could find back home flocked across the border, their dollars firing the region's growth. Tijuana became the entry port for what was termed a "sinful, seamy playground," frequented by Hollywood playboys and the idle rich. Then Prohibition was repealed, Mexico outlawed gambling, and Tijuana's fortunes dwindled. The Agua Caliente Resort fell into ruin and has never been revived.

The flow of travelers from the North slowed to a trickle for a while, but Tijuana still captivated those in search of the sort of fun that was illegal and frowned upon at home. The ever-growing number of servicemen in San Diego, particularly in wartime, kept Tijuana's sordid reputation alive; visitors of a different adventuresome bent kept pushing inward and southward, discovering new scenes, lifestyles, and cultures. Until the toll highway to Ensenada was finished in 1967, travelers going south drove straight through downtown Tijuana, stopping along Avenida Revolución and the side streets for supplies and souvenirs. The free road, still used by those with plenty of time for wandering, curved over the hills through barren ranchland and eventually turned west to the coast at Rosarito

Beach. The toll road, which now bypasses downtown (if you follow the signs carefully), cut down on the traffic through the hills, which have sprouted full-size towns, called *colonias*. Downtown Tijuana wasn't affected much by the toll road, since it took many more years to complete the bypass, and continued carrying on as "sin city" until the early '70's, when local politicians and businessmen began eyeing its resources. Since then, Tijuana has been paying serious attention to tourism.

Throughout the '70s and '80s, Tijuana's population—both resident and tourist—has exploded. The city has spread into canyons and dry riverbeds, over hillsides and ocean cliffs. Many of its residents live in total poverty, in cardboard shacks far from electricity and running water. The city is crowded; services are constantly malfunctioning, and the government is forever dealing with such natural disasters as floods. Still, Tijuana attracts more and more *maquiladoras*—foreign-owned factories and plants that employ thousands of Tijuana's residents. Originally, many of the companies operating in Tijuana were based in the United States; now, the Japanese are leading manufacturers in the area. Prosperity and poverty coexist throughout town.

Tijuana's Cultural Center speaks for the city's presence as Baja Norte's leading region in tourism and business. As the capital of Baja Norte, Mexicali is the state's civic center, but Tijuana is its cultural soul. The Mexican history exhibits at the Cultural Center are a perfect introduction for the thousands of visitors whose first taste of Mexico is at the border. One can wander past models of Maya and Aztec temples, Indian pueblos and missions, and get a true sense of the scope of Mexico's land, people, and history. In a way, Tijuana is representative of all Mexico, its varied cultures, arts, crafts, foods, and faces.

Tijuana's tourist attractions have remained much the same throughout the century. Gambling on horses and greyhounds is legal and popular. The recently renovated Agua Caliente Racetrack speaks of that glamorous decade when Hollywood stars came for amusement. El Palacio Frontón (Jai Alai Palace), where betting is also allowed, offers fast-paced games, cheering fans, and a palatial edifice.

Some of the greatest Mexican and Spanish bullfighters appear at the oceanfront bullring, and nationally celebrated musicians and dancers perform at the Cultural Center. Then there are the restaurants, more than anyone could count: Eating and drinking well are among Tijuana's greatest attractions. A few of the best restaurants from the '20s and '30s still attract a steady clientele with their excellent international cuisine and reasonable prices. On a more moderate scale, there are scores of seafood restaurants and kitchens serving great Mexican food, unadulterated for American tastes. Avenida Revolución resembles one huge cafeteria, with places for every taste and budget. At night the street life often gets rowdy as tourists demonstrate the effects of Mexican margaritas (much stronger than those in the north).

The Río Tijuana area is quickly becoming the city's glamorous zone. Not far from the border, it is just past the dry riverbed of the Tijuana River along Paseo de los Héroes. This boulevard is one of the city's main thoroughfares, and large statues of historical figures grace the *glorietas* (traffic circles). The Plaza

Río Tijuana, built on Paseo de los Héroes in 1982, was Tijuana's first major shopping center. It is an enormous affair, with good restaurants, major department stores, and hundreds of shops. The plaza has become a central square of sorts, where holiday fiestas are sometimes held. The Cultural Center is within easy walking distance; combined with the shopping center it makes a pleasant day's outing. Smaller shopping centers are opening all along Paseo de los Héroes. Pueblo Amigo, a new shopping and entertainment complex at the north end of the Zona Rio and just 300 meters from the border, has a pedestrian walkway from the border to the Plaza and Paseo de los Héroes.

As a tourist spot, Tijuana has traditionally been popular as a day trip or as a layover for trips farther into Mexico. Now wealthy Mexicans from Guadalajara and Mexico City are using Tijuana as a resort destination. Southern Californians take advantage of the lower airfares into Mexico from the Tijuana airport; if you are planning a trip farther into Mexico you might want to compare the rates out of Tijuana. There are plenty of quality hotels in the city, and taxis to and from the airport are economical. With tourism predicted to double again in the next few years, Tijuana is sure to continue adding more and more luxury hotels and attractions.

Essential Information

Important Addresses and Numbers

Tourist Information Reservations in the United States are handled by the San Diego office of **Tijuana's Convention and Tourist Bureau.** *Tijuana/Baja Information, 7860 Mission Center Ct., No. 202, San Diego, CA 92108, tel. 619/299–8518, 800/225–2786 in the U.S., or 800/522–1516 in CA.*

There is a tourism office directly across the border, with maps, newspapers, and English-speaking clerks. Tourist information booths are located at the foot of Calle 1a, just after the pedestrian overpass across the border; at the airport; and at the intersection of Avenida Revolución and Calle 4a. *Tel. 668/3–1310. Open daily 9–5.*

The **Tijuana Chamber of Commerce** is the best source of tourist information. *Av. Revolución and Calle 1a, tel. 66/5–8472. Open daily 8–8.*

The Baja California Norte State tourism office is at Boulevard Díaz Ordaz in the Plaza Patria shopping center (tel. 668/1–9492).

Emergencies **Police** (tel. 134); **Red Cross** (tel. 132); **Fire** (tel. 136); **U.S. Consulate** (tel. 66–3886).

Arriving and Departing by Plane

Tijuana is located just 29 kilometers (18 miles) south of San Diego. The city can be reached from the United States by bus, trolley, or car, and from mainland Mexico by plane, bus, or car. Visitors to this area do not need tourist cards if they are staying less than 72 hours and traveling no more than 16 kilometers (10 miles) south of Ensenada.

Airport and Airlines **Mexicana** (tel. 800/531–7921), **Aeroméxico** (tel. 800/237–6639), and **Aero California** (tel. 800/258–3311) have flights to and from many cities in Mexico, with fares that are often lower than flying from the United State. No U.S. carriers fly into Tijuana. The airport is on the eastern edge of the city, near the Otay Mesa border crossing. The cab fare from the San Ysidro border is about $6 per person; from the Otay Mesa border, $10. Shuttle service is available in Volkswagen vans from the airport to downtown and the borders.

Arriving and Departing by Car, Trolley, and Bus

By Car U.S. I–5 and I–805 end at the border crossing in San Ysidro; Highway 905 leads from I–5 and I–805 to the border crossing at Otay Mesa, near the Tijuana airport. Day-trippers often prefer to park their cars on the U.S. side (lots charge from $5 to $10 per day) and walk across the border. It's worth the extra money to park at a guarded lot, since break-ins are common. Those driving into Tijuana should purchase Mexican auto insurance, available at many stands along the last exit before the border crossing. On holidays and weekends there can be a wait at the border when traveling into Mexico; coming back into the United States the wait can be up to two hours long, but lines are usually shorter at the Otay Mesa crossing.

By Trolley The **San Diego Trolley** (tel. 619/231–8549) to San Ysidro and the border leaves the San Diego Depot in downtown San Diego every 15 minutes until 7:30 PM (every 30 minutes thereafter), and passes through National City, Chula Vista, and San Ysidro. The 45-minute trip costs $1.50. There are taxis on the Mexican side of the border to take you to your destination.

By Bus **Greyhound** (tel. 619/239–3266 or 800/528–0447) serves Tijuana from San Diego several times daily. **Mexicoach** (tel. 619/232–5049) has several departures from the San Diego Depot to Tijuana. **Baja California Tours** (tel. 699/454–7166) has daily buses to Tijuana. Within Mexico, **Turisticos de Baja California** (Ave. Madero and Calle Mexico, tel. 668/8–3981) has charter buses and vans for trips into Baja and is planning to offer tourist buses with air-conditioning and other creature comforts for trips throughout Baja. **Autotransportes de Baja California** (tel. 668/5–8472) links Tijuana with other points in Baja; **Tres Estrellas de Oro** (tel. 668/6–9186) travels into mainland Mexico; and **Autotransportes del Pacífico** (tel. 668/6–9045) travels to the Pacific Coast. The Tijuana Central Bus Station is at Calz. Lázaro Cárdenas and Blvd. Arroyo Alamar, tel. 668/0–9060.

Getting Around

Those spending just a day in Tijuana are advised to park on the U.S. side of the border and walk or take a taxi to their destinations. There is a large lot with scores of taxis just across the border; from there you can reach the airport, the Cultural Center, the Río area, or Avenida Revolución for under $5. The 2-kilometer (1¼-mile) walk to Avenida Revolución and the 3-block walk to the Río area, over the pedestrian bypass, past vendors and restaurants, are easy.

By Car There are plenty of signs at the border to lead you to main highways and downtown, but once you hit the surface streets, Tijuana can be very confusing. It is advisable to leave your car in one of the guarded parking lots along Avenida Revolución and at most major attractions. If you park on the street, pay attention to the signs. Your license plates will be removed if you park illegally.

By Rental Car Avis is the only major U.S. rental company allowing its cars into Baja as far as Guerrero Negro. **Courtesy Rentals** in San Diego (tel. 800/252–3756, or 800/824–3232 in CA) allows their cars to be taken as far as Ensenada. The larger U.S. rental agencies have offices at the Tijuana International Airport. Offices in town include: **Avis** (Av. Agua Caliente 3310, tel. 66/6–4004); **Budget** (Paseo de los Héroes 77, tel. 66/4–0253); and **National** (Av. Agua Caliente 5000, tel. 66/6–2103).

By Taxi Taxis are plentiful and inexpensive in Tijuana. Fares to all parts of the city are less than $5 per person, and considerably less than that if you're good at bargaining.

By Bus The downtown bus station is at Calle 1a and Avenida Madero, tel. 66/6–9515. Most city buses at the border will take you downtown; the bus to the border departs from downtown at Calle Benito Juárez (also called Calle 2a) between Avenidas Revolución and Constitución. All buses marked *Centro Camionera* go through downtown.

Guided Tours

San Diego Mini-Tours has hourly departures from San Diego hotels to Av. Revolución in Tijuana and back and connections with a Mexican-operated trolley tour of Tijuana ($23). *837 47th St., San Diego, CA 921, tel. 619/234–9044.* Assistance with tours of Tijuana and beyond are available at several Tijuana travel agencies including **Servicios Turisticos,** Av. Septiembre 213-B, tel. 668/6–1725; **Viajes Carrousel,** Blvd. Taboada and Orozco, tel. 668/4–0456; and **Viajes Honold,** Av. Revolución 608, 668/8–1111.

Exploring

Numbers in the margin correspond with points of interest on the Tijuana map.

❶ The **San Ysidro Border Crossing** is the typical visitor's entryway to Tijuana. A pedestrian overpass crosses the dry riverbed of the Tijuana River, leads through a mass of stalls with the full spectrum of souvenirs, and then goes up Calle 2a into the center of town. **Mexitlan** (Blvd. Ocampo and Calle 2a, tel. 668/1–8294), a fascinating combination of museum and enterainment/shopping center was due to open at press time, after several years of planning and construction. Designed by architect Pedro Ramírez Vásquez, Mexitlan has scale models of all the major architectural and cultural landmarks throughout Mexico, and is an exciting addition to Tijuana.

❷ Calle 2a intersects **Avenida Revolución,** Tijuana's main tourist street, is lined with designer clothing shops and restaurants, all catering to tourists. Burros painted to look like zebras pose on the street corners for snapshots. Shopkeepers call out from their doorways, offering low prices for an odd, garish assortment of souvenirs. Many shopping arcades open onto Revolución; inside the front doors are mazes of small stands with low-priced pottery and handicrafts.

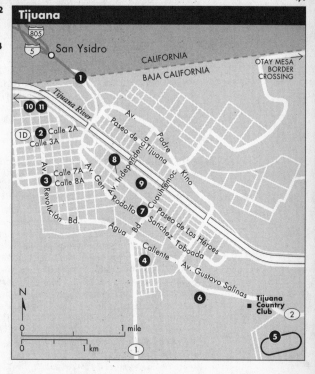

❸ **El Palacio Frontón** (Jai Alai Palace, tel. 668/5–7833) is on Avenida Revolución between Calles 7a and 8a. The Moorish-style palace is a magnificent building and an exciting place to watch and bet on fast-paced jai alai games. The restaurants and bars along Revolución offer excellent and inexpensive meals and drinks. Many of Tijuana's tourists are regulars who have long-time friends and favorite haunts in Tijuana.

Time Out — Among the many restaurants along Revolución, **Bol Corona** (Av. Revolución 520, tel. 668/5–7940) and **La Especial** (Av. Revolución 770, tel. 668/5–6654) are traditional favorites for Mexican food that hasn't been fancied up for the tourists. Head to the **Hotel Caesar** (Av. Revolución 827, tel. 668/8–0550) for Caesar salad, which was invented here. **Tía Juana Tilly's** (Av. Revolución at Calle 7a, tel. 668/5–6024), next to the Jai Alai Palace, can accommodate large parties with varying tastes in food.

❹ At Calle 11a, Avenida Revolución becomes Boulevard Agua Caliente and passes by **Toreo de Tijuana** bullring (tel. 668/4–2126; tickets $4–$6.50), where bullfights are held from May to
❺ September. A few blocks farther is the **Hipódromo de Agua Caliente**, or Agua Caliente Racetrack (tel. 668/6–2002; no admission fee). Since 1985, some $14 million has been spent on renovations and on building the Jockey Club and Turf Club. Horses race on weekend afternoons; greyhounds race nightly except Tuesday. The track also draws bettors to its Foreign Book, where you can place wagers on races televised via satellite from California. Nearby are the two gleaming, mirrored

❻ towers of the **Hotel Fiesta Americana** (tel. 668/1–7000 or 800/ 343–7821), Tijuana's glamor spot.

❼ Between Boulevard Agua Caliente and the border is the **Zona del Río** running parallel to the Tiá Juana riverbed. This zone, along Paseo de los Héroes, is quickly becoming Tijuana's most elegant area, thanks to its impressive Cultural Center and shopping complex. Large statues of historical figures dominate the *glorietas* (traffic circles) on Paseo de los Héroes, one of the city's main thoroughfares. A new pedestrian walkway runs from the San Ysidro border to Pueblo Amigo shopping center at the foot of Paseo de los Héroes.

❽ The **Cultural Center** was designed by architect Pedro Ramírez Vásquez, who also created Mexico City's famous Museum of Anthropology. The Mexican history exhibits at the Cultural Center are a perfect introduction for the thousands of visitors whose first taste of Mexico is at the border. One can wander past models of Maya and Aztec temples, Indian pueblos, and missions, and get a true sense of the scope of Mexico's land, people, and history. Some rotating exhibits focus on specific regions and cultures, others highlight the works of present-day artists. An important part of the center is the globe-shape Omnimax Theater, with a 180-degree screen inside. The film *El Pueblo del Sol* (People of the Sun) is a cinematic tour of Mexico. Guest artists appear at the Cultural Center regularly. The center's bookstore has an excellent selection on Mexican history, culture, and arts in both Spanish and English. *Paseo de los Héroes and Av. Independencia, tel. 668/4–1111. Open daily 9– 8:30. Admission to the Omnimax Theater is $4.50; the film is shown in English at 2 PM daily.*

❾ **Plaza Río Tijuana,** Tijuana's largest shopping complex, is next door to the Cultural Center on Paseo de los Héroes. It is enormous, with good restaurants, department stores, and hundreds of shops. The plaza has become a central square of sorts, where holiday fiestas are held. Smaller shopping centers are opening all along Paseo de los Héroes: Plaza Fiesta and Plaza de los Zapatos are two of the finest. This stretch of Paseo de los Héroes has been landscaped, and there are long, wide sidewalks leading from the shopping complex to the Cultural Center.

❿ **Playas de Tijuana,** at the oceanfront, is the next area slated for development. Now the area is a mix of modest and expensive neighborhoods and a few restaurants and hotels. The long, pleasant beaches are populated mostly by locals. The "Bullring
⓫ by the Sea," **Plaza de Toros Monumental** (tel. 668/4–2126), is at the northwest corner of the beach area, right by the border. Bullfights are held here from June to September on Sunday afternoons. Admission price varies, depending on the fame of the matador and where you sit.

Shopping

Tijuana has always been considered a bargain hunter's haven and is gradually producing more and more shopping centers and stores with high-quality Mexican arts and crafts. The traditional shopping strip is Avenida Revolución, between Calles 1a and 8a. The avenue is lined with shops and arcades displaying a wide range of crafts and curios including wool rugs, serapes, silver jewelry, stained glass lamps, tin mirrors, candelabras and trinkets, pottery dishes and planters, piñatas, paper flowers, leather goods, and wood and wicker furniture. Sellers yell to shoppers in the street, promising low prices. Bargaining is expected. **The Drug Store, Maxim's, Dorian's,** and **Sara's** have good selections of clothing and imported perfumes. **Tolan,** across from the Jai Alai Palace at Revolución 111, has an impressive variety of well-made crafts. **Guess, Eduardo's** (Av. Revolución 1105), and **Maya de México** (Av. Revolución 816) have nice sportswear and resort wear, as does **Ralph Lauren Polo** (Calle 7a). **La Gran Bota** on Avenida Revolución has great cowboy boots; **Espinosa,** with branches on Avenida Revolución and in the Cultural Center, has fine silver, brass, and gold jewelry. Liquor stores dot the avenue; shoppers also get good bargains on tequila, Kahlúa, and Mexican beers and wines.

The Revolución shopping area has spread down Calle 1a to the foot of the pedestrian walkway from the border. The shops in the Plaza Revolución, at the corner of Calle 1a and Avenida Revolución, have high-quality crafts. If you're spending a day shopping, it makes sense to begin at the **Mercado de Artesanías** arcades at the end of the pedestrian border-crossing walkway, gauging prices as you travel toward Avenida Revolución. The best bargains are often found closer to the border.

Plaza Río Tijuana, on Paseo de los Héroes in the Río area near the Cultural Center, is a major shopping center with department stores, specialty shops, and restaurants (*see* Exploring, above). **Plaza Patria** is on Boulevard Díaz Ordaz near the Country Club and Agua Caliente Racetrack; **Lamparas y Vitrales de Baja California,** Tijuana's best-known stained glass store, has an outlet here. **Plaza Fiesta** is located on Boulevard Agua Caliente across from Plaza Río Tijuana. Plaza Fiesta has a collection of well-stocked boutiques and shops selling jewelry and stained glass. Next door, the **Plaza de los Zapatos** houses over a dozen stores offering designer footwear imported from throughout the world; **La Herradura de Oro** sells fine hand-tooled saddles.

Sports

Bullfights Bullfights feature skilled matadors from throughout Mexico and Spain. They are held at **El Toreo de Tijuana,** on Agua Caliente, just outside downtown, Sunday afternoons and holidays. Bullfights are also staged June through September at the **Plaza de Toros Monumental** in the Playas Tijuana area. For ticket information call tel. 66/4–2126 or 66/7–8519.

Charreadas Amateur cowboy associations compete at one of several rings
(Mexican Rodeos) around town Sunday mornings; call tel. 668/4–2126 for information.

Golf The **Tijuana Country Club** (tel. 66/1–7855), on Avenida Agua Caliente, east of downtown, is open to guests at some hotels. It provides rental clubs, electric and hand carts, and caddies for its 18-hole course.

Horse and **Hipódromo de Agua Caliente** (Agua Caliente Racetrack) is
Greyhound Races where the horses race on weekends beginning at noon; greyhounds race nightly (except Tuesday) at 7:45. The new Jockey Club and restaurant—open to the public for $10—are quite lavish. In the Foreign Book area, gamblers can bet on races

taking place in California and shown at Caliente on TV monitors. *Blvd. Agua Caliente at Salinas, tel. 66/6–2002; in San Diego, 619/260–0060.*

Jai Alai This ancient Basque sport is played in **El Palacio Frontón**, the Jai Alai Palace, which is worth seeing even if you don't attend the games. *Av. Revolución and Calle 8a, tel. 66/2–3636. Admission: $2. Closed Thurs.*

Beaches

The **Playas Tijuana** (Tijuana beach area) is located south of town off the toll road, Ensenada Cuota. The area has been under development for years, but as yet there are no major hotels and few restaurants. The beaches are frequented primarily by locals.

Dining

There is no shortage of good eating in Tijuana, from taco stands to gourmet and Continental restaurants. The seafood is unbeatable; beef and pork are excellent, both grilled and marinated. Pheasant, quail, rabbit, and duck are popular in the more expensive places. Lobster and shrimp in the *Puerto Nuevo* style (grilled and served with beans, rice, and tortillas) are fixtures in restaurants modeled after those at the popular seaside fishing village of Puerto Nuevo, south of Rosarito. Some restaurants add a 15% service charge to the bill.

Category	Cost*
Expensive	over $15
Moderate	$10–$15
Inexpensive	under $10

**per person, excluding drinks, service, and sales tax (15%)*

Expensive **Alcazar del Río.** Nouvelle cuisine amid mirrors has hit Tijuana with this upscale, see-and-be-seen restaurant. Patrons are the city's success stories—the casually elegant, sophisticated elite. Everything considered to be exotic in Tijuana is here—smoked salmon with capers, Australian lamb, Serrano ham with sweet cantaloupe, cherries jubilee. The halibut with pine nuts is sublimely simple, and the wine list is excellent. *Paseo de los Héroes, tel. 668/4–2672. Reservations suggested. Jacket and tie suggested. AE, MC, V.*

Cilantro's. Wonderful regional Mexican dishes in a beautiful two-story restaurant. Dishes are described on the English menu—try Chiles Nogada, filled with meat and fruit and topped with pomegranate seeds, or the chicken in almond sauce. *Paseo Tijuana #213, tel. 668/2–8340. MC, V.*

Pedrín's. one of Tijuana best seafood restaurants overlooks the Jai Alai Palace from a second-story garden room. Meals include deep-fried fish appetizers, fish chowder, salad, entrée, and a sweet after-dinner drink of Kahlúa and cream. Recommended dishes include *rajas* shrimp, covered with melted cheese and green chilis, and grilled lobster. *Av. Revolución 1115, tel. 668/ 5–4052. AE, MC, V.*

Reno's. This long-established steak and seafood house is old-fashioned by current Tijuana standards, with leather booths, heavy carved-wood tables and chairs, candlelight, and formal service. The grilled steaks are gargantuan and superbly prepared. *Av. Revolución at Calle 8a, tel. 668/5–9210. Reservations accepted. Dress: casual, though jackets and ties are common. AE, DC, MC, V.*

Moderate **El Abajeño.** This classic Mexican restaurant in an old hacienda is tops for carne asada, tamales, and enchiladas, with hot, hot salsa. The dining room is colorfully decorated with murals and folk art, and the waiters are accommodating. Live mariachi music alternates with a piano bar. *Blvd. Sánchez Taboada and Av. Antonio Caso, tel. 668/4–2788. MC, V.*

La Langosta Loca (The Crazy Lobster). Grilled lobster, refried beans, rice, and tortillas are served here in a happy-go-lucky, anything-goes setting. *Av. Revolución 914, tel. 668/5–13. AE, DC, MC, V.*

La Leña. The sparkling clean white dining room faces an open kitchen where chefs grill such unusual beef dishes as *gaonera*, a tender filet of beef stuffed with cheese and guacamole. The waiters are extremely friendly, and the owner often visits with his guests, getting their opinions on the menu and offering free samples of tripe—a dish meant for those with strong stomachs. *Blvd. Agua Caliente 4560, tel. 668/6–2920. AE, MC, V.*

Margarita's Village. Those who love margaritas have their choice of 14 flavors at this restaurant, which also specializes in cabrito and other Mexican dishes. Singing waiters hold forth in the large indoor dining room and outdoor second-story patio overlooking Avenida Revolución. It's a good place for breakfast or to hang out when you're tired of shopping, and has a bountiful weekend buffet. *Av. Revolución at Calle 3a, tel. 668/5–7362. AE, DC, MC, V.*

Mr. Fish. Cosmopolitan Tijuana is not where you normally find the palapa (beach shack) seafood houses so popular at the coastal resorts. But three blocks from the Fiesta Americana is a 12-table palapa strung with fishing nets, and the ubiquitous mounted marlin on the wall. The corn chips and salsa are fresh, the fish soup is filled with chunks of bass and tomatoes, and the shrimp *al mojo de ajo* comes smothered in garlic, butter, and cilantro. If you like frogs' legs, you've got four styles to choose from. This is definitely the place to go for fish. *Bd. Agua Caliente 6000, tel. 668/6–3603. No reservations. Dress: casual. MC, V.*

Tía Juana Tilly's., Popular with tourists and locals looking for a bustling place to party and dine on generous portions of Mexican specialties, this is one of the few places where you can get *cochinita pibil*, a Yucatecan dish made of roast suckling pig, red onions, and bitter oranges, or the classically bitter and savory chicken mole. Breakfast is also served. (Part of the same chain is Tilly's Fifth Ave., catty-corner to the original.) *Av. Revolución at Calle 7a, tel. 668/5–6024. Reservations accepted. AE, DC, MC, V.*

Inexpensive **Bol Corona.** Its arches and porticos have made Bol Corona an Avenida Revolución landmark since 1934. The bar is a lively place with wide-screen TVs blasting sporting events. Traditional Mexican dishes, including more than a dozen types of burritos, enchiladas, and *chilaquiles* (corn tortillas simmered in chicken broth) are on the menu; breakfast is also served. *Av. Revolución 520, tel. 668/5–7940. No credit cards.*

Carnitas Uruapan. This is a large, noisy restaurant where the main attraction is *carnitas* (marinated pork) sold by the kilo and served with homemade tortillas, salsa, cilantro (coriander), guacamole, and onions. Patrons mingle at long wood tables in rustic surroundings, toasting each other with chilled beer. *Blvd. Díaz Ordaz 550, tel. 668/5–6181. No credit cards.*

Chiki Jai. A tiny Basque place, redolent of the blue cheese served on each table, Chiki Jai is renowned for squid served in its own ink and Basque-style chicken. *Av. Revolución 1042, tel. 668/5–4955. No credit cards. Dinner only.*

La Especial. Located at the foot of the stairs leading to an underground shopping arcade, this restaurant attracts diners in search of home-style Mexican cooking at low prices. There's nothing fancy about the seemingly endless basement room— which is never empty. *Av. Revolución 770, tel. 668/5–6654. No credit cards.*

Lodging

Tijuana's hotels are clustered downtown, along Avenida Revolución, near the Country Club on Boulevard Agua Caliente, and in the Río Tijuana area on Paseo de los Héroes. **International Marketing and Promotions** (7860 Mission Center Court, No. 202, San Diego, CA 92108, tel. 619/298–4105, 800/522–1516 in CA, 800/225–2786 in the U.S.) represents several tourism offices in Baja, makes hotel reservations at a large number of properties, and is a great source of information. **Pan American Hotels International** (P.O. Box 2776, Chula Vista, CA 92012, tel. 619/422–6918 or 800/678–7244) reserves rooms at a large number of properties throughout Baja. **Baja Lodging** (4659 Park Blvd., San Diego, CA 92116, tel. 619/491–0682) reserves rooms in hotels and small, more remote properties throughout Baja.

Category	Cost*
Very Expensive	over $100
Expensive	$50–$100
Moderate	$25–$50
Inexpensive	under $25

All prices are for a standard double room, excluding service charge and sales tax (15%).

Very Expensive **Fiesta Americana.** The two mirrored towers of this property are Tijuana's most ostentatious landmarks, a sign of prosperity and faith in the potential of this lucrative border town. The Fiesta Americana often hosts receptions and parties for Tijuana's elite, and many consider it the city's most glamorous place for a drink or meal. *Blvd. Agua Caliente 4558, tel. 668/1–7000; reservations in the U.S.: tel. 800/343–7821. 422 rooms. Facilities: nightclub, restaurant, health club, tennis courts, pool, travel agency. AE, DC, MC, V.*

Expensive **El Conquistador.** This was the first tourist hotel in Tijuana, close to the racetrack and country club. With a bit of imagination you could say the decor is colonial; the hotel wears its age well. Rooms are large and gloomy, but comfortable. *Blvd. Agua Caliente 7000, tel. 668/6–4801; reservations in the U.S.:*

tel. 619/295–7484. 110 rooms. Facilities: pool, restaurant, disco, sauna, cable TV. AE, MC, V.

Lucerna. This is one of the most charming hotels in Tijuana, with lovely gardens, a large swimming pool surrounded by palms, and comfortable rooms with soft mattresses and pretty tile baths. The hotel's travel agency is particularly helpful with planning trips farther into Mexico. *Blvd. Paseo de los Héroes and Av. Rodríguez, tel. 668/6–1000. 170 rooms, 9 suites. Facilities: pool, restaurant, coffee shop, nightclub, travel agency. AE, DC, V.*

Palacio Azteca. From the outside, this luxurious hotel looks like a bland cement tower. Inside, you'll find a pretty landscaped courtyard and shaded pool, and tastefully decorated pastel rooms. *Av. 16 de Septiembre 2, tel. 668/6–5401; reservations in the U.S.: tel. 903/386–5301. 90 rooms. Facilities: pool, rooftop restaurant, coffee shop, nightclub. AE, MC.*

Moderate **Caesar.** Downtown and noisy, the Caesar is famed for its long bar and for being the home of the Caesar salad. The restaurant is fair and the rooms somewhat run-down, but the hotel has character. *Av. Revolución 827, tel. 668/8–0550. 90 rooms. Facilities: restaurant, bar. AE, MC, V.*

Country Club Motor Hotel. This motel is close to the golf course and racetrack. *Av. Tapachula 1, tel. 668/6–2301. 100 rooms. Facilities: pool, sauna, restaurant, bar. MC, V.*

La Mesa Inn. This is a Best Western property, with nothing much to distinguish it other than reliability. *Blvd. Díaz Ordaz 50, tel. 668/1–6522. 125 rooms. Facilities: pool, coffee shop, bar. MC, V.*

La Villa de Zaragoza. This is a fairly new brown stucco motel with a good downtown location by the Jai Alai Palace, one block from Avenida Revolución. For its price, it has the best rooms downtown. *Av. Madero 1120, tel. 668/5–1832. 42 rooms. Facilities: restaurant, parking. MC, V.*

Inexpensive **CREA Youth Hostel.** The hostel is some distance from downtown, but set in a quiet, peaceful park and sports complex. The 20 beds are in same-sex dorms, and there is a cafeteria. *Av. Padre Kino, no phone. No credit cards.*

León. This downtown hotel just off Avenida Revolución is clean and in the middle of the action, and a bit less noisy than the other properties on the same street. *Calle 7a and Av. Revolución, tel. 668/5–6320. 40 rooms. No credit cards.*

Motel Cortéz. This is a small motel near the beach area. *Paseo de Playas Tijuana 226, tel. 668/0–6617. 51 rooms. Facilities: restaurant, bar. No credit cards.*

Motel La Joya. La Joya has no restaurant or bar, but the rooms are clean and it's near the racetrack. *Blvd. Díaz Ordaz 2900, tel. 668/9–1360. 50 rooms. No credit cards.*

The Arts and Nightlife

The **Tijuana Cultural Center** *(see* Exploring, above) frequently hosts dance and music troupes from throughout Mexico and Latin America. The **Omnimax Theater** (tel. 668/4–1111) has daily showings of *People of the Sun,* an overview of pre-Columbian Mexican history and culture.

Tijuana has toned down its "Sin City" image; much of the night action now takes place at **El Palacio Frontón** and the racetrack *(see* Sports, above). Several hotels, especially the **Lucerna** and

Fiesta Americana, feature live entertainment. Several new discos and clubs have made the Zona del Río a happening night spot. **Iguanas** (Pueblo Amigo, tel. 668/2–4967) is a beyond-hip setting for live music by the latest groups favored by the younger set. For total immersion in the flashy, high-tech disco scene try **OH! Laser Club** (Paseo de los Héroes 56, tel. 688/4–0267), **Heaven & Hell** (Paseo de los Héroes 10501, tel. 668/4–8484), and **Baby Rock** (1482 Diego Rivera, tel. 668/4–9438).

The best Revolución bars for disco dancing are **Club A** (Av. Revolución and Calle 4a, tel. 668/5–2081) and **Regine** (Av. Revolución 1000, tel. 668/2–2761). The **Odyssey** (Av. Revolución between Calles 2a and 3a, tel. 668/7–2477), a watering hole and disco, has a fifth-story terrace overlooking the action on Revolución.

4 Rosarito Beach

Introduction

Not long ago, Rosarito Beach (Playas de Rosarito) was a small seaside community with virtually no tourist trade. Part of the municipality of Tijuana, it was an overlooked suburb on the way to Ensenada. Rosarito now has 80,000 residents and is an important resort area undergoing massive development. Within the next decade Rosarito should gain municipality status, with a local government overseeing a rapidly growing population of Mexicans and transplanted Americans.

Juan Machado was Rosarito Beach's first developer. In 1827, the governor of Baja California granted him 407,000 acres of Baja's coastline, called El Rosario. Machado converted the crumbling Misión del Descanso, near Cantamar, into a rambling ranch. In 1920, 14,000 of those acres were sold to a group of investors headed by Los Angeles attorney Jacob Morris Danziger. Danziger began advertising "El Rosario Resort and Country Club" in California newspapers four years later. A man of generous imagination, he lured tourists with claims of good roads, fishing, camping, bathing, and picnic grounds. In reality, the area was primitive, with no roads to speak of, and no gas, oil, or other essential creature comforts.

Danziger rushed to complete his project as he eyed the competition, Tijuana's new Agua Caliente resort; his resort, he said, would be finished by 1926 and would include a casino, golf course, ballroom, and guest houses, all available through private membership in his Shore Acres Country Club. But when Danziger was hit with a series of lawsuits for back pay and other infractions, he eventually had to sell his shares in Shore Acres. At that point, the resort consisted of a 10-room hotel with one bathroom.

In the early 1930s, Manuel P. Barbachano bought the hotel and surrounding acreage. The '30s were an exciting time in northern Baja—gambling, horse racing, and a continuous flow of alcohol attracted thousands of glamorous Americans eager to escape the restrictions of Prohibition. The Agua Caliente Spa in Tijuana was completed; other investors built the huge Riviera del Pacífico hotel and gambling casino in Ensenada, and the Rosarito Beach Hotel began to grow. Barbachano was instrumental in getting electricity and telephone service for northern Baja. This further encouraged tourism, and smaller hotels and watering holes opened up along the rough road from Tijuana to Ensenada. The end of Prohibition in the United States and the outlawing of gambling in Mexico brought a halt to the weekly migration of Hollywood stars in search of liquor and fun. Before long, Agua Caliente and Riviera del Pacífico closed down. The Rosarito Beach Hotel, however, continued to grow.

Barbachano invested even more in his hotel, hiring a Belgian architect to design the spacious lobby, dining room, and bars. Mexican artist Matias Santoyo covered the lobby walls with intricate, colorful murals depicting Mexican history; another artist, whose name is now unknown, created an elaborate reproduction of the Maya calendar on goat skins affixed to the hallway walls with a tempura made of egg whites. The hotel continued to attract wealthy Americans, some of whom built vacation villas along the beach. As the roads improved, and particularly after completion of Baja's Transpeninsular Highway in 1973, Rosarito Beach boomed. Vacation suites were added along the beach, and timeshare and condo units were put up. As recently as 1980, the Rosarito Beach Hotel was still the only major resort in the area; a few smaller restaurants and hotels had cropped up outside town, but visitors still felt they had discovered an unknown paradise. This sense of solitude and privacy has now disappeared, and Rosarito Beach has become a major resort town.

The '80s brought an amazing building boom to Rosarito. The main street, alternately known as the Old Ensenada Highway and Boulevard Benito Juárez, is packed with restaurants, bars, and shops. The Quinta del Mar resort, with its high-rise condos, restaurants, and sprawling hotels, brought new life to the north end of town, where once there were only a few taco stands and clusters of horses for rent. With the 1987 completion of a major shopping center and convention center by the Quinta del Mar, Rosarito Beach hit the big time.

Still, it is a relaxing place to visit. Southern Californians have practically made Rosarito (and much of Baja Norte) a weekend beach suburb for surfers, swimmers, and sunbathers. The oceanfront seems much wilder and purer south of the border; for long stretches north and south of Rosarito, the coastal cliffs are free of houses and highways, and the watery horizon seems miles away. Whales pass not far from shore on their winter migration; dolphins and sea lions sun on rocky points in the water. Whether you travel the toll road (Ensenada Cuota) or the free road (Ensenada Libre, or the Old Ensenada Highway), the view is startling, soothing, and sensational, particularly on a clear day.

Rosarito Beach is the main stopping point on the way between Tijuana and Ensenada. The beach is one of the longest in northern Baja, an uninterrupted stretch of sand from the power plant at the far north end of town to below the Rosarito Beach Hotel, about 8 kilometers (5 miles) south. This stretch is perfect for horseback riding, jogging, and strolling. The road becomes Boulevard Juárez at the entrance to town; as Rosarito has grown, the main drag has become something of a sideshow, with hotels, restaurants, stores, taco stands, horse pastures, and open-air markets. Rosarito has always attracted a varied crowd. Today's visitors are no exception, an assemblage of prosperous young Californians building villas in vacation developments, retired Americans and Canadians homesteading in trailer parks, and travelers from all over the world. Some say the region has become "yuppified," but the members of the thriving tourism board seem happy. So do the visitors.

Hedonism and health get equal billing in Rosarito. One of the area's major draws is its seafood, especially lobster, shrimp, and abalone. Prohibition may have ended in the States, but many visiting Americans still act as if they've been dry for months—margaritas and beer are the favored thirst-quenchers. People throw off their inhibitions here (at least to the degree permitted by the local constables). A typical Rosarito day might begin with a breakfast of eggs, refried beans, and tortillas, followed by horseback riding on the beach. Lying in the sun or strolling through the shops takes care of midday. Siestas are imperative, and are usually followed by more shopping, strolling, or sunbathing before dinner and dancing and sleep after dinner. Rosarito's developers are trying to build enough hotel rooms to meet the demand; its restaurateurs have acted more quickly. There have to be at least 170 restaurants in the Rosarito area. Most have similar menus—seafood, steak, and Mexican basics—but each has its own style of cooking, clientele, and ambience.

Essential Information

Important Addresses and Numbers

Tourist Information The tourist information office (tel. 661/2–0396 or 661/2–0200) is on Boulevard Juárez, south of La Quinta del Mar Hotel. The office has brochures from several hotels and restaurants and copies of the *Baja Times*, a handy tourist-oriented, English-language newspaper. The staff speaks English and is extremely helpful.

Emergencies **Police** (tel. 134); **Fire** (tel. 136); **Red Cross** (tel. 132).

Arriving and Departing by Car and Bus

Rosarito Beach is 29 kilometers (18 miles) south of Tijuana on the Pacific coast. There is no airport, but **Tres Estrellas de Oro** (tel. 668/8–9186 in Tijuana) has service between Tijuana and Ensenada, stopping at the bus terminal in Rosarito on Boulevard Juárez across from the Rosarito Beach Hotel.

The easiest way to get to Rosarito Beach is to drive. Once you cross the border, follow the signs for Ensenada Cuota, the toll road running south along the coast. Take the Rosarito exit, which leads to what is alternately called the Old Ensenada Highway or Ensenada Libre, and Boulevard Juárez in Rosarito.

Getting Around

Most of Rosarito proper can be explored on foot, particularly on weekends, when Boulevard Juárez has bumper-to-bumper traffic. To reach Puerto Nuevo and points south, continue on Boulevard Juárez through town and head south. There are very few roads leading off the old highway. Taxis travel the stretch regularly, and buses from Tijuana and Ensenada stop across the street from the Rosarito Beach Hotel; if you wish to stop at other beach areas along the way, take a local rather than an express bus.

Exploring

Rosarito Beach has no historic or cultural monuments. Beaches and bars are its main attractions. Sightseeing consists of strolling along the 8-kilometer (5-mile) beach or Boulevard Juárez, the main drag and just about the only paved road in town. An immense PEMEX (gasoline) installation and electric plant anchor the northern end of Boulevard Juárez, which then runs along a collection of taco stands, a huge Tecate beer agency, a baseball field, and some pottery yards. The eight-story **La Quinta del Mar** hotel is the first major landmark, followed by the **Quinta Plaza** shopping center and the **Centro de Convenciones.** The plaza contains a car wash, pharmacy, bakery, specialty shops, restaurants, and the 1,000-seat convention center. Across the street is the **San Fernando Shopping Center.** The **tourism office** is in front of the shopping center.

Rodríguez Park, on the beach at the end of Calle Rene Ortíz about midway between Quinta del Mar and Rosarito Beach hotels, has barbecue pits, picnic tables, and a nice lawn. Tourists and locals congregate here on weekends.

Time Out The long glassed-in bar that sits on a little hill between the pool and the beach at the **Rosarito Beach Hotel** (tel. 661/2–1106) is the best place to absorb the hotel's ambience. To one side, you'll have a view of the tile roof, white adobe balconies, and a flowered courtyard around the pool; to the other, the horseback riders, sunbathers, and ocean. The margaritas are a potent reminder that you're in Mexico, and the nachos are fairly good. Have Sunday brunch ($10) in the dining room, overlooking the pool.

Off the Beaten Track

The most popular side trip from Rosarito Beach, if you go by sheer numbers, is **Puerto Nuevo** (Newport) at Km. 44 on the old highway. A few years ago, the only way to know you'd reached this fishing community was by the huge painting of a 7-Up bottle on the side of a building. You'd drive down the rutted dirt road to a row of restaurants—some just a big room in front of a family's kitchen—where you were served the classic Newport meal: grilled lobster, refried beans, rice, homemade tortillas, butter, salsa, and lime. The meal became a legend, and now it's served at about 30 restaurants on quaint brick-paved lanes on the top of a cliff. **Ortega's** has the most offshoots, with at least four restaurants in the village bearing its name, and another elegant one in Rosarito. Some restaurants have tablecloths, big glass windows, and a view of the water, but they're not typical of the Puerto Nuevo experience. Try one of the family-run places, like **Ponderosa** (*see* Dining, below). Newport is packed on weekends, and now there are Newport T-shirts for sale at a cluster of souvenir shops that seem to constantly grow in size, if not in selection.

Most other sightseeing involves driving down the coast and stopping off at an empty beach. The **Plaza del Mar** (tel. 688/5–9158), at Km. 58 on the Old Ensenada Highway, is a hotel and trailer park with an archaeological garden adorned with replicas of pre-Columbian pyramids and an exhibit of stone art, open to the public. To admire the view, stop for a coffee or beer at **La Fonda, Popotla, Calafia,** or **Bajamar,** all on the road to Ensenada. The **Halfway House** is popular with hang gliders who fly off the high sand dunes nearby, over the scores of dune buggies. At busy times there is at least one car parked at nearly every clifftop clearing while its passengers enjoy the view.

Shopping

The two major resort hotels have shopping arcades with pharmacies, clothing shops, and some good crafts stores. The **Calimax** grocery store on Boulevard Juárez is a good place to stock up on necessities.

The souvenir selection is pretty lackluster, although there is an occasional surprise. The shopping arcade near La Quinta del Mar Hotel has many worthwhile shops. **La Casa del Arte** has wicker and willow furniture, large woven rugs, and hand-carved antique furniture. **Tienda González** carries nice wool serapes (shawls) and rugs. **Muebles Rangel** sells carpeting and wicker furniture; **Oradia Imports** specializes in French perfumes. **Taxco Curios** has a good selection of silver jewelry, and the last shop in the arcade, **Interiores los Ríos,** has exquisite custom furniture, Michoacán pottery, and a selection of delightful ceramic "Tree of Life" candelabras.

Farther south on Boulevard Juárez, midway between the La Quinta and Rosarito Beach hotels, is **Mexicana Viejo y Nuevo,** a shop with museum-quality handcrafts and carved wooden furniture. The nearby **Touch Boutique** has willow chairs with leather trim and some unusual tableware.

Closer to the Rosarito Beach Hotel, still on Boulevard Juárez, is the **Panificadora Bohemia,** a bakery with excellent *bolillos* (hard rolls). **Nuevo Mexico Jewelry** has original designs in silver jewelry and also makes pieces to order. At **Casas Torres,** in the arcade of the Rosarito Beach Hotel, you can purchase fine French perfumes for about one-third less than in the United States.

Just south of town on the Old Ensenada Highway are three large pottery yards—**Maya, Cielito Lindo,** and **Los Hermanos**—all with rows and rows of clay pots, fountains, and fireplaces. Puerto Nuevo has a few good curio shops with silk-screened T-shirts, shell art, and hanging papier-mâché birds and animals.

Sports

Fishing
There is a small fishing pier at Km. 33 on the Old Ensenada Highway; surfcasting is allowed on the beach. You cannot get fishing licenses in Rosarito, but tourism officials say they are not necessary if you fish from shore.

Fitness
The Rosarito Beach Hotel has a new gym open to the public, with racquetball courts, a sauna, and some exercise equipment.

Hang Gliding
An area of large sand dunes just south of Cantamar, at Km. 54 on the Old Ensenada Highway, is a popular spot for hang gliders from California. Informal classes are sometimes held.

Horseback Riding
Horses can be rented next to **Ortega's** on the north end of Boulevard Juárez and on the beach in the early morning. Check the horses carefully; some are pathetically thin. Rates average $4 per half hour.

Surfing
The waves are particularly good at **Popotla,** Km. 33; **Calafia,** Km. 35.5; and **Costa Baja,** Km. 36 on the Old Ensenada Highway.

Spectator Sports

Charreadas
(Mexican Rodeos)
Charreadas are held on summer Sundays at the **Lienzo Tapatío Charro Ring** south of town and at the new **Ejido Mazatlán Charro Ring** on the east side of the toll road. Call 661/84–2126 for dates and times.

Beaches

Rosarito has beautiful beaches, with long sandy stretches for walking, running, and horseback riding, and good waves for swimming and bodysurfing. On weekends, vendors sell crafts and drinks along the sand.

Dining

There may be a shortage of hotel rooms in Rosarito, but the restaurants are abundant. New places open constantly, and though the competition is heavy, nearly all of them have the same items—lobster, shrimp, fresh fish, and steak—at nearly the same prices. Lobster dinners cost about $15; shrimp or steak, $10. The restaurants compete more heavily with their drink prices; many offer free margaritas or a bottle of wine with dinner. Some tack a 15% service charge onto your bill.

Highly recommended restaurants in each price category are indicated by a star ★.

Category	Cost*
Expensive	over $15
Moderate	$10–$15
Inexpensive	under $10

*per person, excluding drinks, service, and sales tax (15%)

Expensive **Dragon del Mar.** This elegant Chinese restaurant is decorated
★ with furniture and paintings imported from China. A miniature waterfall greets guests in the marble foyer and a pianist plays relaxing music. Partitioned with moveable, carved wooden panels, the expansive dining room still creates an intimate dining experience. The food is exquisitely prepared, appealing to the eye as well as the palate. *Blvd. Juárez 20, tel. 661/2–0604. Reservations accepted. Dress: casual. AE, MC, V.*

La Fachada. A quiet place by Rosarito standards, La Fachada is preferred by more subdued diners. The food is good, and the atmosphere is authentic Mexican. At night a guitarist and pianist perform soothing ballads. *Blvd. Juárez 2884, tel. 661/2–1785.*

★ **La Leña.** The cornerstone restaurant of the Quinta Plaza shopping center, La Leña sits on a rise high enough for you to see the ocean from the window tables. La Leña specializes in beef grilled in full view of the diners. The dining room is spacious, and tables are spread far enough apart for privacy. Try any of the beef dishes, especially the tender *carne asada* (grilled steak). *Quinta Plaza, tel. 661/2–0826. Reservations accepted. MC, V.*

La Masia. This is the beach's most elegant restaurant, near the high-rise Quinta del Mar hotel. It's heavy on flaming torches and Polynesian decor, with Continental cuisine. *Quinta del Mar Hotel, Blvd. Juárez 25500, tel. 661/2–1300. AE, MC, V.*

La Misión. A lovely, quiet restaurant, La Misión has white adobe walls, carved wood statues, and high beamed ceilings. Gourmet seafood dishes and steaks are the specialties. La Misión has patio dining in its enclosed courtyard. *Blvd. Juárez 182, tel. 661/2–0202. MC, V.*

Los Pelícanos. One of the few restaurants on the beach, Los Pelícanos has huge windows, a great view, a casual bar overlooking the beach, and a hotel next door with balconies. Lobster is served with vegetables and baked potato rather than rice and beans. Palapas are available for dining and drinking in the summer. *At the end of Calle Ebano, tel. 661/2–1757. MC, V.*

Moderate **El Nido.** A dark, woodsy restaurant with leather booths, this is one of the oldest eateries in Rosarito. Those who are unimpressed with the newer, fancier establishments love it. Steaks are grilled over mesquite wood, and the large central fireplace is a cozy touch. Breakfast is also served. *Blvd. Juárez 67, tel. 661/2–1430. Reservations accepted. MC, V.*

El Oasis. Traditional homemade Mexican food, steaks, and seafood are served here. A bar and rock music for dancing are upstairs. It is open until 2 AM. *Blvd. Juárez 4358, tel. 661/2–1942. MC, V.*

El Rancho Restaurant and Bar. This is a large, airy place popular for its traditional Mexican food and great breakfasts. It offers patio dining and *folklórico* dancing on weekend afternoons. *Blvd. Juárez 255, tel. 661/2–1717. MC, V.*

La Flor de Michoacán. *Carnitas* (marinated pork) roasted over an open pit, Michoacán-style, is the house specialty, served with homemade tortillas, guacamole, and salsa. The tacos, *tortas* (sandwiches made on long, soft rolls), and tostadas are great, and the surroundings are simple but clean. Take-out is available. *Blvd. Juárez 146, no phone. No credit cards.*

Las Cazuelas del Mar. This family restaurant across from Quinta del Mar serves fresh seafood, traditional Mexican dishes, and handmade tortillas. The food is average, but the prices are lower than usual. Upstairs is an authentic Mexican nightclub. *Blvd. Juárez 77, no phone. No credit cards. Closed Tues.*

★ **Las Olas.** Upstairs, this restaurant and bar are worth finding. Specialties are served with a second story view of main street. Live music for dancing on weekends. *Blvd. Juárez 298, no phone. No credit cards. Closed Tues.*

Ortega's. A member of the Ortega's chain of lobster houses, this restaurant has a more varied menu. Lobster is served with beans, rice, and tortillas. The lavish Sunday brunch costs about $8. *Blvd. Juárez 200, tel. 661/2–0022. MC, V.*

★ **René's.** One of the oldest restaurants in Rosarito, René's has been operating since 1924. Specialties include *chorizo* (Mexican sausage), quail, frogs' legs, and lobster. It also boasts an ocean view from the dining room, a lively bar, and mariachi music. *Blvd. Juárez, tel. 661/2–1020. MC, V.*

Vince's Lobster Trap. This seafood restaurant, fish market, and deli is popular with expatriate Americans, who swear Vince's has the best lobster in town. *Blvd. Juárez 39, tel. 661/2–1253. No credit cards.*

Inexpensive **Azteca.** The enormous dining room at the Rosarito Beach Hotel has a view of the pool and beach area. Visitors come to the hotel regularly just for the lavish Sunday brunch, where margaritas are the drink of choice. Both Mexican and American dishes are offered, and the portions make up for the erratic quality of the food. *Rosarito Beach Hotel, Blvd. Juárez, tel. 661/2–1106. Reservations accepted. MC, V.*

Carnitas el Cachanilla. As the name implies, the specialty here is carnitas. The *menudo* (tripe soup) is also great. *Km 20 Old Ensenada Hwy., tel. 661/2–0250. No credit cards.*

Juice 'n Juice. Rosarito's health-food restaurant is a no-frills lunch counter with lots of salads, juices, yogurt, and granola. But you can also order burgers and fries. *Blvd. Juárez 14, tel. 661/2–0338. No credit cards.*

Los Arcos. Next to the Rosarito Beach Hotel, this café serves home-style Mexican food and offers open-air dining in the summer. *Blvd. Juárez 29, tel. 661/2–0491. No reservations. Dress: casual. No credit cards.*

South of Rosarito Beach

Expensive   **Calafia.** This elegant cliff-top restaurant serves up a terrific ocean view with its food. You can dine indoors or sit outside at the tables that perch on terraces down the side of the cliff. Dance floors inside and at the bottom of the cliff are ideal for open-air dancing. *Km 35.5 Old Ensenada Hwy., tel. 661/2–1581. AE, MC, V.*

La Fonda. At this popular restaurant you can sit on an outdoor patio overlooking the beach and sip potent margaritas served with greasy nachos and hot salsa. Fresh lobster, grilled steaks, and traditional Mexican dishes are accompanied by delicious black bean soup. The bar is usually crowded and the patrons boisterous. *Km 59 Old Ensenada Hwy., no phone. MC, V.*

Moderate   **Baja del Sol.** This restaurant and bar has a small area for dancing overlooking the pool. There is live music on weekends. *Km 26.8 Old Ensenada Hwy., tel. 661/2–1350. No credit cards.*

Puerto Nuevo (Newport). Newport is a village of 25–30 restaurants that serve the same dishes—grilled lobster and shrimp, Spanish rice, refried beans, and homemade tortillas with melted butter, lime, and hot sauce. Some places have full bars, others serve only wine and beer. The atmosphere ranges from totally rowdy to family-style, aided by roaming mariachi bands, curio and flower sellers, and photographers. **Ortega's**, which has three branches in Newport and one in Rosarito, is the most crowded; **Ponderosa** is smaller and quieter and run by a gracious family; **Costa Brava** is newer and more elegant, with tablecloths and an ocean view. Lobsters in most places are priced as small, medium, and large—medium is about $10. *Km 44 Old Ensenada Hwy., no phone. Most places are open for lunch and dinner. Some take credit cards.*

Restaurant/Bar Popotla. Breakfast or Sunday champagne brunch on a clear morning is beautiful here, with a lovely ocean view. Dinner includes a sumptuous shrimp-stuffed trout and good Spanish flan. On winter evenings it's fun to sit by the sunken fireplace in the dining room. *Km 33 Old Ensenada Hwy., tel. 661/2–1504. MC, V.*

Lodging

Though Rosarito is in the midst of a resort building boom, there is still a room shortage (at press time there were less than 1,000 rooms). Reservations are a must on holiday weekends. Many hotels require a minimum two-night stay for a confirmed reservation, and inexpensive rooms are hard to find. Many hotels offer reduced rates on weekdays.

Highly recommended lodgings in each price category are indicated by a star ★.

Category	Cost*
Expensive	over $45
Moderate	$35–$45
Inexpensive	under $35

All prices are for standard double rooms, excluding service charge and sales tax (15%).

Expensive **Quinta del Mar.** This large resort complex has three types of accommodations: moderately priced rooms, very expensive town houses near the beach, and high-rise condominiums with ocean views (by far the best). Guest quarters in the hotel are in need of renovation. The resort complex includes rooms with and without TV, and the condominium building has a rooftop hot tub and tennis court. *Blvd. Juárez 25500, tel. 661/2–1145; reservations in the U.S.: Box 4243, San Ysidro, CA 92073, tel. 800/228–7003. Facilities: beach access; pool; tennis, basketball, and volleyball courts; restaurants and bars; children's playground; whirlpool; steam baths; and beauty shop. AE, MC, V.*

★ **Rosarito Beach Hotel.** Dating to the Prohibition era, this resort is beginning to show its age, but it's still a charmer, with huge ballrooms, tiled public rest rooms, and a glassed-in pool deck overlooking a long beach. Rooms and suites in the low-rise buildings that face the beach are not nearly as enchanting as those in the old resort building, but they are more comfortable. The hotel has a good restaurant with a lavish Sunday brunch and powerful margaritas. *Blvd. Juárez at the south end of town, tel. 661/2–1106; reservations in the U.S.: Box 145, San Ysidro, CA 92073. 70 rooms, 80 suites. Facilities: beach, pool, tennis courts, health club, bar, restaurant. MC, V.*

Moderate **Los Pelicanos Hotel.** Completed in 1990, this beachfront hotel's prices vary depending on location of rooms and whether they have a balcony with an ocean view. All rooms have access to the beach. *At the end of Calle Ebano, tel. 661/2–0445; U.S. mailing address: Box 3871, San Ysidro, CA 92073. 39 rooms. Facilities: restaurant, bar, MC, V.*

Motel Quinta Chica. This modern motel at the south end of town has little character but comfortable beds. Rooms in the back are quieter. *Km 26.8 Old Ensenada Hwy, no phone; reservations in the U.S.: tel. 800/228–7003. 90 rooms. Facilities: restaurant and bar across the street. MC, V.*

Inexpensive **Motel Baja Village.** Completed in 1989, this motel is on the main boulevard. Rooms are carpeted and some have color TV. Restaurants, stores and the beach are all within walking distance. *Blvd. Juárez 228 at Via Las Olas, tel. 661/2–0050; U.S. mailing address: Box 309, San Ysidro, CA 92073. MC, V.*

Motel Don Luís. A two-story motel near the entrance to town, it offers rooms, suites, and apartments. *Blvd. Juárez, tel. 661/2–1166. 31 rooms. Facilities: restaurant, pool, bar. MC, V.*

South of Rosarito

Expensive **Hotel New Port Baja.** Within walking distance of the lobster restaurants at Puerto Nuevo, this large hotel sprawls over a clifftop in a horseshoe shape that gives most rooms a great view. Rooms do not have air-conditioning, and the noise from the pool area can be annoying when your windows are open.

The patio restaurant is quite good. *Km. 45 Old Ensenada Hwy., tel. 661/4–1166. 147 rooms. Facilities: pool, restaurant, meeting rooms. MC, V.*

Las Rocas. An elegant addition to this strip of older hotels perched on cliffs above the ocean. At night, the glass-roofed atrium lobby glows against the black sky. Inside, plants hang from balcony flower-boxes three floors up, and guests sip coffee or wine while overlooking the pool and sea. The pale-pink and sea-green rooms have coffee makers and microwave ovens; some have hot tubs and oceanfront balconies. The pool and Jacuzzi seem to spill over the cliffs into the surf. *Km. 37 Old Ensenada Hwy., tel. 661/2–0653. 34 rooms. Facilities: pool, Jacuzzi, restaurant, bar. No credit cards.*

Plaza del Mar. This hotel, spa, and oceanfront resort is set behind an archaeological garden, which is open to the public. The garden's Aztec and Maya ruins are brightly painted (yellow and orange) replicas of the faded and overgrown originals. Accommodations are in long, quonset hut–like buildings clustered around courtyards. *Km 58 Old Ensenada Hwy., ⅗ km. (1 mile) north off the La Misión exit from the toll road, tel. 661/5–9152; reservations in the U.S.: Box 4520, San Ysidro, CA 92073. 180 rooms. Facilities: pool, hot tub, tennis courts, shuffleboard, restaurant, bar. MC, V.*

Moderate **La Fonda.** A longtime favorite with beach-goers, La Fonda has
★ a few older rooms, decorated with carved wood furniture and folk art, with great views of the ocean. The restaurant and bar are immensely popular. If you plan on getting any sleep, ask for a room as far away from the bar as possible. *Km 59 Old Ensenada Hwy., no phone; reservations in the U.S.: Box 268, San Ysidro, CA 92073. 18 rooms. Facilities: beach, restaurant, bar. MC, V.*

Nightlife

The many restaurants in Rosarito Beach keep customers entertained with live music, piano bars, and *folklórico* (folk music and dance) shows; the bar scene is also active. Drinking-and-driving laws are strict—the police will fine you no matter how little you've had. If you plan to drink, take a cab, or assign a driver who won't drink.

Bar La Quinta (Quinta del Mar Hotel, Blvd. Juárez, tel. 661/2–0016) has live music Wednesday through Sunday nights, recorded disco music other nights, and a large dance floor. **Beachcomber Bar and Salón Mexicano** (Rosarito Beach Hotel, Blvd. Juárez, tel. 661/ 2–1106) overlooks the ocean and has live piano music. The cavernous disco has a live band and dancing. **Calafia** (Km. 35.5 Old Ensenada Hwy., tel. 661/2–1581) offers live music and dancing Friday through Sunday afternoons and evenings, with a great view of the ocean. **El Torito** (Blvd. Juárez 318, no phone) has live music for dancing on weekends until 2 AM. **Rosarito Vice** (Blvd. Juárez 4358, tel. 661/2–1942) has rock music, a rowdy atmosphere, and a second-story dance floor. For those who prefer a more subdued ambience, **Las Olas** (Blvd. Juárez 298, upstairs) has tropical music for weekend dancing. **René's** (Blvd. Juárez south of town, tel. 661/2–1061) is a rowdy place with a live dance band, mariachis, and widescreen satellite TV.

5 Ensenada

Introduction

Ensenada is a major port city 104 kilometers (65 miles) south of Tijuana on Bahía de Todos Santos. The paved Transpeninsular Highway (Mexico Highway 1) between the two cities often cuts a path between low mountains and high oceanside cliffs; exits lead to rural roads, campgrounds on the ocean, and an ever-increasing number of resort communities. The Coronado Islands can be clearly seen off the coast, and below Rosarito Beach hang gliders lift off from towering sand dunes. Californians often weekend along this coastline, in clusters of trailer parks, condominium complexes, and housing developments that spring up like mushrooms. Still, much of the coastline is wild and undeveloped.

The small fishing communities of San Miguel and El Sauzal are off the highway just north of Ensenada. The smell of fish from the canneries lining the highway can be overpowering at times. The strip of beaches between San Miguel and Ensenada has long been the domain of moderately priced oceanfront motels and trailer parks, but there are a few luxury hotels under construction now.

Although Ensenada has grown incredibly since 1984, it remains charming and picturesque. Juan Rodríguez Cabrillo first discovered Ensenada, which means "inlet" in Spanish, in 1542. Sebastián Vizcaíno named the region Ensenada–Bahía de Todos Santos (All Saints' Bay) in 1602. Since then, Ensenada has drawn discoverers and developers. First, ranchers made their homes on large tracts along the coast and up into the mountains. Gold miners followed, turning the area into a boomtown during the late 1800s. After the mines were depleted, the area settled back into its pastoral ways. The harbor gradually became a major port for shipping agricultural goods from the surrounding ranches and farms. Now it is one of Mexico's largest seaports and has a thriving fishing fleet and fish-processing industry.

Ensenada is a popular weekend destination for southern Californians. There are no beaches in Ensenada proper, but beaches north and south of town are good for swimming, sunning, surfing, and camping. During the week, Ensenada is just a normal, relatively calm port city with a population of about 150,000. On weekends it turns into a real party town, when the young, rowdy crowd spreads from the *cantinas* into the streets. Many of the hotels have strict rules about having guests and/or alcoholic beverages in the rooms. One look at the crowd and you can understand why. Be sure to ask for a room far from the hotel's entrance if you're planning on sleeping rather than partying.

For decades tourism has seemed incidental to Ensenada's economy. Most hotels and bars have catered to groups of young people intent on drinking and carousing. But now there is a concerted effort to attract conventioneers and business travelers. A group of civic boosters is developing a major convention center near the Riviera del Pacífico, the grand old gambling hall turned civic center that is Ensenada's most stately edifice. The waterfront area has been razed and rebuilt, and elegant restaurants and a new hotel and marina complex are replacing taco stands. Cruise ships anchor regularly offshore, releasing hundreds of passengers eager to drink, dine, and shop.

Ensenada's first full-scale, members-only resort is at Punta Banda, 29 kilometers (18 miles) south of town. The **Baja Beach and Tennis Club** was built on the ruins of another resort that was started in the 1960s, when it was rumored that gambling would again become legal in Baja. The rumors were false, and for 20 years the shell of a grand casino sat half-buried by sand on a desolate point. Now developers have poured close to $15 million into a marina with cabanas and a large health club.

Ensenada is the last major city for hundreds of miles on Mexico Highway 1. The drive from there to Guerrero Negro, on the border between Baja Norte and Baja Sur, is a solitary one, except during holidays. Highway 1 goes past small farming communities, huge ranches, and miles of uninterrupted chaparral. The Valle de Santo Tomás, which has the oldest vineyards in Baja, is about 15 minutes south of Maneadero on Highway 1. A rough dirt road leads west off the highway to **Puerto Santo Tomás** on the coast and some private campgrounds. Bradley's gas station near Colonet is famous for its antique glass reservoir pump. Less than 10 kilometers (6 miles) south is the turnoff for the **San Pedro Mártir National Park and Observatory**, nearly 80 kilometers (50 miles) east on a rough, rutted dirt road. Mike's Sky Ranch and the Meling Guest ranch, two isolated lodges, are located along this road.

San Quintín, 115 kilometers (72 miles) south of Ensenada, is a busy farm town said to be the windiest spot in Baja. Fishing and hunting are good, and the pismo clams found in abundance on the beaches are a tasty treat. The highway south runs through canyons, dry riverbeds, and desert filled with towering boulders and over 800 varieties of cactus. **Cataviña** has a gas station and a few small hotels. Farther south are turnoffs for a paved road to **San Felipe** and another paved road to **Bahía de Los Angeles.** At the end of Baja Norte, 255 kilometers (159 miles) from Ensenada, stands a steel monument in the form of an eagle, 138 feet high. It marks the border between the states of Baja Norte and Baja Sur. The change from Pacific to Mountain time occurs as you cross the 28th parallel. Guerrero Negro, Baja Sur's northernmost town, with hotels and gas stations, is two kilometers (1¼ miles) south. The area is most popular in the winter, when thousands of California gray whales migrate to the lagoons to birth their calves.

Essential Information

Important Addresses and Numbers

The **State Tourist Commission** office (Av. López Mateos 1305, tel. 667/6–2222; open weekdays 9–7, Sat. 9–1, and Sun. 10–1) is near the hotels. The **Convention and Visitors Bureau** (corner of Avs. López Mateos and Espinoza, tel. 667/8–2411) has a small stand with pamphlets and brochures on Boulevard Costera at the waterfront.

Emergencies **Police** (Calle Ortíz Rubio and Av. Libertad, tel. 667/9–1751); **Hospital** (Av. Ruíz and Calle 11a, tel. 667/8–2525); **Red Cross** (tel. 667/8–1212).

Air Evac International (tel. 619/425–4400) is a San Diego–based air ambulance service that travels into Mexico to bring injured tourists back to the United States.

Arriving and Departing by Plane

Airport and Airlines Ensenada has only a small airstrip, **Aeropuerto el Ciprés** (tel. 667/6–6301), for private planes. Most people who visit Ensenada drive. Tourist cards are required only if you are traveling south of Ensenada or staying longer than 72 hours.

Arriving and Departing by Bus, Ship, and Car

By Bus Ensenada can be reached by bus from Tijuana, Mexicali, and Mexico City. **Autotransportes de Baja California** and **Tres Estrellas de Oro** travel throughout Baja, linking all the major cities. The bus station (tel. 667/8–2322) is at Avenida Riveroll between Calles 10a and 11a.

By Ship Ensenada is a year-round port of call for **Carnival Cruise Lines** (tel. 800/232–4666), which sails from Los Angeles twice each week. The **Crown Cruise Lines** ship *Viking Princess* (tel. 800/421–0522) has one-day cruises from San Diego several times a week and some overnight trips; the **Ensenada Express** (tel. 619/232–2109) has day trips to Ensenada from San Diego.

By Car Highway 1, called Ensenada Cuota, is a toll road that runs along the coast from the Tijuana border to Ensenada. The toll booths along the road accept U.S. and Mexican currency; tolls are usually about $2.00. The road is excellent, though it has some hair-raising curves atop the cliffs and is best driven in daylight. The free road, called the Old Ensenada Highway or Ensenada Libre, sometimes runs parallel to the toll road, cutting east of the low hills along the coast. Although free, this road doubles the travel time and is very rough in spots.

Getting Around

Most of Ensenada's attractions are situated within five blocks of the waterfront; it is easy to take a long walking tour of the city. A car is necessary, though, for reaching La Bufadora, the Chapultepec Hills, and most of the beaches. Buses travel the route from Ensenada through Guerrero Negro at the border between Baja Norte and Baja Sur and on down to the southernmost tip of Baja. Addresses can be confusing within the city, particularly along the waterfront, where the road is called Boulevard Costera, Avenida Lázaro Cárdenas, Alternate Highway 1, and Carretera Transpeninsular.

By Bus The main bus station (tel. 667/8–2322) is at Avenida Riveroll between Calles 10a and 11a; **Tres Estrellas de Oro** and **Autotransportes de Baja California** cover the entire Baja route and connect in Mexicali with buses to Guadalajara and Mexico City.

By Taxi There is a sitio (central taxi stand) on Avenida López Mateos by the Bahía Hotel (tel. 667/8–3475). Destinations within the city should cost less than $5.

By Car Ensenada is an easy city to navigate; most streets are marked. If you are traveling south, you can bypass downtown Ensenada on the Highway 1 truck route down Calle 10a. To reach the hotel and waterfront area, stay with Alternate Highway 1 as it hugs the fishing pier and becomes Boulevard Costera, also known as Boulevard Lázaro Cárdenas. Cárdenas ends at Calle Agustín Sangines, also known as Calle Delante, which leads out to Highway 1 traveling south. Highway 3 to Ojos Negros and San Felipe on the south and Guadalupe and Tecate on the north intersects Highway 1 at the north and south ends of the city. The parking meters along Ensenada's main streets are patrolled regularly; parking tickets come in the form of a boot on the car's tires, or license plates being confiscated. Carry some one- and five-peso coins for the meters.

Car Rentals **Ensenada Rent-a-Car** (tel. 667/8–1896) has an office on Avenida Alvarado between Boulevard Lázaro Cárdenas and Avenida López Mateos.

Guided Tours

Baja California Tours (6986 La Jolla Blvd., #204, La Jolla, CA 92037, tel. 619/454–7166) offers comfortable, informative bus trips through all of Baja, and can arrange special-interest tours. Vans depart daily from San Diego to Ensenada; midweek transportation and hotel packages are a real bargain. **Las Bodegas de Santo Tomás** (666 Av. Miramar, tel. 667/ 8–3333), Baja's oldest winery, offers tours and tastings daily at 11 AM and 1 PM. Group tours should be arranged in advance. **Viajes Guaycura** (Av. López Mateos 1089, tel. 667/8–3718) offers half-day bus tours of Ensenada and the surrounding countryside.

Exploring

Numbers in the margin correspond with points of interest on the Ensenada map.

❶ The city of Ensenada, the third largest in Baja, hugs the harbor of **Bahía de Todos Santos**. If you have a car, begin your tour of Ensenada by driving north up Calle 2a or east on the Highway
❷ 1 bypass around town into the Chapultepec Hills to **El Mirador** (The Lookout). From here one can see the entire Bahía de Todos Santos, from the canneries of San Miguel south to Punta Banda and La Bufadora. The city of Ensenada spreads for miles under the hills. By checking the scenery against a map you can figure out how to get anywhere. Behind El Mirador the hills rise even higher, providing breathtaking views from the palatial homes of Ensenada's wealthier residents.

To tour Ensenada's waterfront and downtown, you're better off on foot. As Highway 1 leads into town from the north it becomes Boulevard Costera, running past shipyards filled with massive freighters. To the right, by the water, a new shopping-and-dining complex is under construction. A long sidewalk runs along the waterfront from this point. At the northern-
❸ most point sits an indoor/outdoor **fish market:** Row after row of counters display giant shrimp as well as fresh tuna, dorado, marlin, snapper, and dozens more species of fish caught off Ensenada's coast. Outside, there are stands selling grilled or smoked fish, seafood cocktails, and fish tacos. The market is packed on weekends with buyers and sellers. Browsers can pick up some standard souvenirs, eat well for very little money, and take some great photographs. Boulevard Costera runs
❹ along the waterfront from the market and the **sportfishing pier** past a long stretch of palms and rocky coastline. New hotels and restaurants are changing the face of the waterfront, once a seedy stretch of empty lots. At Boulevard Costera and Avenida
❺ Riveroll is the **Plaza Cívica,** with sculptures of Benito Juárez, Miguel Hidalgo, and Venustiano Carranza. Farther on is the

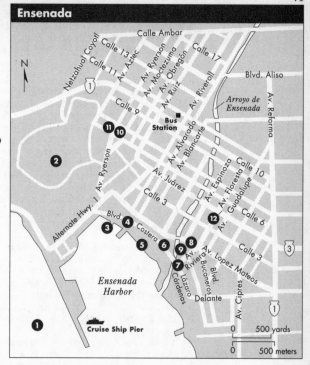

Ensenada

Calle Ambar

Nezahualcoyotl · Calle 13 · Calle 11 · Av. Aztec · Av. Ryerson · Av. Moctezuma · Av. Obregón · Calle 17 · Av. Ruiz · Av. Riveroll · Blvd. Aliso · Av. Reforma

Arroyo de Ensenada

Calle 9

Bus Station

⑪ **⑩**

②

Av. Ryerson · Av. Alvarado · Av. Blancarte · Calle 10 · Av. Espinoza · Av. Floresta · Av. Guadalupe

Av. Juárez

Calle 3

Blvd. Costera · **③** **④** · **⑫** · Calle 6

Alternate Hwy. 1

⑤ **⑥** **⑨** **⑧**

⑦

Calle 3

Av. Riviera · Blvd. Bucaneros · Av. Lopez Mateos · Av. Cipres

Av. Lázaro Cárdenas

Delante

Ensenada Harbor

①

⚓ **Cruise Ship Pier**

0 ___ 500 yards
0 ___ 500 meters

---

⑥ plaza **Artesanía de Ensenada,** with about 20 souvenir shops. Cruise-ship passengers arrive at the foot of the pier here.

Time Out You can't visit the **fish market** without trying at least one fish taco. Strips of fresh snapper, halibut, or other fresh catches are dipped in batter and deep-fried, then wrapped in fresh corn tortillas. You choose your toppings—cilantro (coriander), salsa, tomatoes, onions, pickled carrots—from an array of dishes set out on the counter.

Boulevard Costera becomes Avenida Lázaro Cárdenas at
⑦ Avenida Riviera, site of the **Riviera del Pacífico.** This rambling hacienda-style mansion was built in the 1920s with money raised on both sides of the border. Heavyweight fighter Jack Dempsey was one of the more famous shareholders. An enormous gambling palace, hotel, restaurant, and bar, the glamorous Riviera was frequented by wealthy U.S. citizens and Mexicans, particularly during Prohibition. When gambling was outlawed in Mexico and Prohibition ended in the United States, the palace lost its clientele. In 1977, the Convention and Visitors Bureau began refurbishing the building and its lavish gardens. During daylight hours, visitors can tour the elegant ballrooms and halls, which host occasional art shows and civic events. The Riviera del Pacífico is now officially called the Centro Social, Cívico y Cultural de Ensenada (Social, Civic, and Cultural Center of Ensenada), and there are plans for including it in a major convention-center complex along the waterfront. These days it is used as a convention center or wedding site, and it contains some government offices and a

public library. But most of the time the grand hallways and ballrooms remain empty, and it's not hard to imagine how magnificent they must have been in their heyday. *Blvd. Costera and Av. Riviera, tel. 667/6–4310. Admission free. Open daily 9–5.*

Ensenada's tourist zone is centered one block east of the waterfront along Avenida **López Mateos.** High-rise hotels, souvenir shops, restaurants, and bars line the avenue from its beginning at the foot of the Chapultepec Hills for eight blocks south to the dry channel of the Arroyo de Ensenada. South of the riverbed is a row of inexpensive motels, across the street from the **Tourist** (8) (9) **Office,** the **Fonart** government crafts store, and **Caliente Foreign Book** (corner of Avenidas López Mateos and Castillo, tel. 667/6–2133), where horse-racing fans can place their bets on races televised via satellite. The four-block stretch between Avenidas López Mateos and Juárez is Ensenada's true downtown area, where the locals shop for furniture, clothing, and (10) other necessities. **Parque Revolución,** near the northern end of (11) Juárez at the **Mother's Monument,** is the prettiest of the city parks, with a bandstand, children's playground, and plenty of (12) comfortable benches in the shade. The largest cathedral, **Our Lady of Guadalupe,** is at Avenida Floresta and the south end of Avenida Juárez. The church is undergoing renovation, and has some incredibly detailed stained-glass windows.

Off the Beaten Track

The hillsides and valleys outside Ensenada are known for their grapes and olives; hotels in town can arrange tours of many of the wineries. The **Santo Tomás Winery** is located in town and has tours daily except Sunday. The **Cetto Winery** (tel. 668/8–2581 in Tijuana) is located in the Guadalupe Valley, north on Highway 3 toward Tecate. The valley is about a 30-minute drive from Ensenada on a good, paved highway that runs up into the hills past cattle ranches and orchards. In San Antonio de Las Minas, about 15 minutes from Ensenada, there is an excellent gourmet restaurant, **Mustafa,** known for its lamb and goat dishes (Km. 93 on the Ensenada–Tecate Road, no phone; open Tues.–Sun. 8 AM–9 PM). There's nothing else to do along the road except marvel at the boulders, cliffs, and scenery. **Valle Guadalupe** has a few small markets and a PEMEX station. **Olivares Mexicanos,** which claims to be the world's largest olive plantation (it boasts 120,000 trees), lies just outside town. The Cetto and Calafia vineyards run for miles along the road toward Tecate. The drive is a pleasant half-day adventure, and the view coming back over the hills to the coast is spectacular.

La Bufadora is an impressive blowhole in the coastal cliffs at Punta Banda, off Highway 1 at Maneadero, about 15 minutes south of Ensenada. The drive, 19 kilometers (12 miles) west on Highway 23, is slow and somewhat risky (don't try it at night), but the coastal scenery is worth the effort. The rutted dirt road that curves dramatically along the crumbling seaside cliffs passes small fishing communities, a few trailer parks, and rows of stands selling fresh-cut flowers, honey, fiery-hot olives, peppers, and fragrant homemade tamales. At Punta Banda there is a new resort, the **Baja Beach and Tennis Club,** and a settlement of Americans with modest oceanfront homes.

Shopping

Browsing and bartering are popular Baja pastimes, and the selection of Mexican handicrafts in Ensenada is equal, if not superior, to that in Tijuana. Most of the tourist shops are located along Avenida López Mateos by the hotels and restaurants. Several new two-story shopping arcades have brand-name sportswear stores. Dozens of curio shops on the street offer similar selections of pottery, woven blankets and serapes, embroidered dresses, and onyx chess sets. Four blocks inland from Avenida López Mateos is Avenida Juárez, the center of downtown. Large department stores, pharmacies, and shoe stores catering to locals line the avenue.

La Rana (Av. López Mateos 715) has a wide selection of beach attire and surfing supplies. **Originales Baja** (Av. López Mateos 623) sells large brass and copper birds, wood carvings, and glassware. **Artes de Quijote** (Av. López Mateos 503) has an impressive selection of carved wood doors, huge terra-cotta pots, wood puzzles and games, Oaxaca tablecloths and napkins, and large brass fish and birds. **Joyería Princess,** a few doors down, has a good selection of gold and silver jewelry at reasonable, set prices. In the Mitla Bazaar (Av. López Mateos 405), **Elles** and **Fila** have designer men's and women's clothing. **Mike's Leather** (Av. López Mateos 621) has a nice selection of leather clothing and dyed huaraches (sandals). **Fantasías del Mar** (Av. López Mateos 821) has exotic shells, coral jewelry, and paintings. The government craft store, **Fonart** (Av. López Mateos 1303, next door to the tourism office), is filled with excellent Mexican crafts, notably black pottery from Oaxaca and wood dolls and animals from Michoacán. **La Mina de Solomón** (next to the El Rey Sol restaurant on Av. López Mateos) carries handcrafted gold jewelry. **Artes Bitterlín,** a gallery in the same building, carries antiques, sculptures, paintings, and Sergio Bustamante copper and brass animals.

Hussong's Edificio (Av. Ruíz, next door to Hussong's bar) has a collection of shops selling silk-screened T-shirts, surfboards, and Ensenada bumper stickers and souvenirs. **Avila Imports,** across the street from Hussong's, sells French perfumes, Hummel statues, and crystal. **Beibylandia** (Av. Ruíz 232) has a wide assortment of baby clothing, furniture, and toys. **Librería Banuelos** (Av. Ruíz 370) and **El Spaña** (Av. Ruíz 217) have a good selection of English-language magazines and books. **El Pegaso** (Av. Obregón and Calle 2a) is a bit out of the way but well worth the trip. The store carries beautiful clothing, jewelry, furniture, and crafts from throughout Mexico, and shares its inventory with its sister store in San Miguel de Allende. The items here are a bit higher-priced than at the main curio stands, but the quality is far superior. The **Astra Shopping Center** at Calle Delante and Highway 1 has major department stores and small handicraft shops. **Los Globos,** a large swap meet on Calle 9a, is open weekends.

There is a shopping center on the waterfront, **Centro de Artesenal,** catering to the cruise-ship visitors; the best shop by far is **Unique Art Center,** displaying glossy black pottery in unusual shapes and varied folk art from the Indians of Northern Mexico. There are some nice folk-art galleries amid the T-shirt and souvenir shops.

Sports

Hunting and fishing are popular sports around Ensenada, which calls itself the "Yellowtail Capital of the World."

Golf **Bajamar** (tel. 667/8–1844) is an excellent 18-hole course 32 kilometers (20 miles) north of Ensenada at the Bajamar condominium and housing resort.

Hunting The hunting season for quail and other wildfowl runs from September through December. Trips can be arranged through **Uruapan Lodge** (Gastelum 40, tel. 667/8–2190). The package includes transportation from the border, room, meals, hunting equipment, and licenses for $100 per day.

Sportfishing Fishing boats leave the **Ensenada Sportfishing Pier** regularly. The best angling is from April through November; bottom fishing is good in the winter. Charter vessels and party boats are available from several outfitters along Avenida López Mateos, Boulevard Costera, and off the sportfishing pier. Trips on group boats cost about $35 per day. Most hotels can arrange fishing trips. Licenses are available at the tourist office or from charter companies, and a number of companies organize fishing trips and rent equipment: **Ensenada Clipper Fleet** (Pier, tel. 667/8–2185) has charter and group boats; **Gordo's Sportfishing** (Pier, tel. 667/8–3515) is one of the oldest sportfishing companies in Ensenada with a waterfront motel, charter boats, group boats, and a smokehouse; and **El Royal Pacífico** (26651 Naccome Dr., Mission Viejo, CA 92691, tel. 714/859–4933) offers advance-sale tickets and reservations on sportfishing boats in Ensenada from its U.S. office.

Tennis **Bajamar** (tel. 667/8–1844) and the **Baja Tennis Club** (Calle San Benito 123, no phone) have public courts.

Spectator Sports

Charreadas Rodeos are scheduled sporadically at the ring (Av. Alvarado
(Mexican Rodeos) and Calle 2a, tel. 667/4–0242).

Horse Racing There is no racetrack in Ensenada, but horse-racing fans can place bets and watch televised races from Tijuana's Agua Caliente Racetrack and Los Angeles's Santa Anita and Hollywood tracks at the **Caliente Foreign Book** (Av. López Mateos, behind the Riviera Pacífico building, tel. 667/6–2133).

Beaches

Since the waterfront in Ensenada is taken up by fishing boats, the best swimming beaches are south of town. **Estero Beach** is long and clean, with mild waves. Surfers populate the beaches off Highway 1 north and south of Ensenada, particularly at **San Miguel, California, Tres Marías,** and **La Joya** beaches; scuba divers prefer **Punta Banda,** by La Bufadora. Lifeguards are rare; swimmers should take caution. The tourist office in Ensenada has a map that shows safe beaches.

Dining

Since Ensenada is a sportfishing town, fish is the prime dining choice. The lobster, shrimp, and abalone are great, and a variety of fresh fish is prepared in French, Italian, and Mexican sauces. On the street, at the Fish Market, and in inexpensive restaurants, seafood cocktails, ceviche (marinated seafood), and fish tacos are the main delight. During the winter hunting season, quail and pheasant are popular. Some restaurants add a service charge of 10%–15% to your bill, in addition to the 15% tax.

Highly recommended restaurants in each price category are indicated by a star ★.

Category	Cost*
Expensive	over $15
Moderate	$10–$15
Inexpensive	under $10

*per person, excluding drinks, service, and sales tax (15%)

Expensive **El Rey Sol.** A family-owned French restaurant over 40 years ★ old, El Rey Sol is in a charming building with stained-glass windows, wrought-iron chandeliers, heavy oak tables and chairs, and linen tablecloths. Specialties include French and Mexican presentations of fresh fish, poultry, and vegetables grown at the owner's farm in the Santo Tomás Valley. Appetizers come with the meal; excellent pastries are baked on the premises. *Av. López Mateos 1000, tel. 667/8–1733. AE, MC, V.*

La Bamba. One of the newer buildings on the sportfishing pier, La Bamba is a beautiful, stylish restaurant with gray marble floors, peach cloths and napkins, pale wood furnishings, and lots of gleaming brass. The kitchen area is glassed in so you can see your chateaubriand on the grill, and the upstairs bar has a superb view of the water, comfortable lounge chairs, and a large dance floor. This is by far the classiest place in Ensenada, and most likely the only place where you'll find shrimp pâté. *Sportfishing pier, tel. 667/4–0881. MC, V.*

★ **La Cueva de los Tigres.** A dining room on the beach, with sliding glass windows opening to the ocean air, makes this restaurant especially nice at sunset. The enduring specialty, abalone in crab sauce, has won numerous international awards. Though the prices for seafood are higher here than elsewhere, the preparation is so consistently excellent that patrons regularly drive down from Southern California just for dinner. *Km 112 at Playa Hermosa, tel. 667/6–4650. AE, MC, V.*

Moderate **Casamar.** A long-standing, dependable restaurant, Casamar is ★ known for its wide variety of excellent seafood. Large groups, families, and couples fill the main dining room. Lobster and shrimp are prepared several ways, but taste freshest when grilled *con mojo de ajo* (with garlic and butter). The upstairs bar has live jazz on weekend nights. *Av. Cárdenas 987, tel. 667/ 4–0417. MC, V.*

El Toro. An old favorite with a new location on the main drag, this large adobe and red tile restaurant is considered to be *the* place in town for grilled meats—steak, lamb, and quail—by candlelight. *Blvd. Costera 1790, tel. 667/6–0834. MC, V.*

Enrique's. Known for having the smallest bar in Baja (5 stools and one couch), Enrique's is an out-of-the-way discovery with a loyal clientele. The Los Angeles–trained chef has a way with frogs' legs, salmon, and quail, and believes "the essence of culinary art is time"—meaning this is not the place to eat if you mind waiting for your meal. For the ultimate in decadence, save room for the Mexican Irish coffee and cherries jubilee. *⅘ km (½ mi) north of town on Hwy. 1, tel. 667/4–4061. MC, V.*

Haliotis. Seafood doesn't come any fresher than this, and the owners, originally from Mazatlán, know how to prepare it well. Try the Sopa de Siete Mares (Seven Seas Soup), a giant bowl filled with hearty broth and everything from abalone to squid. The restaurant is a bit out of the way, but every taxi driver knows where it is, since they've probably dined here with their families. Here you can escape your fellow tourists. *Calle Delante 179, tel. 667/6–3720. MC, V.*

Las Cazuelas. A seafood and steak house a short way from town, this place is known for its great Mexican cooking. For breakfast, try the spicy *huevos rancheros* (fried eggs on a tortilla with hot sauce), and for an all-out adventure, have giant shrimp stuffed with lobster for dinner. *Av. Sangines and Blvd. Costera, tel. 667/6–1044. MC, V.*

Smitty González. One of the premier fun spots, Smitty's has tasty Mexican food, Puerto Nuevo lobster, killer daiquiris, and a fireman's pole that guests can use to get from the second-story bar to the dining room. *Avs. Reyerson and López Mateos, tel. 667/4–0636. MC, V.*

Inexpensive **Calmariscos.** Some of Ensenada's best seafood is served in this modest restaurant, with Formica-topped tables and plastic chairs. No frills, but the food is great, plentiful, and inexpensive. *Calle 3a #474, near Av. Ruíz, tel. 667/8–2940. MC, V.*

El Fábula Pizza. This funky, fun place features a mock airplane crashing into the front wall, posters and record album covers hanging inside, and picnic tables where families and friends gather for pizza and beer. *Blvd. Costera and Av. Club Rotario, no phone. No credit cards.*

★ **Fish Market.** The cheapest and tastiest meal in town is available day and night at the many small stands outside the fish market. Adventurous types can sample the pickled squid or octopus cocktails; the more cautious might prefer shrimp cocktails or ceviche. The best meal is fish tacos, costing about $1 for three tacos filled with deep-fried fish. Wander past the stands until you find the one with the widest range of salsas and pickled and fresh vegetables to ladle over your taco.

Señor Taco. This is a clean, inviting storefront with benches and stools along the walls, serving good, basic Mexican food at low prices. *Av. Ruíz 171, no phone. No credit cards.*

Lodging

Ensenada has become a major resort town, with prices to match. Low-cost places are hard to find, and reservations are a must on holiday weekends. The most popular hotels are concentrated in a five-block area along Avenida López Mateos, the center of tourist activity. Most hotels take credit cards; some insist on advance payment. **International Marketing and Promotions** (7860 Mission Center Court, No. 202, San Diego, CA 92108, tel. 619/298–4105, 800/522–1516 in CA, or 800/225–2786 in the U.S.) represents several tourism offices in Baja, makes hotel reservations at a large number of properties, and is a great source of information. **Pan American Hotels International** (P.O. Box 2776, Chula Vista, CA 92012, tel. 619/422–6918 or 800/678–7244) reserves rooms at a large number of properties throughout Baja. **Baja Lodging** (4659 Park Blvd., San Diego, CA 92116, tel. 619/491–0682) reserves rooms in hotels and small, more remote properties throughout Baja. Weekday rates are sometimes lower than those on weekends.

Highly recommended lodgings in each price category are indicated by a star ★ .

Category	Cost*
Expensive	over $55
Moderate	$25–$55
Inexpensive	under $25

All prices are for a standard double room, excluding service charge and sales tax (15%).

Expensive **Corona.** The only hotel on the waterfront, the Corona has one completed hotel building and plans for two more, plus condos and a marina. The building is tastefully done, with white towers and peaks rising over the red-tile roof, resembling a little castle by the sea. The rooms have bleached-wood furnishings, beige carpeting, tile baths, and balconies facing the water or downtown. At press time, the pool, restaurant, and bar were still under construction. *Blvd. Costero 1442, tel. 667/6–4023; reservations in the U.S.: Box 3926, Chula Vista, CA 92011–0255, tel. 800/34–MEXICO. 93 rooms completed, with plans for 320 rooms. Facilities: marina, 2 pools, restaurant, bar. MC, V.*

Estero Beach Hotel Resort. This full-service resort is one of the oldest in Ensenada and a longtime favorite with Southern California families who come for a week or so and rarely leave the grounds. This is one of the few places where you can stay right on the beach; the feeling is laid-back and mellow, heavy on comfort, and light on glitz and glamour. *10 km (6 mi) south of town on Estero Beach, off Hwy. 1, Box 86, Ensenada, BCN, tel. 667/6–6225. 74 rooms, cottages, and suites. Facilities: beach, pool, tennis courts, horseback riding, bar, restaurant, shops, golf driving range, RV park next door. AE, MC, V.*

★ **Las Rosas.** This pretty pink palace just north of town is by far the most modernistic hotel in the area; its green glass–ceilinged atrium lobby glows in the night. All rooms face the ocean and pool, which seems to flow right over the edge of the seaside cliffs. Flowering vines trail down the inner walls; palms tower over the pool. The effect is elegant, with gleaming marble floors, mint green and pink upholstered couches facing the sea, and lots of glass. Some rooms have fireplaces and Jacuzzis, but even the least expensive are gorgeous: they have private balconies, silk flower arrangements on the polished dressers, and light pastel spreads on the queen-size beds. *Hwy. 1 north of town, tel. 667/4–4310. 32 rooms and suites. Facilities: pool, hot tub, restaurant, cocktail lounge, jewelry shop, gallery. AE, MC, V.*

San Nicolás. This is a private place that doesn't look like much from the street but is actually a massive resort behind cement walls painted with Indian murals. The San Nicolás is 20 years old, but much of it has been refurbished. The suites boast large, tiled hot tubs, elegant living rooms with deep-green carpeting, mauve furnishings, beveled glass doors, and mirrored ceilings in the bedrooms. The less extravagant rooms are comfortable and tastefully decorated with folk art and Indian paintings. There is a rushing waterfall over the pool, and a good restaurant overlooking the gardens. *Avs. López Mateos and Guadalupe, tel. 667/9–1901; reservations in U.S.: tel. 800/522–1516. 150 rooms and suites. Facilities: 2 pools, hot tubs, restaurant, cocktail lounge, disco, meeting rooms, shops, cable TV. AE, MC, V.*

Villa Marina Hotel. Ensenada's only high-rise is either a symbol of prosperity or an eyesore, depending on your vantage point. The hotel is near finished, except for the top-floor restaurant; the rooms have a spectacular view of the waterfront and are modern, bright, and comfortable. There's not a lot of character to the place, but when it's all completed it may just be the most luxurious hotel in town. *Avs. López Mateos and Blancarte, tel. 667/8–3321. 130 rooms. Facilities: pool, restaurant, bar. MC, V.*

Moderate **Cortéz Motor Hotel.** This is a dependable, if lackluster, Best Western Motel right in town, with tired orange drapes on the windows and somewhat lumpy mattresses. *Av. López Mateos 1089, tel. 667/8–2307; reservations in the U.S.: tel. 800/528–1234. 62 rooms. Facilities: pool, restaurant, bar, meeting rooms. MC, V.*

La Pinta. The first in a chain of six La Pinta hotels, which offer discounted rates for travelers using the La Pinta properties throughout their Baja sojourns. This branch is recovering from a 1990 fire; when complete, the rooms will have new furnishings. *Av. Floresta and Blvd. Bucaneros, tel. 667/6–2601; reservations in the U.S.: tel. 800/336–5454. 52 rooms. Facilities: pool, restaurant, bar, tennis courts, shops. MC, V.*

Las Dunas. Billed as a "hometel," Las Dunas provides rooms that are more like apartments, with kitchenettes, laundry facilities, and barbecue grills outside your door. It's a good place if you're staying a while and want to set up housekeeping. One block from the water, a few blocks south of town. *Calle Caracoles 169, tel. 667/6–3095. 28 kitchenette suites. Facilities: pool, hot tub, cable TV, laundry. MC, V.*

★ **Misión Santa Isabel.** Ensenada's only colonial-style hotel is a pretty place, with a nice central courtyard and pool area, tiled hallways, and carved wood furniture in the rooms. *Av. López Mateos at Av. Castillo, Box 76, Ensenada, tel. 667/8–3616. 31 rooms. Facilities: pool, bar, restaurant, tour desk. MC, V.*

★ **Quintas Papagayo.** A bungalow and low-rise establishment opened by the Hussong family in 1947, Quintas Papagayo is a place where couples honeymoon and come back each year for their anniversaries. The accommodations are far from spectacular—rustic and homey are better descriptions—but it feels like a special hideaway, and the staff remembers your name. Fireplaces, kitchens, patios, and decks are available. *Hwy. 1 north of town, tel. 667/8–3675; reservations: Box 150, Ensenada; reservations in the U.S.: tel. 619/491–0682. 50 rooms. Facilities: pool, tennis courts, restaurant, bar, beach. MC, V.*

TraveLodge. If you're looking for dependability, reliability, and no surprises, this American-affiliated hotel is your place. The rooms are dull but clean, with mini-bars, cable TVs, and

VCRs. *Av. López Mateos at Av. Blancarte 130, Box 1467, Ensenada, BCN, tel. 667/8–1601 or 800/255–3050 in the U.S. 50 rooms. Facilities: pool, restaurant, bar. MC, V.*

Inexpensive **America Motel.** This plain motel is well-located across from the Fonart government craft store and tourism office, a few blocks from the center of town. Check the room before agreeing to it, as some have dreadfully uncomfortable beds and dripping showers. *Av. López Mateos 1309, tel. 667/6–1333. 20 rooms. No credit cards.*

California Trailer Park and Motel. This is a new motel with trailer park, concrete spaces, and hookups. *8 km (5 mi) north of Ensenada on Hwy. 1, tel. 667/6–2037. Reservations: Box 262, Ensenada. MC, V.*

Joker Hotel. A bizarre, brightly colored mish-mash of styles makes it hard to miss this hotel, conveniently located for those traveling south of Ensenada. Spacious rooms have private balconies, satellite TV, and phones. *3 miles south of Ensenada on Hwy 1, tel. 667/6–7201; reservations in the U.S. 800/678–7244. 20 rooms. Facilities: pool, Jacuzzi. MC, V.*

La Bufadora

Inexpensive **La Jolla Beach Camp.** Rest rooms and showers. *On Punta Banda, just off the road to La Bufadora. Reservations: Alejandro Pabloff, Box 953, Ensenada, no tel. No credit cards.*

Rancho la Bufadora. Campsites, no hookups. *26 km (16 mi) south of Ensenada on the road to La Bufadora. Box 300, Ensenada, no tel. No credit cards.*

Villarino Camp. 60 RV sites with hookups. *On the road to La Bufadora, no tel. No credit cards.*

Cataviña

Expensive **Hotel La Pinta.** This is a small, solitary hotel in the middle of Baja's Desert National Park. *Off Hwy. 1, 1.6 km (1 mi) north of Rancho Santa Inés. Box 179, San Quintín, tel. 667/6–2601, 800/678–7244 in U.S. 28 rooms. Facilities: restaurant, bar, tennis, pool. AE, MC, V.*

Inexpensive **Cataviña Campground.** Trailer and tent sites, showers, rest rooms, gas station, electricity, restaurant. *Next to Hotel La Pinta, 1.6 km (1 mi) north of Ranch Santa Inés, off Hwy. 1, no phone. No credit cards.*

San Quintín

Hotel La Pinta. Another in the La Pinta's chain, this one is by the beach. *Box 168, San Quintín, BCN, tel. 667/6–2601, 800/678–7244 in U.S. Facilities: pool, tennis, bar, restaurant. MC, V. Expensive.*

Cielito Lindo Motel. This is a small establishment next to a campground with 100 RV sites, electricity, rest rooms, showers, and restaurant. *3 km (2 mi) west of Hwy. 1, APDO N7, Valle de San Quintín, B.C., no phone. 24 rooms. MC, V. Moderate.*

The Arts and Nightlife

The **Teatro de la Ciudad** (Calle Diamante) holds occasional dance shows and plays. **The International Spanish Institute of Ensenada** (Blvd. Rodríguez 377, tel. 667/6–0109; information in the U.S.: Box 536, Bonita, CA 92002–0536, tel. 619/472–0600) offers week-long and weekend Spanish-language immersion programs, with accommodations provided by local families.

Ensenada is not a place for arts and culture—rather, it's a party town for college students, surfers, and young tourists. The bars, particularly along Avenidas López Mateos and Ruíz, are rowdy at night. Most of the expensive hotels have bars and discos that are less frenetic. **La Taberna Española** (Blvd. Costero 1982) is a great place to gather for a night-long feast of tapas and sangria, along with Flamenco shows.

Hussong's (Av. Ruíz) is perhaps Ensenada's most prominent landmark. No trip is complete without entering this dark, dingy, noisy, enormous saloon where vendors hawk rugs, roses, and Polaroid photos, and the crowd of patrons never seems to diminish.

Papas and Beer, across the street, is newer, cleaner, and trendier, but the crowd is just as rowdy. On the same block, **Bandito's** is a boisterous disco. Billiard parlors line Calle 2a between Avenidas Ruíz and Gastelum—this is definitely men-only territory. **Tortilla Flats,** on the harbor with a view of the fishing boats, has dining and dancing of a more mellow sort. **Carlos 'n Charlie's** (Blvd. Costera) is more family-oriented, but rowdy. **Club Bananas,** nearby, is a neon/video/disco bar popular with the college crowd, as is **Tequila Connection** (Av. Alvarado 12 just off Blvd. Costera). **Smitty Gonzales** (Av. Reyerson) attracts devoted disco dancers. **Joy's Disco** (Avs. López Mateos and Balboa) is popular with the locals, as is **Xanadu Disco** (Ejército Nacional).

6 Northeastern Baja: Mexicali, San Felipe, and Tecate

Introduction

The northeastern region of Baja California Norte is a land of surprises, of new and startling vistas in its cities, mountains, lakes, and deserts. There are the comforts of luxurious resorts, the excitement of the big city, and the awesome presence of varied landscapes—the blazing orange sun rising in the east over deserted islands in the Sea of Cortés, the rugged crags in the volcanic mountains, the sweeping plateaus of productive ranchland; and the rich, black soil of the Imperial Valley farms.

Mexicali, the capital of Baja California Norte, shares the Imperial Valley farmland and the border crossing with Calexico, a small California city. Mexicali is an expanding city. New *colonias* (neighborhoods) crop up steadily in the far-reaching suburbs. Massive new government buildings and sprawling shopping centers appear throughout the city. *Maquiladoras* (manufacturing plants operated by companies from the United States and Japan) bring new jobs for the steady stream of workers from mainland Mexico. The current population of Mexicali is estimated at 800,000. As a capital city, Mexicali sees a great deal of government activity. In the southern part of the city, a new civic and commercial center has been built with a hospital, government offices, and shopping center, reflecting both Mexicali's importance as an administrative seat and its rapid growth.

The construction of the Imperial Canal in 1902 brought an influx of Chinese immigrants to the region. Their presence is strongly seen in the faces of many inhabitants; Mexicali is a good place to sample Chinese cuisine, and Chinese imports fill the curio shops.

During Prohibition, Mexicali earned a reputation as a seamy border town; liquor was plentiful and gambling and prostitution were common. The first highway to Tijuana—an impressive engineering feat in itself—was financed from taxes imposed on these activities. A steady stream of gringos took advantage of Mexicali's permissive environment until 1935, when gambling was outlawed. Since then, the town has toned down considerably.

Though water is scarce in these largely desert lands, the Mexicali area is blessed with some of the world's richest topsoil; agriculture is the primary source of income in this part of the country. Mexicali has its own salt lake, the beautiful and serene Laguna Salada, the tip of which lies 24 kilometers (15 miles) east of town; but this lake is a natural lake, an extension of sorts of the Sea of Cortés (Gulf of California). Since water is so scarce here, it is wise to travel with a plentiful supply in the hot summer months. The climate is more or less typical of that found in the low desert regions of the southwestern United States—the region is at sea level, and the average rainfall is three inches per year. In summer, the temperature can hit 120°F.

As a tourist town, Mexicali is not very popular. It lacks the fine museums, parks, and attractions of Mexico's larger cities, and does not have the charm of the small colonial towns. It is more a business-oriented place or a stopover en route to the mainland. A train that reaches points throughout Mexico originates in Mexicali. Sometimes referred to as "The Gateway to the Sea of

Cortés," Mexicali is the port of entry for travelers to the beaches of San Felipe.

At the end of Highway 5, 200 kilometers (125 miles) south of Mexicali along solitary stretches of desert and salt marshes, lies the fishing village of **San Felipe,** on the Sea of Cortés. San Felipe has been a popular getaway spot for years, a place where hardy travelers in recreational vehicles and campers hide out for weeks on end. Gradually, it is gaining in popularity with those seeking hotels, swimming pools, and good restaurants.

Not until 1948, when the first paved road was completed from the northern capital, did San Felipe become a town where people actually lived. Now it is the home of an impressive fishing and shrimping fleet. The largest boats are docked 5 kilometers (3 miles) south of town within a man-made breakwater enclosure. A hurricane nearly destroyed San Felipe in 1967. The residents rebuilt most of the town, and the new housing was of much higher quality than it had been before the tragedy. Since then, San Felipe has continued to grow steadily. Today it boasts an international airport (scheduled to open in 1991) and an increasing number of hotels. On the way into town there are at least a dozen campgrounds on the beach. These are quite popular and fill up quickly during the winter and spring holidays. There are more campgrounds in town as well—two large trailer parks between the Hotel Cortés and the popular *malecón* (boardwalk). Dune buggies, motorcycles, and off-road vehicles abound. On weekends, San Felipe can be quite boisterous.

San Felipe draws many fishermen, especially in the spring. Launches, bait, and supplies are readily available. Game wardens regularly check for valid fishing licenses, which are available through fishing charters and Mexicali travel agencies. The tides at Bahía San Felipe change dramatically. They crest at 20 feet, and since the beach is so shallow, the water line can move in and out up to 1⅛ kilometers (about ½ mile). This has caused problems for more than one fisherman who tied his boat on shore, stopped in town for a few beers, and hours later found his craft high and dry. The sea here is often unpredictable. What begins as a glassy smooth surface in the morning can quickly turn rough and high-running before noon. The local fishermen are well aware of the peculiarities of this section of the Sea of Cortés. Many of them visit the shrine to the Virgin of Guadalupe (Cerro de la Virgen) before setting sail. This shrine sits 940 feet high on a hill at the north end of the bay and offers a view of the town and the desert mountains behind it.

West of San Felipe, on the way to Ensenada, the highway winds through an imposing mountain range, the Sierra San Pedro Mártir, with the highest peak in Baja, Picacho del Diablo, at 10,126 feet. Farther south along the Gulf coast, approximately halfway down the peninsula, lies the beautiful Bahía de los Angeles, a secluded bay perfect for fishing, camping, and relaxing.

Tecate is about 144 kilometers (90 miles) west of Mexicali on Highway 2. It is a quiet community, a typical Mexican small town that happens to be on the border. Tecate never offered the vices on which many other border towns thrive. So incidental is the border to local life that its gates are closed from midnight until 7 AM. Absent are the cheap curio shops that are so thick in

Tijuana and, to a lesser degree, Mexicali. Once across the border, the *zócalo* (main square) and the church appear, and a pleasant country atmosphere prevails.

Only about 50,000 people live in and around Tecate, yet despite its relatively small size the town is known throughout Mexico for the beer that bears its name. (In restaurants, Tecate beer seems to be the only one served with wedges of lime; also, some say this brand, in its familiar red can, connotes more machismo than various other brands.)

Although the brewery is the biggest industry, farming is also good in this area. A bit farther south, the valleys of Guadalupe and Califia boast some of Mexico's lushest vineyards. Olives and grain also grow in profusion. At 1,600 feet above sea level, Tecate's climate is warm in the summer and cool in the winter.

The Mexican government has elected not to develop this area for tourism and has instead declared it part of a special industrial zone.

Tecate's main tourist draw is Rancho la Puerta, a fitness resort catering to well-heeled southern Californians. But many residents of San Diego enjoy driving down for the day to savor the foreign atmosphere, dine at one of the many good restaurants, and then stroll around the shops.

Essential Information

Important Addresses and Numbers

Mexicali
Tourist Information
Information is available at the Tourist Commission and Mexicali Chamber of Commerce offices (Blvd. Lopez Mateos and Calle Camelias, tel. 65/2–9795).

Emergencies
Police (Centro Cívico, tel. 65/2–4443); **Hospital** (Durango and Salina Cruz, tel. 65/5–1666).

San Felipe
Tourist Information
The **State Tourism Office** (Av. Mar de Cortés, tel. 657/7–1155) is open weekdays 9–7, weekends 10–2.

Emergencies
Police (Calle Ortíz Rubio and Av. Libertad, tel. 657/7–1006), **Hospital** (tel. 657/7–1001).

Tecate
Tourist Information
The **Tourist Information Booth** (Madero Alley and Calle Cárdenas) is open Tuesday through Sunday from 9 to 2 and from 3 to 5 PM. Enlist staff members at the **State Tourism Office** (1305 Libertad Alley, tel. 65/4–1095), if you need more help.

Arriving and Departing by Plane

There are no flights from the United States to the Mexicali International Airport, but flights within Mexico are available on **Mexicana** (tel. 800/531–7921), **Aeromexico** (tel. 800/237–6639), and regional carriers.

San Felipe has an international airport, but at press time it was not open to commercial carriers. **Air Resorts** (800/522–1516 in CA, 800/225–2781 in the U.S.) is expected to have flights from San Diego to San Felipe soon.

Arriving and Departing by Car, Bus, and Train

By Car Mexicali is located on the border, opposite Calexico, California, approximately 184 kilometers (115 miles) east of San Diego and 88 kilometers (55 miles) west of Yuma, Arizona. Tecate lies on the border between Tijuana and Mexicali on Highway 2. The journey from Tecate east to Mexicali (134 kilometers, or 84 miles) on La Rumorosa, as the road is known, is as exciting as a roller coaster ride: The highway twists and turns down steep mountain grades over endless stretches of flat, barren desert. San Felipe is on the coast, 200 kilometers (125 miles) south of Mexicali via Highway 5. That highway ends in town; the road farther south is not recommended for passenger cars or RVs. Most travelers to this section of Baja prefer to drive, but Mexican bus service is frequent. Visitors will not need tourist cards, but should purchase Mexican car insurance at agencies near the border.

By Bus Four Mexican bus lines run out of the Mexicali Station: **Tres Estrellas de Oro** goes through Tecate on its way to Tijuana; **Transportes del Pacífico** goes to Mexico City and other points on the mainland; **Transportes Norte de Sonora** frequents border towns in Baja and on the mainland; and **Autotransportes de Baja California** goes to San Felipe, Tijuana, and Ensenada. Reserved seats can be purchased on all buses the day before departure, but only at the bus station on Av. Independencia (tel. 65/7–2410 or 65/7–2420).

Mexicali **Central Bus Station** (Centro Cívico, Av. Independencia, tel. 65/7–2451).

San Felipe **Autotransportes de Baja California** (Av. Mar de Cortés, tel. 65/7–1039).

Tecate **Central Bus Station** (Av. Benito Juárez and Calle Abelardo Rodríguez, tel. 665/4–1221).

By Train Although there is no train service through Baja, the **Sonora–Baja California Railroad** (Ferrocarríl Sonora–Baja California) runs from Mexicali to points south in the mainland interior. The station is located at the south end of Calle Ulises Irigoyen, a few blocks north of the intersection of Avenidas López Mateos and Independencia. Trains leave twice daily. The first is the express with sleeping and dining cars; the other is the local, coach only. Fares are reasonable, and there are several different price options. *Camarines* are sleepers for one or two people and have an adjoining rest room. *Alcobas* have twin bunk beds and are large enough for four people, also with adjoining rest rooms. *Primera clase* is fairly comfortable; travelers sleep in their seats. But *segunda clase* is not recommended, since it is packed full, with no running water. At press time, a double sleeping room for one person to Mexico City cost about $55. *For advance reservations write to: Estación de Ferrocarríl, Box 3-182, Mexicali, tel. 65/7–2101.*

Getting Around

By Car The ideal way to see the northeastern part of Baja is to drive your own car or to rent one in Mexicali. Most U.S. car rental agencies do not allow their cars to be taken into Mexico. Be sure to buy Mexican auto insurance before driving into Baja.

Four major rental agencies operate out of the Mexicali airport: **Avis** (tel. 800/331–1212), **Budget** (tel. 800/527–0700), **Hertz** (tel. 800/654–3131), and **National** (tel. 800/227–7368).

By Taxi Taxis are easy to find in downtown Mexicali, especially around the intersection of Avenidas Azueta and Reforma. Negotiate your fare before you start the trip. Fewer taxis are available in Tecate and San Felipe, but your hotel should be able to arrange for one if you wish to explore outside town.

Guided Tours

Baja California Tours offers comfortable, informative bus trips through all of Baja, and can arrange special-interest tours. Vans depart daily from San Diego to San Felipe; midweek transportation and hotel packages are a real bargain. *6986 La Jolla Blvd., #204, La Jolla, CA 92037, tel. 619/454–7166.*

VTC Tours (237 Rockwood Dr., Suite 210, Calexico, CA 92231, tel. 619/357–0342) offers one-day and overnight tours of Mexicali and San Felipe.

Exploring

Mexicali's sights are few and far between, and most visitors are engaged in business. A tourist-oriented strip of curio shops and sleazy bars is located along Avenida Francisco Madero, one block south of the border. The old state capitol building, **El Antiguo Palacio de Gobierno,** sits closer to the center of town, almost two blocks from the border, at the intersection of Avenida Obregón and Calle Ulises Irigoyen. The architecture of the Palacio is reflective of Mexicali's past, with archways, balconies, and a quiet park. The **State Library** (Avs. Obregón and E) often doubles as an art museum with exhibits of paintings and sculptures.

The **Regional Museum** administered by the Autonomous University of Baja California (UABC) provides a comprehensive introduction to the natural and cultural history of Baja. Exhibits on indigenous tribes, missions, and wildlife are especially good. *Av. Reforma 1998 near Calle L, tel. 65/2–5717. Admission free. Open Tues.–Sat. 9–6.*

Parque Obregón (Av. Reforma and Calle Irigoyen) and **Parque Constitución** (Avs. México and Zuazua) are the only two parks in downtown Mexicali. Both are attractive and restful during the day. Avenida Obregón is one street away from the border, next to the House of Culture; Constitución is farther into the downtown area, built around a large music pavilion. The **Mexicali Zoo** is in the City Park, **Bosque de la Ciudad,** south of town; the entrance is at the south end of Calle Victoria, between Cárdenas and Avenida Independencia. The zoo is pleasant enough, but hardly to be compared with other Mexican zoos. Adjoining the park is the **Xochimilco Lagoon** (the Mexicali reservoir), where there are picnic facilities and boat rentals. **Laguna Salada,** 21 kilometers (miles) west of town, is an impressive desert lake with boating, picnic facilities, and camping at Centinela Beach, just off the highway across from the deserted PEMEX station.

If you allocate an hour for exploring **Tecate** you'll be hard put to fill your time. **Parque Hidalgo,** in the center of town, is a typical

Mexican village plaza, with a small gazebo and a few wrought-iron benches. Dance and band concerts are held at **Parque López Mateos,** on Highway 3 south of town, on summer evenings.

San Felipe is the quintessential dusty fishing village, with one main street (two, if you count the highway into town). The malecón is little more than a cement sidewalk beside a seawall, with a collection of fishing *pangas* (boats) clustered at one end. The one landmark in town is the Shrine to the Virgin of Guadalupe, at the north end of the malecón on a hill overlooking the Sea of Cortés and San Felipe Bay.

Shopping

Northeastern Baja is not renowned for its shopping. **Baldini Importers** in Mexicali (Calles F and Reforma) offer a fine selection of imported items, ranging from perfumes and cosmetics to porcelain and cut crystal. There are also dozens of shoe stores in Mexicali; **Tres Hermanos** and **Canada** are the best (boots are a bargain). Two outdoor markets sell produce in Mexicali, one at Avenida Obregón and Calle del Comercio and the other at the end of Calle Aldama, a block south of Parque Constitución. In Tecate, shopping is limited to daily necessities and household items. In San Felipe, there's the typical array of sombreros, sundresses, and T-shirts, and a large supply of fireworks. **Curios Oaxaca** has some handsome rugs and dresses from Oaxaca, and **Roberta's** is practically a department store, where you can get supplies and souvenirs.

Sports

San Felipe

Fishing The Sea of Cortés offers plentiful sea bass, snapper, corbina, halibut, and other game fish. Most hotels can arrange fishing trips. Licenses and trips can also be arranged at the **Fishing Cooperative** office on Calle Zihuatanejo and at the bright blue ramshackle house at the north end of the malecón. Clamming is good as well, and grunion (tiny silvery fish) come up on shore to spawn at San Felipe.

Baja Fishing Tours (2143 San Diego Ave., San Diego, CA 92110, tel. 800/832–BAJA, fax 619/295–2539) has fishing trips on long-range boats out of San Felipe in May and June, as does Tony Reyes (tel. 714/538–8010).

Mexicali

Baseball Baseball is played at the **Estadio de Beisból** (Av. Cuauhtémoc, 5 km or 3 mi east of the border, tel. 656/2–4709) by Mexicali's team in the Triple A Pacific League from mid-October through December. Many American players sharpen their talents in this league during their off-season, and the games are exciting.

Bullfights Bullfights are held usually twice a month from October through May at the **Calafia Bullring** (tel. 65/7–0681), near the civic center on Calle Calafia.

Golf Golf is played at the **Mexicali Campestre Golf Course** (Km. 11.5 on Hwy. 5 south of town, tel. 65/1–7130), which stays open

Tuesday through Sunday. The 18-hole course, open year-round, is private, but anyone can use it. Greens fees are around $10.

Dining

Northeastern Baja is not known for fine dining, but there is good seafood and steak. Mexicali is best known for its abundant Chinese restaurants, while Tecate boasts one of the better Italian eateries in the region. Lobster, shrimp, and fresh fish abound in San Felipe.

Highly recommended restaurants in each price category are indicated by a star ★.

Category	Cost*
Expensive	over $15
Moderate	$10–$15
Inexpensive	under $10

per person, excluding drinks, service, and sales tax (15%)

Mexicali

Expensive ★ **La Misión Dragón.** An eclectically landscaped restaurant, the Misión Dragón combines features of a mission and a Chinese palace. Behind its gates are fountains, a garden, and Asian and Mexican artifacts. The locals hold large dinner celebrations here, and the Chinese food is top-notch. *Av. Lázaro Cárdenas 555, tel. 65/6–4320 or 65/6–4451. MC, V.*

Moderate ★ **Cenaduría Selecta.** This charming restaurant has been serving traditional Mexican food since 1945. The waiters are formal and efficient, the menus come in wooden folders, and the booths always seem filled with locals enjoying themselves. *Av. Arista and Calle C 1510, tel. 65/2–4047. MC, V.*
Chu-Lim. This spacious yet quiet Chinese restaurant is a welcome haven from the bustle of downtown shopping. The walls and ceilings are decorated in detailed Oriental-style paneling. *Calle Morelos 251; tel. 65/2–8695. MC, V.*
Sanborn's. Always dependable for good American and Mexican breakfasts, Sanborn's has a wide selection of recipes from throughout Mexico. The adjoining shop has a nice selection of folk art, and the bakery is a plus. *Calzada Independencía, tel. 65/7–5262. AE, MC, V.*

Inexpensive ★ **Casita de Pátzcuaro.** A good place for tacos and burritos, this is a favorite with regulars headed for San Felipe. *Calzada López Mateos 648, tel. 65/2–9707. No credit cards.*
Gloria. The specialties here are home-cooked Mexican food—tacos, tostadas, chiles rellenos, *menudo* (tripe soup), and *pozole* (corn, meat, and chili stew). *Blvd. de las Américas 502, tel. 65/6–5530. No credit cards.*
Las Cazuelas. A nice, clean restaurant, Las Cazuelas serves traditional Mexican dishes and good combination meals. *Av. Juárez 56, tel. 65/4–0649. No credit cards.*

San Felipe

Expensive **Alfredo's.** Located in La Trucha Vagabunda Hotel, Alfredo's is
★ run by the daughter of Mexico City restaurateur Alfredo
Bellinghieri. With its crystal chandeliers, the dining area resembles a large ballroom. The fettuccine Alfredo and lasagna
are first-rate, and the tender, tasty *carne asada Siciliano*
(grilled beef) is marinated in olive oil and oregano. *Calle Mar
Báltico, tel. 65/7–1333. No lunch. MC, V.*

Moderate **El Nido, Puerto Padre, Las Redes,** and **George's,** are lined up in
an informal restaurant row on Avenida Mar de Cortés south of
town. All serve good steaks, Mexican dishes, and seafood. *MC,
V.*

El Rubén's. The large and popular restaurant and bar in Rubén's Trailer Park is a great place for breakfast, which many
regular customers accompany with Rubén's Coco Loco, a potent blend of liquors and coconut milk. The restaurant is a local
hangout day and night. Try the shrimp omelette. *North of town
on Av. Golfo de California, tel. 65/7–1091. No credit cards.*

★ **John's Place.** Two blocks east of the waterfront is this homey,
comfortable, family-run restaurant with excellent food. The
catch of the day is grilled and comes with vegetables—but ask
for beans, rice, and the wonderful homemade tortillas instead.
Off Calle de Ensenada, no phone. No lunch. MC, V.

Inexpensive **Los Mandiles.** Americans gather here at plain Formica-topped
tables to drink beer, watch sports on TV, and munch on free
appetizers. The meals are basic and good, but don't splurge on
steak and shrimp here. *Av. Mar de Cortés and Chetumal, tel.
65/7–1168. MC, V.*

★ **Tacos La Gaviota** and **Tacos La Bonita.** Both are in the downtown area and serve great fish, clam, shrimp, or pork tacos at
outdoor stands. Straddle a stool at the counter, order one of
each, and enjoy a $2 feast. *Av. Mar de Cortés, no phone. No
credit cards.*

Tecate

Moderate **El Passetto.** This could be the best Italian restaurant in all of
★ Baja, with superb garlic bread and homemade pasta. The proprietor makes his own wines, which are pretty good, and there
is live music on the weekends. *Callejón Libertad 200, tel. 665/
4–1361. MC, V.*

El Tucán. By Tecate standards, this steak house is fancy. It is
four blocks from the border. *Av. Juárez 1100, tel. 665/4–1333.
MC, V.*

Inexpensive **Restaurant Intimo.** The seafood is very good at this friendly,
family-run café. *Av. Juárez, no phone. No credit cards.*

Restaurant 70. This is the finest Chinese restaurant in Tecate.
Av. Hidalgo 350, tel. 65/4–1675. No credit cards.

Lodging

Hotels are abundant in Mexicali, but scarce in San Felipe and
Tecate. Rates are lower than in the rest of Baja, but as a rule,
accommodations are modest and plain.

Highly recommended lodgings in each price category are indicated by a star ★.

Category	Cost*
Expensive	over $45
Moderate	$20–$45
Inexpensive	under $20

All prices are for a standard double room, excluding service charge and sales tax (15%).

Mexicali

Expensive   **Holiday Inn.** This is the perennial favorite of business travelers, with standard rooms and services and no surprises. *Blvd. Juárez 2220, tel. 65/6–1300; reservations in the U.S.: tel. 800/465–4329. 173 rooms. Facilities: pool, restaurant, coffee shop, bar. AE, MC, V.*

★   **La Lucerna.** The prettiest hotel in Mexicali, La Lucerna has lots of palms and fountains around the pool and colonial decor in the rooms. *Blvd. Juárez 2151, tel. 66/6–1000; reservations in the U.S.: Box 2300, Calexico, CA 92231. 200 rooms. Facilities: pool, restaurant, coffee shop, bar. MC, V.*

Moderate   **Castel Calafia.** This is one of the newest hotels in town; the rooms are clean and comfortable, but plain. *Calzada Justo Sierra 1495, tel. 66/8–3311; reservations in the U.S.: Box 947, Calexico, CA 92231. 173 rooms. Facilities: pool, restaurant, bar. MC, V.*

La Siesta. The rooms here are adequate, with all the amenities, including movies on cable TV. *Calzada Justo Sierra 899, tel. 66/8–2001. 85 rooms. No credit cards.*

Inexpensive   **Del Norte.** In the midst of noisy downtown, this is the first hotel one sees upon crossing the border. The location is convenient and the rooms have recently been remodeled, but don't stay here if you're a light sleeper. *Av. Madero and Calle Melgar, tel. 65/2–8101. 52 rooms. Facilities: restaurant, bar. MC, V.*

Plaza. This air-conditioned hotel is in the heart of the city near the international border and the House of Culture. *Av. Madero 366, tel. 65/2–9757 or 65/2–9759. 54 rooms. Facility: restaurant. MC, V.*

San Felipe

Expensive   **Aquamarina.** The most luxurious hotel in San Felipe is also the
★   most troubled, with frequent changes in ownership. The setting, on a high bluff over the beach, is lovely, but the buildings are in various stages of disrepair—check your room closely before unpacking. *9 km (5.5 mi) south of town on the Puertecitos Hwy., tel. 66/7–1349; reservations in the U.S.: 619/422–6918, 800/678–7244. Facilities: 2 pools, tennis courts, restaurant, coffee shop. AE, MC, V.*

Las Misiones. A combination of two hotels—the older Castel San Felipe, a long-time favorite, and the newer Las Misiones. This is the largest hotel complex in town, with a central courtyard, private beach, and two pools with swim-up bars. The rooms in the newer section are bright and clean; those in the older section need refurbishing, but face the courtyard and landscaping. Most of the bus and group tours to San Felipe stay here, though the smaller hotels in town are more convenient if you don't have a car. *Av. Misión de Loreto, tel. 65/7–1280; res-*

ervations in the U.S.: 619/298–4105, 800/522–1516 in CA, 800/ 225–2786. 241 rooms. Facilities: 2 pools, restaurant, bar, cable TV. AE, MC, V.

Moderate **El Cortés.** This is probably the most popular hotel in San
★ Felipe, with a lively bar; a long, clean beach; and a small pool and hot tub. Some of the rooms have beachfront patios. There is also a newer 77-room annex. *Av. Mar de Cortez, tel. 657/7–1055; reservations in the U.S.: Box 1227, Calexico, CA 92231, tel. 706/566–8324. 167 rooms. Facilities: pool, beach, boat launch, restaurant, bar. MC, V.*

Hotel Riviera. On the hill overlooking the bay, this hotel has a pretty central courtyard, a long lap pool, and large rooms. *Calle Isla de los Cedros, tel. 65/7–1185. Facilities: pool, restaurant, bar. MC, V.*

La Trucha Vagabunda. You can't miss this pretty blue and white hotel on a hill overlooking the bay, a short walk from town. The rooms are spacious, simple, and clean, and the restaurant is one of San Felipe's best. *Av. de los Cedros Sur, tel. 657/7–1333; reservations in the U.S.: Box 5484, Calexico, CA 92231, tel. 619/298–4105, 800/522–1516 in CA, 800/225–2786 in the U.S. 45 rooms. Facilities: pool, restaurant, bar, disco. MC, V.*

Inexpensive **El Capitán.** This brick and adobe two-story motel is across the street from the beach and popular with families. The rooms are basic, and the small grounds are nothing more than a parking lot. *Av. Mar de Cortés 298, tel. 65/7–1303. 40 rooms. Facilities: pool, laundry room. MC, V.*

Tecate

Expensive **Hacienda Santa Veronica.** An unusual resort on the Brave Bull Ranch, where guests can watch matadors at practice. The hacienda's main attraction, though, is its Santa Veronica Off Road Park and Raceway, with seven tracks for motocross racers. The Colonial-style rooms (far away from the roaring race cars) have queen beds, tile floors, and folk art on the walls; a huge river stone fireplace is a gathering spot in the lounge and dining area. *15 mi (24 km) east of Tecate off Hwy. 2, tel. 68/5–9667; reservations in the U.S.: 619/298–4105, 800/522–1516 in CA, 800/225–2786 in U.S. 87 rooms and 105-space RV park. Facilities: pool, racetrack, restaurant, bar. MC, V.*

Rancho la Puerta. For those who can afford $1,500 or more a week, Rancho La Puerta is a peaceful, isolated health spa and resort 5 kilometers (3 miles) west of Tecate. Spanish-style buildings with red-tile roofs and more modern glass and wood structures are spread throughout the sprawling ranch. Hiking trails lead off into scrub pine hills surrounding the resort, and a large pool is the central gathering spot for those intent on relaxation. Guests stay in luxurious private cottages and usually check in for a week or more, taking advantage of the special diet and exercise regimen in order to lose weight and get in shape. Overnight guests are accepted when space is available. *Hwy. 2, tel. 65/4–1005 or 619/744–4222 in CA. Facilities: health club, massage, beauty salon, pool, tennis courts, restaurant. AE, MC, V.*

Moderate **El Dorado.** A pleasant in-town motel, El Dorado has carpeted, air-conditioned rooms. *Av. Juárez 1100, tel. 66/4–1102. 47 rooms. Facilities: pool, restaurant. MC, V.*

RV Parks, Trailer Parks, and Campgrounds

San Felipe is a popular place for campers and RV travelers who often settle in along the coast for the winter. Parks and campgrounds fill quickly during Christmas and Easter vacations, so make reservations early.

San Felipe **Club de Pesca Trailer Park.** A large, well-groomed facility with 120 RV and tent sites and all amenities, including boat launch and store. *9/10 km (1 mi) south of town on the beach off Av. Mar de Cortés, tel. 65/7–1180. Reservations: Apdo. 90, San Felipe, BCN.*

Mar del Sol RV Park. All amenities, including hotel facilities, are available here. *Av. Misión de Loreto, tel. 65/7–1280. Reservations: 664 Broadway, Suite G, Chula Vista, CA 92010, tel. 619/422–6900, 800/336–5454. Reservations required.*

Rubén's Trailer Park. One of the oldest and most popular parks in town, Rubén's has a good restaurant and a strong sense of community among the repeat visitors. It is located on the beach and boasts 50 sites, hookups, and most amenities, including restaurant and bar. *9/10 km (1 mi) north of town on Av. Mar de Cortés; tel. 657/7–1091. No reservations.*

The Arts and Nightlife

Mexicali **Teatro del Estado** (The State Theater) (tel. 65/4–0757) is on Calle López Mateos near the government center. Stage hits from Mexico City are often performed, and dance troupes and musical groups, both classical and modern, appear here. Much of the entertainment would be hard to find in the United States, particularly the excellent jazz and dance from Cuba and Russia.

There is nightly entertainment in the **Lucerna** (tel. 65/6–1000) and **Holiday Inn** (tel. 65/6–1300) hotels as well as at several places along Avenida Juárez, including the **Cadillac, El Zarape,** and **Chic's.** Also on Avenida Juárez is **La Capilla,** a discotheque with live entertainment, and **El Guaycura.**

San Felipe The bar at the **El Cortés Hotel** (tel. 65/7–1055) is always crowded. **La Misión** (tel. 65/7–1280) has live music and dancing on weekend nights.

Tecate For all its sleepy, provincial atmosphere, Tecate has one disco called **Los Candiles** (Hidalgo 327) and another at **Club Fandango** (Av. Revolución and Av. Juárez). **El Tucán Bar** (Blvd. Benito Juárez and Esteban Cantú) often has live entertainment.

Excursions in Northeastern Baja

The **Bahía de los Angeles,** located some 640 kilometers (400 miles) from the border, is one of the most beautiful spots on the entire peninsula. For fishing, relaxation, and getting away from it all, there are few places in Baja that can top this secluded Gulf Coast paradise. To get there, take Mexico Highway 1 south from Tijuana through Ensenada and the Santo Tomás Valley, past the Pacific Coast towns of Colonet and San Quintín, and turn inland at El Rosario, through Cataviña to the junction kilometers (8 miles) north of Punta Prieta. The turnoff is paved and easily passable by passenger vehicle. The bay itself is backed by mountains, and there are a number of islands offshore. Boats can be rented for spectacular sportfishing. The shelling is excellent, and there are beds of oysters and clams offshore. Trips to the nearby islands are also recommended. The two motels are good, but reservations should be made, particularly during the peak season from late October until May. **Casa Díaz** is adequate, built of rough-hewn stone, offering 15 units and electricity until 9 PM. *Reservations: Apdo. 579, Ensenada, BC, tel. 66/8–6070. No credit cards. Moderate.*

The **Villa Vitta Motel** is nice-looking and modern; its 40 units have air-conditioning, and the motel provides guide service for fishing. *Reservations: Jimsair, 2904 Pacific Hwy., San Diego, CA 92101, tel. 619/298–7704. No credit cards. Moderate.*

On Highway 2 between Tecate and Mexicali, there are turnoffs for two fascinating spots: the **Constitución de 1857 Parque Nacional** (Constitution of 1857 National Park), and **Cañon de Guadalupe** (Guadalupe Canyon). Only the most adventurous and properly equipped travelers should take on the dirt roads leading into these areas. West of Tecate, the same road that leads to the Hacienda Santa Verónica eventually passes through the national park, the beautiful Laguna Hanson, and ends in Los Ojos, connecting with Highway 3, which runs east and west from Ensenada to San Felipe. If taking this side trip, be sure to bring extra gas, water, and food. The sprawling pine forests, verdant meadows, and pleasant lake make this a good place for hiking and camping. The turnoff for Guadalupe Canyon is 26 kilometers (16 miles) east toward Mexicali from the top of the La Rumerosa Road; at the PEMEX station turn right and follow the signs to Cantú Palms (30 kilometers or 19 miles from the highway) and Cañón de Guadalupe (56 kilometers or 35 miles from the highway). The Cocopah Indians once congregated in Cantú Palms, and evidence of their presence— petroglyphs and grinding holes—can still be found among the rocks. Cantú Palms is beautiful, but not as startling as Guadalupe Canyon, with its hot springs and cool stream rushing in from the nearby 6,000-foot-high mountains. Palm trees abound in this oasislike setting, and the campground can accommodate about 30 campers. Visit the area in the spring, when the flowers are blooming and the weather is not yet unbearable.

Between San Felipe and Ensenada, south of Highway 3, lies the **Sierra de San Pedro Mártir National Park.** In this mountain range stands the highest peak in Baja, Picacho del Diablo, at over 10,000 feet. Its snow-covered summit can sometimes be seen from both Pacific and Gulf coast vantage points. The high plateau in this area contains dense forests and streams that run all year through mountain meadows. Some say the air here is clearer than anywhere else in the world, which may be why the Mexican government has an observatory here. There are two relatively popular places to stay in this area: the **Meling Ranch** and **Mike's Sky Rancho.** About 141 kilometers (88 miles) east of Ensenada on Highway 3 (also known as Baja California 16), a dirt-road turnoff leads 34 kilometers (21 miles) to Mike's Sky Rancho, a resort with cabins, pool, bar, café, and horses (reservations: Box 5376, San Ysidro, CA 92073, tel. 668/5–4995). About 18 kilometers (11 miles) farther south lies the Meling

Ranch (reservations: tel. 619/758–2719). This is a working cattle operation that takes in up to 12 guests at a time and arranges pack trips into the mountains. To avoid winter storms, plan trips from May through October.

7 Loreto

Introduction

The original capital of the Californias, Loreto now aspires to be simply a "capital" resort area. A start has been made, but it still has far to go. In the late '70s, when Mexico was oil-rich, Fonatur—the Mexican government agency charged with creating master-plan resorts—tapped the Loreto area for development. Streets were paved in the dusty little village, and nearly 2,000 acres were urbanized to allow for future development. Telephone service was brought in, along with electricity, potable water, and sewage systems. The little town of 8,000 inhabitants got an international airport. One big luxury hotel was built, as was a championship tennis center, where John McEnroe was signed as a touring pro.

Then everything came to a halt. No new hotels have opened since 1980. The Loreto Tennis Tournament moved to Ixtapa. In 1986 George Bush spent Christmas in Loreto, but only because he wanted to hold an unpublicized meeting with the then-president of Mexico, Miguel de la Madrid. Loreto was the perfect site.

Today, Loreto is a good place to escape the crowds and relax, then do nothing for awhile and relax some more. In between, there may be some time for fishing. Long before Fonatur arrived, Loreto was a favorite getaway for a few knowing American sports enthusiasts. Their fears that it would be spoiled have thus far been unfounded. Loreto is much as it was a decade or two ago, except that now it is more accessible.

Located on the Sea of Cortés some 1,200 kilometers (750 miles) south of the California border, Loreto's setting is truly spectacular. The gold and green hills of the Sierra Gigante seem to tumble into the cobalt sea. Rain is rare. According to local promoters, the skies are clear 360 days of the year. There are not even any bugs—or at least there are few—to plague vacationers. The dry, desert climate is not one in which insects thrive.

Loreto was the site of the first California mission. Jesuit Fathers Eusebio Kino and Juan María Salvatierra settled the area in 1683 and started building the mission in 1697. It was from Loreto that Father Junípero Serra, a Franciscan monk from Mallorca, Spain, set out in 1769 to found missions from San Diego to San Francisco in the land then known as Alta California.

Mexico won its independence from Spain in 1821, and the missions were gradually abandoned. The priests, who in many cases were Spanish, were ordered to return home. Loreto had been the administrative as well as the religious center of the Californias, but with the decline of the mission and the virtual destruction of the settlement by a hurricane in 1829, the capital of the Californias was moved to La Paz. A severe earthquake struck the Loreto area in 1877, further destroying the town.

The village languished for the next century. The U.S. fishermen who rediscovered the town after World War II were a hearty breed, flying down in their own aircraft to go out after marlin and sailfish in open launches. Loreto's several small hotels were built to serve this rough-and-ready set; most of the properties were built before 1960, when no highway came down this far and there was no airport worthy of the name.

Fonatur is a more recent arrival. Its projects take in not only the village, but some 24 kilometers (15 miles) of coastline. An area known as Nopoló is slated to be the address of swank hotels, and Puerto Escondido is to host a major marina and large hotels in addition to an existing trailer park. The little town is destined to become a bedroom community for all the people who will work at the hotels, shops, and restaurants that have yet to be built. The infrastructure has been completed, and Loreto sits waiting. Only the financing is missing.

Essential Information

Important Addresses and Numbers

Tourist Office (Calle Salvatierra across from the mission, tel. 683/3–0035) Closed Sundays.

Police, who may not speak English (tel. 683/3–0035).

Arriving and Departing by Plane

There is an international airport in Loreto serviced by **Aero California** (800/258–3311) from Los Angeles and La Paz. At press time, **Air Resorts** (619/298–4105, 800/522–1516 in CA, or 800/225–2786 in the U.S.) was scheduled to start flights into Loreto from San Diego and Tucson.

Arriving and Departing by Car

Loreto is 1,200 kilometers (750 miles) south of the U.S. border via Mexico Highway 1; **La Pinta Hotel at Guerrero Negro** is a good place to stay overnight. Early starts are recommended to avoid nighttime driving. **Tres Estrellas de Oro** (tel. 662/6–1146 in Tijuana) provides bus service along this route.

By Rental Car

There is a car rental agency at the airport and in the **Stouffer Presidente** hotel (tel. 683/3–0700), but only a few vehicles (all with standard shift) are available. There are two gas stations in Loreto; be sure to fill your tank before heading out on any long jaunts.

Getting Around

By Taxi Taxis are in good supply, and fares are inexpensive. It is wise, however, to establish the fare in advance.

Guided Tours

Sightseeing in the area means dropping by the little **Museo de las Misiónes** (Museum of the Missions) at Our Lady of Loreto church on the plaza late in the morning, popping over to the **Stouffer Presidente hotel** for a bit of refreshment, then continuing on to the RV park Tripui for lunch (the restaurant is quite good). Many variations on the theme are possible; use taxis for transportation.

Picnic cruises to **Carmen Island,** excursions into the mountains to visit the **San Javier Mission** and view prehistoric rock paintings, and day trips to **Mulegé** can be arranged through hotels. Call the local tour operator, **Turismo los Candeleros** (tel. 683/3–0700).

Exploring

One could allocate 15 minutes for a tour of downtown Loreto and still have time left over. The *malecón* (waterfront promenade) is a high seawall (a new one is now under construction); to see the water you have to walk on top of it. The small **zócalo** (square) and town center is one block west on Calle Salvatierra. The church, **La Misión de Nuestra Señora de Loreto,** is the only historic sight. Founded in 1697 by Jesuit Father Juan María Salvatierra, the church was the first mission in the Californias, the beginning of a chain of missions that eventually stretched as far as Sonoma, California, in what is now the United States. The church was nearly destroyed in the hurricane of 1829, and has only been restored in the past decade. The carved stone walls, wood-beam ceilings, gilded altar, and primitive portraits of the priests who have served there are worth seeing. The **Museum of Anthropology and History,** also called **El Museo de los Misiones,** next door to the church, contains religious relics, tooled leather saddles used in the 19th century, and displays of Baja's history. The museum has erratic hours and no phone, but is usually open Sunday morning and closed on Tuesday. Adjacent to the church is a new shopping complex, with boutiques selling fine silver and crafts.

Nopoló, where the luxury resorts are scheduled to go up, is about 8 kilometers (5 miles) south of town. Already in operation is the five-star Stouffer Presidente, complete with Hobie Cats and sailboats on its beach, a coffee shop, restaurant, lobby bar, and lively discotheque. Across the way is the nine-court tennis complex that is slated to more than double in size. An 18-hole golf course designed by Desmond Muirhead is supposed to be built just beyond the tennis complex.

According to Fonatur's plans, within 10 years there will be 5,700 hotel rooms in the Nopoló area, along with about 1,000 private homes and condo units. Whether this will actually come to pass depends on the willingness of private investors. For now, sidewalks and concrete foundation slabs run through fields of weeds and shrubs. **Juncalito,** a few miles south, is a pretty, isolated beach down a passable dirt road. There are public beaches, and camping is allowed, but there are no facilities.

More progress has been made 16 kilometers (10 miles) down the road in **Puerto Escondido,** where the marina, still under construction in the well-protected harbor, already contains 100 boat slips. Nearby is the RV park called **Tripui,** which has expanded to include motel rooms. Facilities for motorists and sailors include a snack shop, bar and restaurant, stores, showers, laundry, pool, and tennis courts. A boat ramp has been completed; just ask around for David Hernández, the port captain, to pay your fees and get permission to launch your boat. **Isla Danzante,** 5 kilometers (3 miles) southeast of Puerto Escondido, has good diving and some deep black coral reefs.

Picnic trips to nearby **Isla Coronado** may be arranged in Loreto proper, at Nopoló, or in Puerto Escondido. The island is inhabited only by sea lions. Snorkeling and scuba diving are excellent both here and off **Isla del Carmen,** site of a large volcano.

The second of the California missions, **San Javier,** is 35 kilometers (22 miles) southwest of Loreto. It is in many ways more imposing than the first. Construction of the stone church was started in 1720 and completed nearly 50 years later. The gilded altar was shipped from Mexico City via burro and boat, and the church is one of the most spectacular on the peninsula, its white Moorish domes rising high above the valley floor. Near San Javier, **Piedras Pintas** (painted rocks) is one of the few places where it is easy to view the 2,000-year-old prehistoric paintings found in remote areas throughout Baja California. Tours to San Javier and the cave paintings are available from Loreto hotels. The road to the mission is steep but graded, and the trip is rough for sedans.

Off the Beaten Track

A longer excursion involves driving some 134 kilometers (84 miles) north on Highway 1 to **Mulegé** (moo-leh-HAY), an old mission that was frequented by U.S. sportfishermen long before the current building boom. Many fishermen still fly in. The 32-room Hotel La Serenidad has a 4,000-foot landing strip outside its front door. Mulegé is a pretty, tropical town on the Sea of Cortés, with idyllic beaches along Bahía Concepción, the largest protected bay in Baja.

Santa Rosalia, 64 kilometers (40 miles) north, is known for its **Iglesia Santa Bárbara,** a prefabricated iron church designed by Alexandre-Gustave Eiffel, creator of the Eiffel Tower. Just south of Santa Rosalia there are groves of 60-foot-high cardon cactus, which resembles the saguaro cactus in the southwestern United States. The drive to Santa Rosalia and Mulegé and back, with the cobalt sea on one side and the craggy hills of Sierra Gigante on the other, is truly spectacular.

Shopping

There are few opportunities for browsing and buying in Loreto. **Kino's** and **La Choya,** near each other on the waterfront, handle an assortment of handicrafts from all over Mexico, including ceramics, sweaters, and serapes. Resort wear is also available. There is a smaller selection in the shop at the **Stouffer Presidente** (tel. 683/3–0700), which also stocks reading material in English. The small shopping complex near the church houses some newer boutiques, with a fine selection of silver jewelry.

Sports

Fishing Fishing is what put Loreto on the map, especially for Americans. Cabrillo and snapper are caught year-round; yellowtail in the spring; and dorado, marlin, and sailfish in the summer. Sports enthusiasts should bring tackle with them because local tackle is likely to be primitive and worn. All Loreto-area hotels can arrange fishing, and many own their own skiffs; the local fishermen congregate with their small boats, called *pangas*, at the beach on the north end of town. **Alfredo's Sportsfishing** (tel. 683/3–0016) takes anglers out and has good guides.

Scuba Diving The coral reefs off Coronado and Carmen islands are an undersea adventure. The scuba specialist is **Fantasia Divers** at the Hotel Stouffer Presidente (tel. 683/3–0700).

Sailing The best sailing is off the beach by the **Stouffer Presidente** on Nopoló Bay. Hobie Cats and similar craft may be rented at the hotel (tel. 683/3–0700).

Tennis The **Loreto Tennis Center** (tel. 683/3–0700), adjoining the Stouffer Presidente in Nopoló, 8 kilometers (5 miles) south of Loreto, is open to the public. The center, where John McEnroe is touring pro, is operated by All American Sports; it has expert instructors and nine illuminated courts.

Beaches

All Loreto-area hotels are on the waterfront, but the beaches are disappointing, being more stones than sand. The beach in front of the La Pinta hotel is probably the best place to swim. The setting everywhere is spectacular: The craggy hills tumble into the gentle surf in such a way that Fonatur can promote Loreto as the place where "even the mountains swim."

Dining

There aren't many restaurants in Loreto, but the seafood is excellent no matter where you go.

Highly recommended restaurants in each category are indicated by a star ★.

Category	Cost*
Expensive	over $10
Moderate	$5–$10
Inexpensive	under $5

per person, excluding drinks, service, and tax (15%)

Moderate
★ **Caesar's.** One block east of the church, it's the best restaurant in town, with good seafood and traditional Mexican dishes. Try giant shrimp stuffed with cheese, wrapped with bacon, and grilled. The most expensive dinner won't be more than $12. *Salvatierra at Zapata, tel. 683/3–0203. MC, V.*
Tripui. The recreational vehicle park in Puerto Escondido is the best place outside Loreto for seafood, with prices somewhat higher than at Caesar's. *At the RV park, tel. 683/3–0818. MC, V.*

Inexpensive **Cafe Olé.** The best taquitos in town are found here, as well as good burgers and delicious chocolate shakes. *Calle Francisco Madero, tel. 683/3–0496.*

Lodging

The choices are good, but limited. The most luxurious hotels are out of town and isolated.

Highly recommended lodgings in each price category are indicated by a star ★.

Category	Cost*
Very Expensive	over $100
Moderate	$40–$50
Inexpensive	under $40

All prices are for a standard double room, excluding 15% sales tax.

Very Expensive **Stouffer Presidente.** A modern all-inclusive hotel across from
★ the tennis center, the Presidente features all water sports, including fishing and sailing. This is by far the most lavish resort in the area, with modern rooms, carpeting, and air-conditioning. *Nopoló Beach, tel. 683/3-0700; reservations in the U.S.: tel. 800/472-2427. 250 rooms. Facilities: pool, beach, tennis, restaurant, bar, disco, tour desk, TV. AE, MC, V.*

Moderate **La Pinta.** Part of a chain of Baja California hotels, this property is a much-remodeled fishing camp on the beach. It has its own fleet of launches. *Blvd. Misión de Loreto, tel. 683/3-0025; reservations in the U.S.: tel. 800/678-7244. 48 rooms. Facilities: pool, 2 tennis courts. MC, V.*

Misión. An old favorite, this is the only hotel right in Loreto. It has a view of the sea beyond the seawall. The beach across the street is stony, but most guests come to fish; arrangements for fishing may be made at the hotel. *Calle de la Playa, in town, tel. 683/3-0048. Facilities: pool, restaurant, bar. MC, V.*

★ **Oasis.** This is one of the original fishing camps, a favorite with those who want to spend as much time as possible on the water. Many of the rooms, set amid a tropical oasis of palms, have a view of the water. The hotel has its own fleet of skiffs. *Loreto Beach, tel. 683/3-0112; reservations in the U.S.: tel. 619/491-0682. 60 rooms. Facilities: pool, tennis, fishing, boats. MC, V.*

Inexpensive **Serenidad.** Some 130 kilometers (80 miles) north of Loreto, this
★ hotel is worth the trip. The rooms have fireplaces (nights can be chilly), and the Saturday barbecue is a Baja institution. *In Mulegé, tel. 685/3-0111. 27 rooms. Facilities: pool, restaurant, airstrip. MC, V.*

Nightlife

After-dark entertainment is pretty much limited to the lobby bar and disco at the **Stouffer Presidente;** this is also the only place with TVs in the rooms and a satellite dish to pick up U.S. programs. The **Playa Blanca** (Av. Madero) has live music nightly at 8 PM. The bars at the other hotels usually attract a congenial crowd, but the fishermen drawn to the Loreto area turn in early.

8 La Paz

Introduction

La Paz is one of those cities that makes you wish you'd been there 20 years ago, when its population was half the current 170,000, before the highway and airport maligned the moniker "City of Peace." Even in the slowest of times, late summer, when the heat tops 120°F, you can easily see how commerce competes with the city's charms.

It was commerce of a sort that first attracted Hernán Cortés and his soldiers in 1535: The beautiful bay was rich with oysters and pearls. The Jesuits arrived in 1720, aiming to civilize and convert the Indians. Instead, the missionaries inadvertently decimated the local populace by introducing smallpox and syphilis. Within 30 years, there was no one left to convert.

While the rest of Mexico was being torn apart by the struggle for independence, La Paz became a refuge for those escaping the mainland wars. In 1829, after the then-capital Loreto was leveled by a hurricane, La Paz became the capital of the Californias. Troops from the United States occasionally invaded it, but sent word to Washington that the whole peninsula was not worth fighting for. In 1853, a different group of invaders arrived from the United States: southerners, led by William Walker, who were intent on making La Paz a slave state. The Mexicans disliked Walker's plans, and he was soon banished from La Paz. Peace reigned for the next century, and the oysters and their pearls continued to attract prospectors. But in 1940 disease wiped out the oyster beds; with the pearls gone, La Paz was once again left to its own devices.

La Paz officially became the capital of Baja Sur in 1974, and is now the state's largest settlement. It is the site of the state power plant, a fleet of cruise ships, the ferry to Mazatlán, the state bureaucracy, the governor's home, and the state jail. It is the stopping-off point for fishermen and divers headed for Cerralvo, La Partida, and Espíritu Santo islands, where parrot fish, manta rays, neons, and angels blur the clear waters by shore, and marlin, dorado, and yellowtail leap out of the sea. Mexicans from the mainland come on shopping sprees (until 1989, Baja had a 6% sales tax, as compared to 15% in the rest of the country) to buy goods from Europe and the Orient. For much of the day and night the waterfront and downtown are filled with the crush of buyers, sellers, residents, and visitors.

La Paz's charm is evident in the early morning. The faded brown hills surrounding the sprawling city turn golden amber; the sea turns aqua blue. The plaza on the malecón is empty, except for kittens, joggers, and a trickle of workers. In the plaza downtown—Jardín Velazco (Velazco Garden)—the pink quartz gazebo shines in the sunlight: Dense trees and blooming hibiscus shade the freshly swept tile paths. Bells ring in the Catedral de Nuestra Señora de La Paz, and uniformed children stroll arm in arm to school. At sunset, the city grows calm, and *los Paceños*, as the residents are called, pause at the waterfront to watch the sea grow dark.

Essential Information

Important Addresses and Numbers

Tourist Information
The main tourism office is across from the **Fidepaz** on Paseo Obregón (Box 419, La Paz 23010, tel. 682/2–1199).

Emergencies
Police (tel. 682/2–6610); **Fire** (tel. 682/2–0054); **Red Cross** (tel. 682/2–1111); **Clínica La Paz** (461 Calle Revolución tel. 682/2–0685 or 682/2–2800) has English-speaking doctors on staff and can handle most medical emergencies, including lab work. Doctors will make house calls and are on call for after-hours emergencies.

Arriving and Departing by Plane

The La Paz airport, about 16 kilometers (10 miles) north of town, is home to **Aero California** (tel. 800/258–3311), which flies from Los Angeles, Phoenix, and San Diego to La Paz. **Aeroméxico** (tel. 800/237–6639) flies in from Tijuana and Guadalajara. At press time there were no flights to La Paz on U.S. carriers.

Arriving and Departing by Car, Bus, and Ferry

By Car
La Paz is 1,474 kilometers (921 miles) south of the U.S. border at Tijuana on the Transpeninsular Highway (Mexico Highway 1), and 211 kilometers (132 miles) north of Los Cabos, on the southern tip of the peninsula. Highway 1 makes a gentle, hardly noticeable U-turn as it nears La Paz, so the city looks north when you expect it to look east. This can be disconcerting at dawn and sunset, when the sun seems to be on the wrong side of the sky.

By Bus
Tres Estrellas de Oro (tel. 682/2–3063) operates buses along Highway 1 north to the border and south to Los Cabos.

By Ferry
The ferry system connecting Baja to mainland Mexico has been privatized, and is constantly undergoing changes in rates and schedules. Currently, there are ferries from La Paz to Mazatlán and La Paz to Topolobampo. The ferry office is at the dock on the road to Pichilingue (tel. 682/5–3833). Go to the office and purchase your ticket personally, in advance of your trip, and expect confusion. **Baja Express** is a new ferry system using hydrofoils, or fast catamarans, for daily departures from La Paz to Topolobampo/Los Mochis. Future plans include ferries to Los Cabos, Guaymas, and Santa Rosalia. Reservations can be made in the U.S. by calling 213/578–9680 or 800/829–0510.

Getting Around

By Rental Car
A car is not necessary if you plan to stay in town, since taxis are readily available. But to explore the more remote beaches, a car is a must. Rental prices are about $70 per day for a Volkswagen Beetle, including insurance and unlimited mileage. The rates are about the same no matter which company you use, and all have desks at the airport. If you want a sedan or air-conditioning, call ahead to reserve a car.

Rental agencies include: **Budget** (Paseo Obregón at Calle Hidalgo, tel. 682/2–1097) and **Servitur Autorento** (5 de Febrero at Calle Abasolo, tel. 682/2–1448).

By Taxi Taxis are inexpensive, but be sure to decide on a price with the driver before the cab gets going.

Guided Tours

Travel agencies in the hotels and along the malecón offer tours of the city, day-long trips to Los Cabos, sportfishing, and boating excursions.

Exploring

Numbers in the margin correspond with points of interest on the La Paz map.

The Malecón

① The **malecón** is La Paz's boardwalk, tourist zone, and the main drag. Entering town from the north, you'll know when **Paseo Obregón** has become the malecón when you spot boutiques and hotels rather than auto parts stores and funeral parlors. By mid-1990, there is supposed to be a more official entry point to **②** the city—the 500-acre **Fidepaz**, about 10 blocks north of the current center of activity. So convinced are the tourism officials and developers of the marina's eventual success that the **③** **State Tourism Department** headquarters is across the street from the marina. The location is not of much use to tourists without cars, but there is eventually supposed to be a tourist information booth in the center of the malecón.

The malecón is at its best at night, when the real action starts at Paseo Obregón and Calle Márquez de León and rock 'n roll **④** blares from **La Paz-Lapa,** a classic hybrid of the Carlos 'n Charlie's restaurant chain. Be sure to peek in if you've never seen the chain's special breed of tourist trap—cavernous rooms claustrophobically cluttered with a mass of billboards, road signs, hanging model planes, and clients' business cards stapled on the walls.

Time Out If you begin your tour in the evening and can handle frenetic activity, have your first margarita and some nachos at **La Paz-Lapa.** The portions are gargantuan, and the quality consistently good. *Paseo Obregón at Calle Márquez de León, tel. 682/2–6025. MC, V. Closed Tuesday.*

⑤ La Paz's only true colonial Mexican hotel is **Los Arcos** (Paseo Obregón and Calle Allende, tel. 682/2–2744). The central courtyard has a fountain surrounded by flowers and, if no one is playing Ping-Pong nearby, is a pleasant place for a short quiet rest. The Los Arcos lobby is a good place to gather information from hotel guests, the tour desk, and the fishing-tour desk. The adjacent travel agency is extremely helpful as well.

Shops carrying the predictable assortment of sombreros, onyx chess sets, and painted plaster curios line the next few blocks. Wander through **Artesanías La Antigua California** (220 Paseo Obregón) for a sampling of better Mexican crafts—colorful woven baskets from Michoacán, carved masks from Guerrero, and

replicas of Aztec and Mayan artifacts. When you tire of walking and shopping, choose one of the front-row tables at **La Perla Hotel**'s second-story bar—the best seats on the malecón for watching teens cruising through town in their cars, with red and yellow lights twinkling around their license plates and the latest American hits blaring from their radios.

A white arch over the street at the foot of Calle 16 de Septiembre marks the entrance to the center-city area. Across the street, a two-story white gazebo is the focus of the **malecón plaza.** Military bands and mariachis play in the gazebo on weekend nights, when you can barely make it through the crowd of children chasing balloons and young men eyeing the parade of young women in miniskirts and high heels. Indian women spread their worn blankets on the sidewalk and sell gum, candy bars, and cigarettes, while the aroma of steaming corn drifts in from the wagons lining the curb. A visit to the plaza should also include a stroll farther north on the malecón, past the children's playground. Those too young to join in the ritualistic flirting along the sidewalk watch their brothers and sisters from the swing sets, while the grown-ups look on. The crowd thins out within a few blocks, until couples seeking the solitude of park benches are all that remain along the walkway.

Central La Paz

To reach the real business district walk a few blocks east on Calle 16 de Septiembre, then turn left on Calle Madero or Calle Revolución. Here the crush of window-shoppers, street vendors, and businesspeople becomes nearly overwhelming. Grab onto your purse and the arm of whomever you're with and plunge in past bridal boutiques, furniture stores, and myriad specialty shops. Though the street sights are mesmerizing, be sure to watch your feet as well—some sidewalks ascend abruptly into overpasses, then end in steep steps.

This downtown district is where mainland Mexicans do their shopping, but as most of the goods are imported, they are no bargain for those from the United States. Browse through **Dorian's,** a large chain department store at the corner of Avenidas 16 de Septiembre and Agosto to see what the mainlanders buy.

8 **La Catedral de Nuestra Señora de La Paz** (Our Lady of La Paz Cathedral) is the big attraction downtown, though it's not nearly as gilded as the churches in the colonial cities on the mainland. La Paz's original Catholic church was a mission built by Jesuit Padre Jaime Bravo in 1720. The Indians weren't fond of him, and the mission was soon abandoned. The cathedral was built near the mission site in 1860, and it's obvious this was a struggling settlement at the time. The plain brick and mortar church with a few primitive stained-glass windows attests to how difficult life was for the early settlement. The interior white cement walls are devoid of the elaborately dressed saints one sees elsewhere, and instead bear only small wooden stations of the cross, labeled in English. The cathedral faces the

9 zócalo, also known as **Plaza Constitución and Jardín Velazco.** The plaza is heavily landscaped in a haphazard sort of way, but lacks the sense of community evident in the sidewalk cafés surrounding the plazas in Oaxaca or Veracruz.

10 On the opposite end of the plaza is the **Biblioteca de las Californias,** a library specializing in the history of Baja California, with reproductions of local prehistoric cave paintings, oil paintings of the missions, and the best collection of historical documents on the peninsula. *Calle Madero at Calle 5 de Mayo, tel. 682/2–2640. Open by appointment.*

One gets an excellent sense of La Paz's culture and heritage at

11 the **Museum of Anthropology**, at the corner of Calles Altamirano and 5 de Mayo. The cactus garden at the entrance reflects careful restoration of the city's former natural dignity. The spiny cardon is juxtaposed against the mud-colored cement of the museum's walls, reminiscent of what La Paz was like when settlers lived in simple adobe homes amid the desert cacti and dust. Exhibits include a diorama of the early city, complete with yellow toy bulldozers and cranes; gypsum arrowheads and re-creations of Comondo and Las Palmas Indian villages; sparkling chunks of quartz from the now-defunct mines; photos of the cave paintings found in remote Baja; copies of Cortés's writings on first sighting La Paz; handicrafts from outlying settlements, including huaraches and palm hammocks (which look too scratchy and stiff to be comfortable); and a large collection of leather chaps, branding irons, and tools used by the cowboys. Many of the exhibit descriptions are written only in Spanish, but the museum staff will do their best to translate for you. *Calles Ignacio and 5 de Mayo, tel. 682/2–0162. Admission free. Open daily 8–6.*

The museum's original building at the corner of Avenidas Altamirano and Constitución, on the same block as the muse-

⑫ um, is now the **Biblioteca Justo Sierra**, a children's library that contains a workroom decorated with drawings made by youngsters. *Calle Altamirano at Av. Constitución, tel. 682/2–2852. Admission free. Open weekdays 8–8, Sat. 9–2.*

Pichilingue

North of town, Paseo Obregón—the malecón—becomes what is commonly known as the Pichilingue Road, which leads about 16 kilometers (10 miles) south to the sportfishing and former ferry terminals. Just outside town the road divides, and outbound traffic climbs up a steep cliff overlooking deserted
⑬ beaches. The road passes over **Playa Coromuel** and its bright blue water slide, called El Torrero (The Lighthouse Keeper). A few kilometers south is the most deluxe resort in town, La Concha. The beach at the north end of the hotel is clean, un-
⑭ crowded, and open to the public. Next door is the **Governor's House,** surrounded by guards and gates. A road sign points out the site, certainly the largest and most impressive home in the area, with its own secluded beach and view of the islands.

Just 10 kilometers (6 miles) out of town is the Baja outback; the west side of the road looks out over barren desert, while to the east are lagoons and bays where brown pelicans and delicate white egrets dive for fish. The scenery is less inviting as you
⑮ pass the **Ferry Terminal**, where warehouses serve as waiting rooms, and the state's main power plant. Roadside stands serve oysters and grilled fish along the highway, across the street from the terminal, but if you're traveling by car, wait for a
⑯ snack until you reach **Pichilingue Beach**, just past a few more pretty coves.

Since the time of pirate ships and Spanish invaders, Pichilingue was known for oysters bearing black pearls. In 1940, they were killed off by an unknown disease, leaving the beach deserted. Now Pichilingue is a pleasant place to sunbathe and watch the sportfishing boats bring in their haul. A
⑰ dirt road leads away from the beach to **Punta Balandra**, a secluded point where some of La Paz's prettiest beaches and best diving spots are located. You'll need a car to reach these beaches.

Time Out Two large *palapa* (open-air) restaurants on the beach serve icy cold beer and oysters *diablo*, raw oysters steeped in a fiery hot sauce. The palapas are open from sunrise to sunset and serve some of the freshest and least expensive grilled fish in town—a full meal with drinks won't cost more than $5. The palapas are unnamed and there are no phones on the point, but taxi drivers will know what you're talking about if you say you want oysters diablo in Pichilingue.

What to See and Do with Children

Children are quite obviously cherished in La Paz. Residents speak proudly of their version of Boy's Town, an orphanage called **La Ciudad de los Niños y Niñas,** where orphans from throughout the state are housed and trained in printing and carpentry skills. Playgrounds are plentiful; the biggest and best is at the beach, near the foot of Calle 16 de Septiembre. A giant slide extends a few feet out in the water, candy-striped balance beams rise over the sand, and at the water's edge, a trapeze of sorts is stretched between two high poles. You climb the stairs by a pole, grab the rope hanging from the trapeze line, and swoop across the beach, dangling in the air. At night the playground is positively packed with parents and children, and it's a great place to find playmates. There is another beach for children at Coromuel, with its gigantic water slide, shallow surf, and swings. The children's library (*see* Central La Paz in Exploring, above) has regular arts and crafts workshops for the little ones. Teens will enjoy hanging out on the malecón, watching the Paceños cruise and flirt.

Off the Beaten Track

The workshop of weaver **Fortunada Silva** (3315 Calle Abasolo, tel. 682/2–4575) sits on a dirt lot just outside town, on the way to the airport. Silva, an elderly man who speaks no English, demonstrates his craft in a large workroom filled with looms and spinning wheels. In the back lot, he boils cotton from local gins in huge bathtubs over wood fires until the yarn turns vivid shades of green and blue, then soaks the yarn in vats dug into the ground till the dye sets. Indoors, his siblings and children (some of whom speak English) weave the yarn into simple rugs, place mats, and tablecloths that are sold in a small shop at the front of the workshop. Bargaining is unnecessary, since the prices are incredibly low—about 50¢ for a durable, colorful place mat. Silva's shop is just about the only place in La Paz where you get a true picture of Mexican folk arts. Silva says his workshop is open daily. If the doors are shut, just wander around the lot; someone is sure to appear and let you in.

Shopping

Souvenir shopping is pretty basic in La Paz. There are straw sombreros, onyx chess sets, Disney character piñatas, and embroidered dresses in the shops along the malecón, with a few genuine finds thrown in. **Soko's** (corner of Paseo Obregón and Calle 16 de Septiembre, next to the arch) has rooms filled with classic curios of the velvet painting genre. **Bazaar del Sol** on the next block north has a more imaginative selection, with brightly painted *animalitos* (small wood animals) from Oaxaca and pastel-glazed pottery from Guanajuato. **Artesaniás la Antigua California** (220 Paseo Obregón) has more imports from the mainland, including pottery from Guadalajara, carved and painted gourds from Olinala, and replicas of Aztec and Maya artifacts arranged gallery-style. The prices are higher than elsewhere, but the selection is far more extensive. **Curios La Carreta** (Paseo Obregón between Calles Muelle and Tejada) has three large showrooms with carved wood tables and chairs, heavy blue and purple glassware, woven baskets, appliquéd clothing, and much more. The selection of English-language books on Baja is excellent.

For high-quality souvenir T-shirts and shorts silk-screened with vivid fish and birds, try **Bye-Bye,** whose chain of shops has expanded throughout Mexico's tourist regions. **El Delfín,** next to La Perla hotel, has shells strung, mounted, and lacquered in mobiles, mirrors, and jewelry. **El Dios del Sol,** inside La Perla, carries Baja-made leather furniture, pottery, jewelry, and handicrafts, which it also exports to the United States.

Deportes Ortíz (260 Calle Degollado) has sportfishing equipment. The downtown stores are a jumble of bridal, baby, furniture, appliance, and shoe shops. For the best selection, go to Dorian's chain department store (Calles 16 de Septiembre and Agosto) or **La Perla** (Calle Mutualismo 39).

Sports

Diving, windsurfing, sportfishing, and yachting are La Paz's major sports, with the warm waters of the Sea of Cortés offering ideal conditions for those who prefer calm waters, little or no surf, and visibility that reaches 50 feet and more.

Diving Popular dive spots include the white coral banks off Isla Espíritu Santo, the sea lion colony off Isla Partida, and the seamount 14 kilometers (9 miles) farther east, where schools of hammerhead sharks circle the divers.

Scuba Aguilar gives windsurfing and sailing lessons, rents equipment, and operates dives. Tours skirt the coast to Espíritu Santo and take in the *Salvatierra* wreck, a sunken, 270-foot-long ferryboat. A two-tank dive costs $55. *107 Av. Independencia, Box 179–B. tel. 682/2–0719. Open daily 9:30–1:30 and 4:30–7:30.*

Fishing The considerable fleet of private boats in La Paz now has more
and Boating room for docking at two marinas, the **Fidepaz** at the north end of town, and the **Hotel Palmira marina** south of town. Fishing is a big draw in La Paz, and several U.S. and Mexican companies run long-range and one-day fishing charters from La Paz. Most hotels have fishing operations. The **Dorado Velez Fleet** (Box 402, La Paz, tel. 682/2–2744) operated by Jack Velez in Los Arcos hotel, has 25- and 32-foot cabin cruisers, which can be chartered for about $200 per day. **Roberto's Boats** (tel. 682/5–2816), also out of Los Arcos, has similar boats and prices.

Spectator Sports

Boat and The town is all eyes every spring as fleets of yachts go by during
Auto Races races from Long Beach, Newport Beach, and Los Angeles, California to Los Cabos, and up the Sea of Cortés to La Paz. Fishing tournaments in August and November bring marlin admirers out, while the Baja 1,000-mile road race in November creates a mighty roar.

Parachuting Parachutists and hang gliders from the United States have recently discovered La Paz, and during the summer come to town by the hundreds, filling the skies for days on end as their parachutes float to the ground in impromptu air shows.

Beaches

With no surf, great visibility, and miles of white sand, La Paz has enough beach space for all visitors. The beaches off the malecón are best suited for strolling and playing at the beach playground by Calle 16 de Septiembre. Swimming and snorkeling are best north of town, on the way to Pichilingue. Near the La Concha resort is **Playa Coromuel**, home of the bright blue El Torrero, a gigantic water slide that seems *at least* five stories high and ends in the ocean—best to try it when the tide is in, or you'll end up scraping your bottom in the sand. There's a U-turn just north of the beach that leads back to the entrance. El Coromuel is definitely designed for children, with trash cans covered with plaster bear and lion heads and a beach that slopes gradually into the shallow water. A large palapa-style restaurant serves beer and tacos in the shade, but many signs admonish the clientele to keep the furniture off the beach.

Playa de Pichilingue, between the former ferry landing and the end of the point, seems miles long; it has plenty of private space and two palapa restaurants serving cold drinks and fish. Beyond the palapas, off a dirt road, is **Punta Balandra,** with scores of secluded coves and the popular **Playa Tecolote** and **El Coyote.** Campers in Volkswagen buses stay put at El Coyote for days, watching the city lights from across the water.

Travel agencies and fishing and diving charter boat companies offer day trips to Isla Espíritu Santo, where the snorkeling is great in the white coral banks, natural springs form pools amid the palms, and there are no footprints in the white sand.

Dining

The specialties here are fresh fish and oysters *diablo*, served with fiery hot sauce. Most of the restaurants are clustered along the malecón, though there are some finds in other parts of the city. Some restaurants, particularly in the hotels, add a service charge of 10%–15% on top of the 15% tax.

Highly recommended restaurants in each price category are indicated by a star ★.

Category	Cost*
Expensive	over $15
Moderate	$10–$15
Inexpensive	under $10

*per person excluding drinks, service, and sales tax (15%)

Expensive
★ **El Bismark.** You've got to wander a bit out of your way to reach El Bismark, where locals and repeat visitors go for good, home-style Mexican food. The chips are whole, deep-fried corn tortillas served with a mayonnaiselike guacamole that's best avoided. Instead, try the ceviche—a large cocktail glass stuffed with fresh shredded fish, lime juice, onions, tomatoes, and chilis. Specialties include *cochinita pibil* (marinated pork chunks) served with homemade tortillas, *carne asada* (marinated and grilled steak served with beans, guacamole, and tortillas), and enormous grilled lobsters. Families settle down for hours at long wood tables, while waitresses divide their attention between the patrons and the soap operas on the TV above the bar. *Calle Degollado and Altamirano, tel. 682/2-4854. MC, V.*

El Moro. This stark, white Moorish palace near the Hotel Palmira looks like it would serve Basque or Middle Eastern dishes, but the menu is mostly Italian. The setting is more elegant than at most La Paz establishments, with heavy tablecloths, real silver and china, and candles on the tables. *2 km (1.2 mi) from town on Pichilingue Rd., no phone. MC, V.*

★ **Las Brisas.** A few blocks past the malecón's concentration of blaring music is a quiet, romantic restaurant where two male guitarists and a female vocalist softly croon Mexican ballads. The popular palapa theme is upscale here, with white linen tablecloths, woven leather chairs, and candles in hurricane lamps—which cast just enough light for you to read the menu without setting it on fire. The fresh salsa with chunks of onion and tomato and lots of pungent cilantro is a sign of good things to come. Try a plate of fresh *cabrillo* (sea bass) grilled over mesquite, encrusted with toasted garlic, and served with steak fries, homegrown tomatoes, and a basket of homemade tortillas. *Paseo Obregón at Calle Heróico Colegio Militar, no phone. AE, MC, V. No lunch.*

Moderate **El Camarón Feliz.** On the quieter end of the malecón, by the park on Calle Bravo, you can hang out at the open-air tables by the window and watch the sunset, drink beer or coffee, have some good lobster or shrimp, and gather your forces for the night. The ambience is casual and friendly—lots of playful flirting goes on between the window sitters and the street strollers, and the skateboarders practicing in the park put on a good show. *Paseo Obregón at Calle Bravo, tel. 682/2–9011. MC, V.*

La Paz-Lapa. Ask locals where to dine and they will inevitably point to La Paz-Lapa, which seems popular mostly because it's different. The noise level here is deafening, but it's a fun place, with lots of clutter on the walls, wide-screen TV in the bar, waiters so jolly you expect them to break into song, and an air of excitement. Families like it, as do those preparing for a wild night of drinking and carousing. The sunset view of the ocean is lovely, and it's easy to make friends with fellow diners. The food—basic beef, chicken, fish, and Mexican selections—is tasty and plentiful. *Paseo Obregón at León, tel. 682/2–6025. AE, MC, V. Closed Tues.*

La Terraza. On the malecón under the waterfront rooms of La Perla hotel is a combination coffee shop, piano bar, Italian bistro, and tourist hangout where the strong coffee is poured and re-poured without extra charge. The menu caters to both snackers and big eaters; tacos and enchiladas share the bill with pastas and T-bone steaks. The guacamole is an unusual blend of avocado and grated cheese—actually, it comes off quite well. *Paseo Obregón 1570, tel. 682/2–0777. MC, V.*

Restaurante Yate. The location is ideal—on the waterfront by the malecón plaza. One of a score of palapas on the malecón, the Yate is distinguished by its cappuccino, a rarity in La Paz, and by its generous, inexpensive breakfasts. *Paseo Obregón at Septiembre, no phone. No credit cards.*

★ **Samalu.** Owners Santos and Manuel Mompala put the first two letters of their names together, tacked on a "lu" for "euphonic effect," and opened their A-frame palapa restaurant in an overgrown garden of palms and vines on a marginally paved back road near the butane plant. The brothers have a faithful following among cab drivers, hotel clerks, and shop owners—ask where to eat, and often enough you'll hear about Samalu's *chiles rellenos* and turtle steaks. Stick with anything prepared "Samalu style"—giant shrimp stuffed with cheese, wrapped in bacon, dipped in batter and deep-fried, or a thin steak filet served with grilled onion and pepper strips, guacamole, beans, and a cheese enchilada. Be sure to check out the "Maligator" (half-marlin, half-alligator) mounted in the bar—the sight is much more believable if you've had a few shots of Cuervo Gold. Real mounted marlin, parrot fish, and giant turtle shells hang on the restaurant walls beneath wagon-wheel chandeliers with twinkling lights tucked in conch shells. Samalu becomes downright charming in the evening; French windows open to the garden and the hurricane lamps flicker in the breeze (the mosquitoes like the setting as well). *Calle Rangel between Colima and Calle Jalisco, tel. 682/2–2481. MC, V.*

Inexpensive **El Quinto Sol Restaurante Vegetariano.** Like a bit of Berkeley
★ transplanted south, El Quinto's bright yellow exterior walls are painted with Indian snake symbols and smiling suns. Inside, bright blue tablecloths cover metal folding tables, clay suns and moons hang on the walls, and healthy vines and palms grow beside bookshelves filled with herbs and teas. The natural foods store in the back room stocks grains, soaps, lotions, oils, and books, while the restaurant serves yogurt smoothies with bananas and wheat germ, ceviche tostadas, and *machaca* (marinated shredded beef) made with meat substitutes. Customers linger over tea and philosophize; browsing is encouraged. *Calle Belisario Domínguez and Av. Independencia, tel. 682/2–1692. No credit cards.*

La Fabula Pizza. With its turrets and lacy white trim, this building resembles a bright yellow, two-story midwestern victorian frame home. The pizza parlor inside, crowded and fun, could be in Ohio: It has posters of Tom Selleck, Burt Reynolds, and the like; old 45 records hanging from the walls; and plastic red and white checked tablecloths. But we're not talking just your basic pepperoni here. They've got pizza with sausage, beans, and jalapeño peppers; smoked oysters and tuna; and Hawaiian ham and bananas. *Paseo Obregón at Calle 16 de Septiembre, no phone. No credit cards.*

Lodging

La Paz has hotels clustered along the malecón, although a few of the more expensive places are outside town on the roads to Pichilingue and the airport. If you're interested in sunbathing and relaxing on the beach, stay outside town.

Highly recommended lodgings in each price category are indicated by a star ★.

Category	Cost*
Expensive	over $55
Moderate	$25–$55
Inexpensive	under $25

*All prices are for a standard double room, excluding service charge and sales tax (15%).

Expensive **Hotel Gran Baja.** This solitary high rise (called the "Ivory Tower" by cynics in the trailer parks down the road) is in its fourth or fifth incarnation, having already been a Ramada and a Sheraton, and the bellboys seem ready to change uniforms again if need be. It's a pleasant enough hotel, with great views of the town, desert, and islands, large white rooms with pastel spreads and sketches, and good piano music in the bar, but somehow it seems out of place in La Paz. If you're oblivious to the location and interested in lounging by the pool, playing shuffleboard and tennis, walking on a pristine beach that could be almost anywhere, or watching HBO and ordering room service, this is your spot in La Paz. *Calle Rangel at Playa Sur, tel. 682/2–3900; reservations in the U.S.: 4422 Cerritos Ave., Los Alamitos, CA 90720, tel 213/583–3930 or 800/347–2252. 250 rooms. Facilities: pool, beach, tennis, miniature golf, restaurant, lobby and palapa bars, gift shop. AE, MC, V.*

★ **La Concha Beach Resort.** La Concha has taken over the old El Presidente Hotel on the road to Pichilingue and turned it into a first-class resort. Low white buildings with red-tile roofs are surrounded by towering palms, and the long white beach is the cleanest in La Paz. Except for a jaunt into town for shopping or a change of scenery, you could stay put for a week and not be bored: Tennis, scuba diving, snorkeling, waterskiing, widescreen TV, movies, and a large swimming pool are all available. *Km 5 on the Pichilingue Rd., tel. 682/2–6544; reservations in the U.S.: tel. 800/999–2252. 109 rooms. Facilities: pool, 2 tennis courts, restaurant, palapa and lobby bars, gift shop, meeting and banquet rooms. AE, MC, V.*

Los Arcos. Many say Los Arcos is the nicest hotel in La Paz, but that depends on the location of your room. Resist the waterfront view and request a room in the central courtyard, where the rush of water in the fountain drowns out the music from the street and the noise from the pool area. All rooms have balconies and TV; some have squeaky, lumpy mattresses. The self-service coffee shop opens early so that those headed out on fishing boats can eat and pick up a box lunch. The upstairs bar is cavernous and dark, and looks out over the malecón. *Paseo Obregón between Calles Rosales and Allende, tel. 682/2–2744; reservations in the U.S.: 4422 Cerritos Ave., Los Alamitos, CA 90720, tel 213/583–3930 or 800/347–2252. 150 rooms. Facilities: pool, sauna, coffee shop, restaurant, bar, store, sportfishing tours. AE, MC, V.*

Moderate **Acuario's Mar de Cortés.** There's a definite emphasis on astrological signs here—the bus station-style restaurant is called Tauro, the bar is Libra, and the floors are called Cancer, Pisces, etc. Aquario's is a good home base for those who want modest accommodations—brown and beige predominate—away from the center-city noise. The plain, monochromatic rooms have TVs, bathtubs, and dime-store oil paintings with a bathing-beauty theme. *Calle Ignacio Ramírez 1665, tel. 682/2–9266 or 682/2–9133. 60 rooms with bath. Facilities: pool, restaurant, bar. MC, V.*

La Misión. By far the most peaceful place in town, La Misión literally handles the overflow from La Posada hotel, since the guests can reach their rooms only by boat from the beach at La Posada. The rooms are simple in style, and the small restaurant has a limited menu, but it's a delightful place, almost like a private island. La Misión is open only when needed, and reservations are a must during the winter months. *Box 152, La Paz, 23000, tel. 682/2-4011 or 682/2-0663. 25 rooms. Facilities: beach, restaurant, shuttle boat service. MC, V.*

La Perla. Smack in the center of the malecón, La Perla was once a great hotel, and with recent renovations it is coming back from a long stage as a dark and dreary place. The rooms on the higher floors are filled with light and furnished in cool pastels. The waterfront view is great, but if you're a light sleeper, ask for a room at the back, away from the malecón noise. *Paseo*

*Obregón 1570, tel. 682/2–0777; reservations in the U.S.: 800/
458–6888 or 800/227–0212 in CA. 100 rooms. Facilities: restaurant, bar, shops. MC, V.*

★ **La Posada.** For 25 years, divers on their way to and from
lengthy sea trips have stayed at La Posada for their last chance
to straddle a stool at the poolside palapa bar and swap stories
about hammerheads, sea lions, and manta rays. They stay in
casitas—cottages with wood shutters, haphazardly tiled bathrooms and fireplaces, worn couches in the living rooms, and
rocking chairs on the tile porches. At night, miniature lights
twinkle in the palm trees, guitarists stroll between the blue patio umbrellas, and underwater lights illuminate the holiday displays on the cement island in the middle of the pool. Past and
future boat mates joke over grilled fish and lobster dinners,
then dance and drink like the best of friends. Saturday night
entertainment alternates between the ballet *folklórico* and a
Hawaiian luau with respectable island dances performed by local girls. The noise dies down early, though, since nearly everyone will be playing hard in the water the next day. La Posada
also operates a 25-room inn on a small jetty across the water;
it opens only when the main hotel is full. *Nueva Reforma
and Playa Sur, tel. 682/2–4011. Box 152, La Paz, 23000. 25
rooms. Facilities: private beach, pool, restaurant, palapa bar.
MC, V.*

★ **Las Cabañas de Los Arcos.** These small, thatched-roof brick
cottages on a side street beside Los Arcos are surrounded by
trees and flowering hibiscus bushes, with lawn chairs set out
in the shade. Sidewalks lead through the small complex to a
pool nearly hidden by the trees. The cabanas are a bit rundown, but private; for more modern surroundings, stay in the
low-rise hotel building by the pool. *Just off Paseo Obregón
on the short street (no name) at the corner of Calle Rosales;
reservations in the U.S.: 4422 Cerritos Ave., Los Alamitos,
CA 90720, tel. 213/583–3930 or 800/347–2252. 30 rooms. Facilities: pool, access to other facilities at Los Arcos hotel. AE,
MC, V.*

Palmira. The main convention center in La Paz, the Palmira is
deceptively plain at first glance. But once you walk past the
low-rise meeting room buildings, the central courtyard looks
like a tropical oasis with palm trees and massive scheffleras and
aralias. The bright blue pool is long enough for laps; padded
lounges under the palms are perfect for naps. There's a large
children's playground far enough away to keep the peace. The
restaurant and bar open out to the pool area, which serves
as the stage for a Mexican fiesta on Thursday nights and a
generous Sunday buffet brunch. The rooms have phones,
TVs, and tables and chairs for those with more paperwork in
mind—the clashing blue and orange bedspreads should keep
you awake. *Blvd. Arámburu 23010, tel. 682/2–4000 or 682/2–
2950; reservations in the U.S.: tel. 800/336–5454. 120 rooms.
Facilities: convention center, pool, disco, restaurant, bar,
tennis courts, playground, store, travel agency, car rental.
AE, MC, V.*

Inexpensive **Gardenias.** By far the most pleasant of the budget hotels, Gardenias has lovely gardens, a pool and patio, and clean, spacious
rooms. The drawback is its distance from the malecón (about a
half-hour walk). *Calle Serdán Norte 520, tel. 682/2–3088. 56
rooms. Facilities: pool, restaurant. MC, V.*

Pension California. Backpackers and low-budget travelers find an old, run-down hacienda with clean blue and white rooms with baths, a courtyard with picnic tables and a TV, and a general laid-back, friendly camaraderie. *Av. Degollado 209, tel. 682/2-2896. Facilities: cooking privileges. No credit cards.*

The Arts and Nightlife

El Teatro de la Ciudad, (Calle Altamirano and Av. Nevarro), built in 1986, is La Paz's new cultural center. The long low-rise building, with a towering cement slab higher than almost any other building in La Paz, looks a lot like the archaeological museum in Mexico City, though it was designed by a local architect. Four red and silver windmills mark the front entrance, a reminder of the windmills that once provided energy to the city. A theater seating 1,500 is used for stage shows by local and visiting performers. At the theater's back entrance, a stark, circular tiled plaza memorializes the city's founders and heroes. Stone pillars with brass plaques describe their deeds, and the ashes of each person—some of whom died 100 years ago or more—are supposedly buried beneath the pillars. Ceremonies honoring the dead are held regularly for schoolchildren, to impress upon them the importance of following such good examples.

Nightlife in La Paz centers around the malecón and the **OK Maguey** disco (Paseo Obregón, tel. 682/2-3133) near La Perla. The mirrored **Disco El Rollo,** at the Hotel Palmira (tel. 682/2-4000), plays music videos on wide-screen TVs, recorded salsa and disco tunes, and occasionally has live entertainment. A raised circular bar surrounds the large dance floor, where strobe and black lights pulse with the beat. The **Old West** bar (at Paseo Obregón and Calle Tejada) lives up to its name; a stuffed coyote (so mangy it's hard to tell the species) hangs over the bar, and saddles, spurs, and antlers grace the walls. It's a good place to watch football, drink beer, and howl at the moon.

Excursions from La Paz

The drive from La Paz to Los Cabos is one of the most scenic in Baja, through the mountain passes of the Sierra Gigante, past old mining towns and remote villages to primitive fishing camps and secluded beaches. The most direct route is on the 184-kilometer (115-mile) Transpeninsular Highway, or Mexico Highway 1, a paved four-lane road. The highway passes through **El Triunfo,** once the largest mining town in Baja California. In 1862, when the Triunfo Gold and Silver Company operated the mines, there were over 10,000 people living in El Triunfo; now, there are about 500. The bright blue church is across the street from the town's only restaurant, also called El Triunfo. Highway 1 continues on through **San Antonio,** another ghost town from the silver mining era, to **Los Barriles,** near the coast. The winds are considered to be among the best in the world for windsurfing, and there are a few small hotels in the area.

As an alternative to Highway 1, Highway 286 travels along the coast from La Paz to Los Barriles. The road is paved for the first 49 kilometers (30 miles), twisting through the mountains and then dipping down to sea level and becoming a rutted dirt road at the small village of **San Juan de los Planes.** The road is still being paved; take it slow over the arroyos (small riverbeds) and ruts.

After another 10 kilometers (6 miles) or so there is a sign to the left for the **Hotel Las Arenas,** a full-scale fishing resort set off by itself on a 19-kilometer (12-mile) stretch along Bahía de las Ventana. The hotel is only 70 kilometers (44 miles) from La Paz, but farther removed from civilization. **Cerralvo Island,** not far offshore, is a famed game-fishing area, while the property's beach offers some of the best snorkeling and diving on the coast. The hotel has tennis courts, its own airstrip, a fine dining room, swimming pool, sportfishing boats, and large suites with balconies over the beach. For information and reservations contact *Box 3766, Santa Fe Springs, CA 90670, tel. 2/921–0109, 800/423–4785, or 800/352–4334 in CA.*

Ensenada de los Muertos, a beautiful shallow bay, is nearby. The road continues south to **Bahía las Palmas** and the beginning of a coastal stretch called the **East Cape.** There are two large bays here, with spectacular fishing and snorkeling, called **Punta Pescadora** (at the north end) and **Punta Colorada** (at the south end). The **Hotel Palmas** at Punta Pescadora, and **Hotel Punta Colorada** at the south are lovely old resorts with parrots squawking in the trees, hammocks hanging outside the cabanas, and fishing boats hauling in huge marlin. For information on both hotels, contact *Box 9388, Canoga Park, CA 91309, tel. 818/703–1002.*

Highways 1 and 286 meet up at Los Barriles, and Highway 1 then runs inland to San José del Cabo via **Santiago,** and past the golfball-like sign marking the **Tropic of Cancer.** At Los Barriles an unnamed dirt road runs along the coast. This stretch of the East Cape is a popular one for day trips from Los Cabos. The road is passable with rented cars or Jeeps and heads from empty desert and lush palm groves to one perfect beach after another. The peninsula's only coral reef is located off the white beaches of **Cabo Pulmo,** 46 kilometers (22 miles) northwest of San Jose del Cabo. Hundreds of fish are visible in the clear, shallow water just a few steps from the beach. The area has campgrounds and one small restaurant, Tito's. There are signs of development along this road, particularly near **Los Frailes,** where the bay is nearly 400 feet deep, and tuna and marlin can be caught within a few hundred yards of the shoreline. There are no hotels yet, but campers in tents and RVs set up housekeeping along the coast for weeks. Within an hour's drive, after the road crosses a small stream surrounded by mangrove trees, you will enter San José del Cabo.

Highway 19 offers an alternative to Route 1 north to La Paz, along the Pacific coast. The scenery is a bit different along the sea: The rough ocean surf pounds into the long shores, and the mountains are to the east instead of the west. There are a few campgrounds and small towns along the way, but the major settlement is **Todos Santos,** a small agricultural town with a population of 1,000, about 120 kilometers (75 miles) from Cabo San Lucas. The town's only hotel is the Hotel California (Calle Juárez, tel. 684/4–0002; reservations in the U.S.: tel. 415/768–0614). The place is colonial in style and has a small pool; rooms are about $20 per night double and credit cards are not accepted. At the entrance to town is the **Santa Monica Restaurant,** a good place to stop for a snack. Don't splurge on any large meals—the food is not outstanding. Better to wait and eat in La Paz, about 80 kilometers (50 miles) northeast.

9   Los Cabos

Introduction

At the southern tip of the 1,600-kilometer (1,000-mile) peninsula of Baja California, the land ends in a rocky point called Los Arcos (The Arches). The waters of the Sea of Cortés swirl into the pounding surf of the Pacific Ocean as marlin and sailfish leap above the waves. The desert gives way to white sand coves, with cactus standing sentry under soaring palm trees. Although it has become a haven for sportfishermen, boaters, and sun-seekers, the land's end has retained its stark beauty and mystery.

Cabo San Lucas and San José del Cabo are only 32 kilometers (20 miles) apart, but the ambience is palpably different. Cabo San Lucas has a large expatriate community and dozens of hotels, bars, and restaurants that cater to the rowdy young set. San José del Cabo has the golf course, massive condominium developments, and a low-key hotel zone. Both have an unfinished quality, but ambitious expansion plans continue and, on the down side, timeshare hustlers—those unfortunate byproducts of large resort areas—have become a constant nuisance to tourists.

Pirates placed great value on the capes at the end of the peninsula as an ideal lookout for spotting Spanish galleons traveling from the Philippines to Spain's empire in central Mexico. Missionaries soon followed, seeking to save the souls of the few thousand local Indians who lived off the sea. They established the missions of San José del Cabo and Cabo San Lucas in the mid-1700s, but their colonies did not last long. The missionaries had brought syphilis and smallpox with their preachings, and by the end of the century the indigenous population was nearly wiped out. A different sort of native brought the explorers back. They came for the massive gamefish that appeared to be almost trapped in the swirl of surf where the ocean meets the sea. In the '40s and '50s the capes became a haven for millionaires who built lodges on rocky gray cliffs overlooking the secluded coves and bays. By the '60s, lavish resorts began to rise in the barren landscape, and in the 1980s, Baja's southern tip became a government-sponsored resort area. Today Los Cabos has an international airport, a marina, shopping centers, and dozens of hotels. Long swaths of ancient desert have been bulldozed smooth, ready to bear more traffic and homes. The towns of San José del Cabo and Cabo San Lucas are being spruced up, restaurants and specialty shops replacing humble homes and empty lots. But the towns still feel small and have maintained their charm.

The area remains a rugged outback, a solitary place where telephones and TVs are the exception rather than the rule. Go a few kilometers down any small road off the highway and you'll feel as if civilization is an illusion and survival a challenge. You discover solitary beaches and dive into waters where angelfish, manta rays, and wrasses swim about as far as the eye can see. You don't come here to wind up and party down, you come here to escape, and to marvel at nature's simplicity.

Essential Information

Important Addresses and Numbers

Tourist Information There is no tourism office in Los Cabos, but there are plenty of makeshift stands where timeshare operators seek new clients under the guise of offering information. Unless you have hours to spend listening to sales spiels, you're better off using the tour desk or concierge at your hotel.

Emergencies **Police:** Cabo San Lucas (tel. 684/3–0057); San José del Cabo (tel. 684/2–0361). **Hospital:** Cabo San Lucas (tel. 684/3–0102); San José del Cabo (tel. 684/2–0316).

Arriving and Departing by Plane

Airport and Airlines The **Los Cabos International Airport** is about 11 kilometers (7 miles) north of San José del Cabo and about 48 kilometers (30 miles) from Cabo San Lucas. **Aero California** (tel. 800/258–3311 in Cabo San Lucas) flies to Los Cabos from Los Angeles, San Diego, and Phoenix; **Alaska** (tel. 800/426–0333), from Anchorage, Fairbanks, Portland, Seattle, San Francisco, Los Angeles, and San Diego; **Mexicana** (tel. 800/531–7921), from Denver, Los Angeles, San Francisco, and Seattle; and **Aeroméxico** (tel. 800/237–6639), from Los Angeles.

Vans shuttle passengers from the airport to the hotels in both towns, but not back to the airport. Many of the hotels have sign-up sheets for guests who wish to share a cab and the $30 or so fare to the airport.

Arriving and Departing by Car, Bus, and Boat

By Car Highway 1, also known as the Transpeninsular Highway, runs the entire 1,600 kilometers (1,000 miles) from Tijuana to Cabo San Lucas. The highway is in excellent condition, but some drivers will find the lack of road lights and guardrails unnerving, especially through the steep mountain passes.

By Bus **Tres Estrellas de Oro** (tel. 684/2–0200) travels from Tijuana to Los Cabos and between San José and Cabo San Lucas daily. The peninsula-long trip takes about 22 hours.

By Boat Several cruise lines, including **Carnival** (tel. 800/327–9051), **Princess** (tel. 800/421–0522), and **Admiral** (tel. 800/327–0271), use Cabo San Lucas as a port of call.

Getting Around

By Bus Buses now run between the two towns on an erratic schedule, and will stop at the hotels along the way. The fare between the towns is about $1.50. Ask at your hotel for the latest schedule.

By Car The best way to see the sights is on foot. The downtown areas are small and compact, with the *zócalo* (main square), church, shops, and restaurants within a few blocks of each other. But if you want to travel frequently between the two towns or to remote beaches and coves, you'll need a car. Most hotels and resorts have car rentals. A Volkswagen Beetle or Jeep starts at $35 per day including tax and insurance, plus 18¢ per kilometer. The following car-rental agencies all have desks at the airport and in one or both towns: **Budget** (tel. 684/3–0241), **Dollar** (tel. 684/2–0671), **Hertz** (tel. 684/ 3–0211), and **Servitour** (tel. 684/3–0897).

By Taxi Cab fares are standardized by the government, but you should still confirm the price before the driver starts up. The fare between the two towns is about $8.

Guided Tours

With the water as the main attraction, most tours involve getting in a boat and diving or fishing. Nearly everyone takes a ride to Los Arcos, the natural rock arches at land's end, and Playa del Amor (Love Beach), where the Sea of Cortés blends into the Pacific. Nearly all hotels have frequent boat trips to Los Arcos; the fare depends on how far it is from your hotel.

Chubasco's (22 Blvd. de la Marina, Cabo San Lucas, tel. 684/ 3–0404) offers guided tours on motorcycles and 3-wheel off-road motorbikes to remote areas around Los Cabos, including the old lighthouse.

Pez Gato (tel. 684/3–1396) has sailing tours to Los Arcos and sunset cruises on a 42-foot catamaran, departing from the main dock of the Cabo San Lucas marina. Tours cost $20 per person.

Tours and Activities Store (Blvd. Marina at Madero) is the most reliable of the various information booths. They sell tickets for all the tour and fishing companies, and are very helpful with restaurant suggestions and the like.

Exploring

Numbers in the margin correspond with points of interest on the Los Cabos maps.

You needn't worry about reserving lots of time for sightseeing here—each town can easily be toured in an hour or so. Only a few streets are named, but the towns are small enough that you'll find what you're looking for without wandering very far.

Cabo San Lucas and **San José del Cabo** are about 32 kilometers (20 miles) from each other on Highway 1. Some hotels in one town offer tours to the other, which is a good way to see the sights, or you can take a taxi between the towns. To check out the lavish fishing resorts or the beaches, you're best off renting a car and stopping for lunch or a swim along the way.

There are some spectacular beaches off dirt roads on both sides of the peninsula around Los Cabos, including the areas of Cabo Falso on the Pacific side and Los Barriles and Cabo Pulmo on the Sea of Cortés.

San José del Cabo, the larger of the two towns, has about 10,000 inhabitants (increasing by a thousand or so more in the winter when roving bands of RVs settle in for a few months). The main **❶** street is **Boulevard Mijares.** The south end of the boulevard has **❷** been designated as the tourist zone, with the **Los Cabos Club de Golf** as its centerpiece. Fonatur owns 4,000 acres along this **❸** stretch and has built the **Commercial and Cultural Center** in the middle; condo complexes rise like giant sand sculptures around the golf course. A few reasonably priced hotels are situated along this strip, on a beautiful long beach where the surf, un-

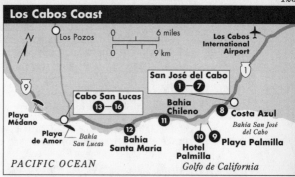

Los Cabos Coast

Los Pozos

0 — 6 miles
0 — 9 km

Los Cabos International Airport

San José del Cabo
1 – 7

Cabo San Lucas
13 – 16

Bahía Chileno

8 Costa Azul

Playa Médano

Playa de Amor

Bahía San Lucas

12

11

Bahía San José del Cabo

10 9 Playa Palmilla

Bahía Santa María

Hotel Palmilla

PACIFIC OCEAN

Golfo de California

Boulevard Mijares, **1**
Church, **7**
City Hall, **5**
Commercial and
Cultural Center, **3**
Estuary, **4**
Los Cabos Club de
Golf, **2**
Zócalo, **6**

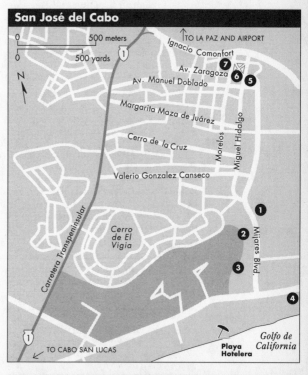

San José del Cabo

0 — 500 meters
0 — 500 yards

TO LA PAZ AND AIRPORT

1

Ignacio Comonfort

Av. Zaragoza
7
6 5

Av. Manuel Doblado

N

Margarita Maza de Juárez

Cerro de la Cruz

Morelos

Miguel Hidalgo

Valerio Gonzalez Canseco

Carretera Transpeninsular

Cerro de El Vigía

1

2

Mijares Blvd.

3

4

1

TO CABO SAN LUCAS

Playa Hotelera

Golfo de California

Bahía de Cabo
San Lucas, **15**
Handicrafts
Market, **14**
Los Arcos, **16**
Zócalo, **13**

Cabo San Lucas

N

Matamoros
M. Hidalgo
Cabo San Lucas
Morelos
Lázaro Cárdenas

Golfo de California

13

14 15

Blvd. Marina

0 — 500 meters
0 — 500 yards

16 Los Arcos

PACIFIC OCEAN

fortunately, is too dangerous for swimming. At the end of the strip, on the unnamed road by the Stouffer Presidente hotel, is ❹ the **estuary,** a freshwater preserve filled with more than 200 species of birds. There is a small stand at the road's end where you can rent a boat to paddle around through the thick swamp grass.

Take Boulevard Mijares north into town, past a stretch of res-❺ taurants and shops. **City Hall** is on your left near Avenida Zaragoza, where Mijares ends. A long fountain lit at night by colored lights marks the end of the boulevard. There is a small, shaded plaza here and, in front of a small public library, a mural painted by the children of San José.

❻ One block east on Avenida Zaragoza is a large **zócalo,** with a white wrought-iron gazebo and green benches set in the shade. ❼ The town's **church** looms over the zócalo: See the curious tile mural out front of a captured priest being dragged toward a fire by Indians. Mexicana and Aeroméxico airlines have offices by the zócalo. The bus station, hospital, market, and pharmacies are all located one block south on Avenida Manuel Doblado. Most of the town's souvenir shops and restaurants are clustered in the surrounding streets.

As you drive south on Highway 1 toward Cabo San Lucas you ❽ ❾ first pass **Costa Azul,** a good surfing beach, and **Playa Palmilla,** San José's best swimming beach, where townsfolk and travel-❿ ers congregate. Above the beach is the **Hotel Palmilla,** a rambling, hacienda-style resort with its own small white adobe chapel. Farther south are some nice beaches for swimming and snorkeling and some spectacular hotels; worth visiting are the ⓫ ⓬ **Bahía Chileno** at the **Hotel Cabo San Lucas,** and the **Bahiá Santa María** at the **Twin Dolphin** hotel. The beaches at both bays have white sand, clear blue water, and schools of fish just offshore.

Highway 1 leads into the center of **Cabo San Lucas,** ending at Km. 1 on the 1,000-mile long Transpeninsular Highway. The main downtown street, Avenida Lázaro Cárdenas, passes a ⓭ small **zócalo.** Most of the shops, services, and restaurants are located between Avenida Lázaro Cárdenas and the waterfront.

Time Out If you've had all the tacos and flan you can stand and crave good old gringo food, head for **Salazar's** on Lázaro Cárdenas at Ocampo. The brownies, carrot cake, and peanut butter cookies are outstanding, and you won't find biscuits and gravy anywhere else.

Boulevard Marina has been transformed from a dusty main drag into a busy paved thoroughfare lined with hotels and cafés. Paved walkways now run from Blvd. Marina to the hotels ⓮ and beaches on the east end of town and west to the **Handicrafts Market** that caters to cruise-ship passengers at the **marina.** ⓯ The sportfishing fleet is docked in the **Bahía de Cabo San Lucas,** and glass-bottom-boat rides are available at the water's edge.

⓰ The most spectacular sight in Cabo San Lucas is **Los Arcos.** The natural rock arches are visible from the marina and some of the hotels, but are more impressive from the water. A little farther on, and visible from the water, is **El Faro de Cabo Falso** (Lighthouse of the False Cape). You need a four-wheel drive to reach the lighthouse by land. If you don't take at least a short boat ride out to the arches and **Playa de Amor,** the beach underneath, you haven't fully appreciated Cabo.

Shopping

Cabo San Lucas Though there aren't many places to shop in Los Cabos, the selection of handicrafts and sportswear is excellent. In Cabo San Lucas, the sportswear shops—**Guess, Ferrioni, Bye-Bye, Cotton Club,** and the like—are clustered at Plaza Cabo San Lucas on Avenida Madero near the waterfront and at Plaza Candido on Calle Guerrero at Avenida Lázaro Cárdenas.

Several high-class resortwear boutiques have opened. The best are **Temptations** (Av. Lázaro Cárdenas at Calle Guerrero, tel. 684/3–1015), **Dos Lunas** (Blvd. Marina, tel. 684/3–1280) and **La Bamba** (Calle Guerrero, tel. 684/3–1545). Across Avenida Hidalgo from the zócalo is **La Bugambilia** (tel. 684/3–0625), a gallery with brass and copper animals by Sergio Bustamante and one-of-a-kind belts, purses, and jewelry. **La Paloma,** a few doors down, has beautiful embroidered and appliquéd clothing from Tlaquepaque, an artisan's colony near Guadalajara.

Galería Rostros de México (Faces of Mexico Gallery) is a must-see. Located on Avenida Lázaro Cárdenas about one block from the zócalo, the gallery has two large rooms filled with old and new masks—some garish and frightening, some fanciful and delightful—from all over Mexico. **Antigüedades del Oraciones,** off Avenida Lázaro Cárdenas near the waterfront, has an intriguing collection of antique wood statues, cow skulls, and carved animals. High-quality folk art from throughout Mexico is also available at **Nekri** (no phone) and **Galería El Dorado** (tel. 684/3–0817) on Blvd. Marina.

At the **Handicrafts Market** in the marina, you can pose for a photo with an iguana, go for a ride in a glass-bottom boat, or browse through dusty stalls packed with blankets, sombreros, T-shirts, and pottery.

San José del Cabo Shopping in San José is limited to the few streets around the zócalo and City Hall. There's a large market across Boulevard Mijares from City Hall, where you can get film, postcards, groceries, and liquor. **Antigua Los Cabos** (Av. Hidalgo) has handsome carved wood furniture, woven rugs, and wrought-iron chandeliers. Along Boulevard Mijares, **La Casa Vieja Boutique** (tel. 684/2–0270) has beautiful hand-knit sweaters, designer dresses, and embroidered *guayaberas* (loose-fitting cotton shirts) for men; **Bye-Bye** has high-quality souvenir T-shirts; **La Mina** displays beautiful silver jewelry and leather bags; and **La Bamba** has colorful hand-painted T-shirts and coveralls. **Galería El Dorado,** across from the City Hall on Blvd. Mijares, displays paintings and sculptures from local artists. For fresh produce, flowers, meat, fish, and a sampling of local life in San José, visit the **Mercado Municipal** off Calle Doblado, behind the bus station.

Sports

Fishing, diving, snorkeling, surfing, windsurfing, and boating are nearly mandatory in Los Cabos, and there are dozens of charter companies, tour agencies, and scuba shops catering to every water sport. Many companies have stands at the marina, where you can check out the boats and operators and haggle over prices.

Diving Los Arcos is prime diving and snorkeling territory, as are several rocky points off the coast. Most hotels offer diving trips and equipment rental.

Companies in Cabo San Lucas serving divers include: **Amigos del Mar** (near the sportfishing docks at the harbor, tel. 684/3–0022), **Palmilla Divers** (at the Hotel Palmilla, tel. 684/2–0582), **Cabo Acuadeportes** (at the Hotel Hacienda and at Playa Chileno, tel. 684/3–0117), and **Tio Watersports** (at the Meliá San Lucas, tel. 684/3–1000).

Fishing Striped, blue, and black marlin are the big catch here, along with sailfish, wahoo, bonito, pompano, roosterfish, and yellowtail. In all, there are over 800 species of fish in these waters. Black marlin, weighing around 200 pounds, are best from October to June; blue marlin are present year-round, but most plentiful in June and July; striped marlin are always plentiful. Dorado (also called dolphin fish and mahi-mahi) are present year-round, and most plentiful from September to December. Wahoo are present from October through January. Unless you are planning to mount your catch, it is advised that you turn marlin and sailfish back to the water, in the interest of conservation.

Most of the hotels, particularly those scattered along the highway between the two towns, can arrange fishing charters and have your catch mounted, frozen, or smoked. Charters include a captain and mate, tackle, bait, licenses, and drinks. Prices start at $250 per day for a 7.5-meter (25-foot) cruiser. Some charters provide lunch. Most of the boats leave from the sportfishing docks in the Cabo San Lucas marina. Usually, there are a fair number of *pangas* (small boats) for rent at about $25 per hour with a five-hour minimum. If you go this route, check out the boat and equipment first, and make sure the boat operator knows which kind of fish you're looking for and how long you want to stay out.

Dependable companies include: **Pesca Deportiva Solmar** (Hotel Solmar in Cabo San Lucas, tel. 684/3–0022), **La Gaviota** (tel. 684/3–0430), the **Palmilla Fleet** (at the Hotel Palmilla, tel. 684/2–0582), and **Pices Sportfishing Fleet** (tel. 684/3–0588, or in the Stouffer Presidente hotel, San José del Cabo, tel. 684/2–0211).

Golf The **Los Cabos Campo de Golf,** completed in 1988, is a nine-hole course and country club that is the pride of Los Cabos. The course, on Boulevard Mijares in San José, is surrounded by villas and condos. The clubhouse restaurant is open from 8 AM until 1 AM; there is also a pro shop. The greens fee is $24 for 18 holes and $12 for nine holes; club rentals are $10 per day.

Tennis The **Los Cabos Campo de Golf** has lighted tennis courts open to the public; fees are $6 per hour during the day and $10 per hour at night.

Beaches

The beaches are the main draw at Los Cabos, and there's plenty of room for all to spread out and stake out their own secluded spot. Having a car greatly enhances your ability to appreciate the coastline, since some of the finest snorkeling, diving, and surfing spots are located along the dirt roads going up the coasts of the Sea of Cortés and the Pacific. As a rule, the beaches on the east side of the peninsula are best for diving, while those on the west have great surf. Most of the beaches around Cabo San Lucas and the arches are part of a marine preserve, where spearfishing and shell collecting are prohibited.

Cabo San Lucas **Playa Médano,** just north of Cabo San Lucas, is the most popular stretch in Los Cabos (and possibly in all Baja) for sunbathing and people-watching. The 3.2-kilometer (2-mile) span of white sand is always crowded, especially on holiday weekends, and rarely if ever totally deserted. A long line of palapa restaurants keeps the crowd going, and vendors parade their wares back and forth along the beach all day long. There's an aquatic center at the south end and ongoing volleyball games at the north, by Las Palmas restaurant.

Playa Hacienda, in the inner harbor by the Hacienda Hotel, has the calmest waters of any beach in town and good snorkeling around the rocky point. **Playa Solmar,** by the Solmar Hotel, is a beautiful wide beach at the base of the mountains leading into the Pacific, but the undertow is dangerously strong. The mountains are shaped so dramatically because the surf has pounded away at them until cliffs have become mere piles of rocks. There is a steep drop-off just offshore where the waves break with tremendous force, wiping out unsuspecting swimmers. Stick to sunbathing here.

Playa de Amor is a secluded cove at the very end of the peninsula, with the Sea of Cortés on one side and the Pacific on the other. It is possible to walk to this beach on a rocky, hilly path south of the Solmar, but most people get there on tour boats, so at least you can spot the invaders as they approach and scurry for privacy. The difference between the peaceful, azure cove on the Sea of Cortés and the pounding white surf on the Pacific is dramatic.

San José del Cabo **Playa Hotelera,** used by the better hotels, is beautiful, but the current is dangerously rough and the water a long walk from the hotel. At the east end of the beach, near the Stouffer Presidente hotel, a freshwater lagoon is filled with tropical birds and plants; sometimes there are boats for rent at the lagoon. If you plan to spend time here, be sure to wear insect repellent. The best swimming beach in San José is **Playa Palmilla,** protected from the surf by a rocky point just south of San José. The northern part of the beach is cluttered with boats and shacks, but as you walk south you reach the Hotel Palmilla beach, a long stretch of white sand and calm sea.

Between San José del Cabo and Cabo San Lucas Some of Los Cabos's best resorts are situated off the highway between the two towns, set on some of the area's loveliest beaches. **Playa Bahía Santa María,** by the Twin Dolphins hotel, is a snow-white cove protected by towering brown cliffs. The snorkeling is superb, with hundreds of colorful fish swarming through chunks of white coral. Just north of the hotel is a public access trail to the beach. **Bahía Chileno,** by the Hotel Cabo San

Lucas, is an underwater preserve teeming with marine life and a great place for snorkeling and diving. The beach is rocky in parts and smoothest in front of the hotel.

At **Playa Barco Varado** (Shipwreck Beach), small bays are formed between the boulders out in the water, making great tide pools filled with sea urchins, starfish, and crabs. The rusted wreck of a Japanese freighter sits jammed up against the rocks, and makes a great snorkeling spot. The beach is located just north of Cabo San Lucas at Km. 8 on the highway.

Dining

Fresh fish, lobster, and shrimp are the dining draws here, along with more exotic abalone and quail. Even in the most expensive establishments, lobster and steak will rarely run more than $25. Prices tend to be highest at the hotel restaurants, and lowest in downtown San José.

Highly recommended restaurants in each price category are indicated by a star ★.

Category	Cost*
Expensive	over $20
Moderate	$10–$20
Inexpensive	under $10

**per person, excluding drinks, service, and sales tax (15%)*

Cabo San Lucas

Expensive   **Alfonso's.** You get the feeling you're in a private dining room
★   feasting on a meal prepared just for you at this small, elegant restaurant within a hacienda-style hotel. The fixed-price meals include six sublime courses served in a leisurely yet attentive manner. There's no more romantic room in town. *On the road to Playa Médano, tel. 684/3-0739. Reservations recommended. AE, MC, V. Dinner only.*

★   **El Faro Viejo Trailer Park Restaurant.** It may seem like an unlikely spot for a fine meal, but this plain restaurant deep inside a trailer park is one of the most popular in town. Lines form at the door almost every night, with regulars coming back weekly for great barbecued ribs or enormous grilled lobsters. If you want to meet Americans who've made Cabo their home, just hang out at the circular bar—they all seem to come by eventually. *Calles Abasalo and Morelos, no phone. No credit cards. Dinner only. Closed Wed.*

El Galeón. Considered the most distinguished restaurant in town, El Galeón is located across from the marina. The choice seats face the water; the inside is decorated with heavy wood furniture. Spanish, Mexican, and U.S. dishes are prepared with an emphasis on thick, tender cuts of beef. The bar is nice for a latenight brandy. *Across from the marina by the road to the Finisterra hotel, tel. 684/3-0443. AE, MC, V.*

Moderate   **El Rey Sol.** By far one of the best and most authentically Mexican restaurants in Cabo San Lucas, El Rey Sol is on the road to Playa Médano. The abalone is succulent and the seafood combination—lobster, oysters, crab, and fish—incredibly generous and outrageously good, though expensive. The 7-Mares soup, with 7 varieties of seafood from octopus to clams, is guranteed to *levanta muertos* (raise the dead) or, at the very least, cure tequila hangovers. This large, brick restaurant is warm and cozy, and the Mexican breakfasts are popular with both townfolk and tourists. *On the road to Playa Médano, tel. 684/3–1117. MC, V.*

The Giggling Marlin. El Marlín Sonriente (as it is also known) is designed for fun, with flowers, vines, hot-air balloons, and parrots painted on the white walls of its high-ceilinged room, dominated by a steep blue stairway and platform where rowdier clientele are hung by their feet like marlin being weighed on shore. A sign at the door reads "Perfect English Broken Here," and other witticisms are painted on the walls. Though the menu is extensive—burgers, sandwiches, tostadas, burritos, and steaks—the regulars advise sticking with tacos, appetizers, and drinks. This is a popular watering hole for gringos, and a place to catch the latest sporting event from the United States on wide-screen satellite TV. *Av. Matamoros and Blvd. Marina, tel. 684/3–0606. MC, V.*

Las Palmas. The most popular restaurant and bar at Playa Medano, Las Palmas is the headquarters for volleyball teams competing on the beach, groups of dune-buggy enthusiasts, and beach bums of all ages. The barbecued ribs are great, but better yet is the quail, lobster, and steak combo, or the abalone marinated in tequila. It's a great place to find out what's going on around town and meet people. *Playa Médano, no phone. MC, V.*

The One That Got Away. A San Diegan and a Canadian have combined talents to create a laid-back spot for watching football games on TV, playing pool, and munching on chicken wings. Try the tamales or garlic mushrooms with fresh tortillas. The tables on the second-story balconies are good spots for watching street action. *Calle Guerrero and Av. Cárdenas, tel. 684/3–0447. No credit cards.*

Inexpensive **El Pollo de Oro.** Roasted chicken served with rice, beans, and tortillas makes for a satisfying feast at budget prices. It's hard to resist the savory smell of the chickens roasting on an open grill on the sidewalk, and there's always a line at the counter. *Av. Cárdenas east of town, tel. 684/3–0310). No credit cards.*

★ **Restaurant San Lucas.** Also known as the Taquería San Lucas, this small palapa just a block from the zócalo has the best breakfast and tacos in town. You place your order at a long Formica counter by the open-air kitchen, help yourself to a cup of coffee, then settle in at one of the five picnic tables until your *huevos rancheros* are ready. Spread some fiery hot sauce over your eggs—it's a real eye-opener. For lunch or dinner, try the grilled fish. *Av. Hidalgo and Calle Zapata, no phone. No credit cards.*

Squid Roe. The Carlos 'n' Charlie chain hits new heights in zaniness and rowdiness with this double-layer, neon-festooned, open-air madhouse. Waiters dressed as bulls charge customers down the aisles, tequila shooters are the drink of choice, and conversation is out of the question. The food—burgers, barbecue, and fish—is always plentiful and good. *Av. Cárdenas on the east end of town, tel. 684/3–0655. MC, V.*

San José del Cabo

Expensive **Da Giorgio.** This large hacienda on a hillside south of town has long been a prime spot for fine Italian dining. The second-story dining room looks out to the sea; the bars and walls are decorated with hand-painted tiles. Try the scampi with pasta, spinach-stuffed ravioli, or first-rate pizzas from the wood-burning oven. *On the Transpeninsular Highway south of San José, no phone. MC, V. Open for lunch and dinner only.*

★ **Damiana.** For a special night out, visit this small hacienda tucked beside the zócalo, past the center of town. The lounge area has overstuffed couches where you can unwind before claiming your table on the patio. Fuchsia bougainvillea wraps around the tall pines shading the wrought-iron tables, and the pink adobe walls glow in the candlelight. Start with fiery oysters *diablo*, then move on to the tender chateaubriand or charbroiled lobster. You'll find the setting so relaxing and charming that you may want to linger on into the night. *Blvd. Mijares 8, tel. 684/2–0499. AE, MC, V. Dinner only.*

Moderate **La Fogata.** Joel Davida and his family, who operate this friendly,
★ comfortable restaurant, have a real knack for catering to their customers without smothering them with attention. Gringos love the first-rate grilled steaks served with baked potatoes and sour cream and gather here annually for the Thanksgiving feast, complete with roast turkey, pumpkin pie, and Irish coffee. The New York steak with basil butter and anchovies is superb, as is the *fettuccine al frutti di mare*, made with assorted seafood in a rich marinara sauce. The meal ends with a complimentary after-dinner concoction of Kahlúa, cream, and whatever else sounds good at the time. *Calles Zaragoza and Morelos, tel. 684/2–0480. MC, V.*

★ **La Paloma.** Don't miss the Sunday brunch—a lavish spread of seafood, salads, and divine pastries. Every meal is a treat on the patio above the pool or in the spacious dining room decorated with Mexican pottery and textiles. Work up a bodacious appetite, then order the mixed grill—a heaping stack of beef, chicken, and pork on a table-top hibachi. This is a great spot for a quiet, romantic evening. *In the Hotel Palmilla on Hwy. 1 near San José, tel. 684/2–0582. AE, MC, V.*

Le Bistrot. Thierry and Veronique Paguet left their native Belgium for San José, where they operate this tiny café in a residential neigborhood. Omelets and crepes are good choices at the breakfast buffet, and by all means try the fish pâté at dinner, but save room for chocolate mousse. *Calle Morelos 4, tel. 684/2–1174. MC, V. Open on Mon. for dinner only.*

Pepe's Playa Palmilla. This large palapa on the beach south of San José is the most popular restaurant on the sand. It serves excellent grilled fish, lobster, and shrimp, and is the best spot for a sunset dinner. *Km 27.5 on the road to Cabo San Lucas, no phone. No credit cards.*

Tropicana. Though the large bar at the front of this restaurant can get noisy and crowded, especially during happy hour when a bountiful, free buffet is served, the garden at the back is a tranquil place. Blue cloths cover the white wrought-iron tables, a fountain gurgles quietly, soft jazz plays over the speakers, and candles flicker in the breeze. Grilled steaks and fish are prepared at the open-air kitchen at the far end of the garden, and the aroma gets the appetite in gear. *Blvd. Mijares 30, tel. 684/2–0907. MC, V.*

Inexpensive **El Californiano.** Real Mexican food—sopes, tamales, sopa mariscos—in a casual spot that's very popular with the locals. While there's nothing fancy about the immaculately clean dining room and deck, the food is straightforward, substantial, and reasonably priced. If you're craving burritos or enchiladas, this is your place, and it's open from 8 AM–10 PM every day of the year. *Calle Doblado, no phone. No credit cards.*

Smokehouse Gordo's. Smoked fish is the specialty at this little palapa near the bus station. Try the smoked marlin or the fresh fish tacos. The burgers are also good. *Av. 5 de Mayo, no phone. No credit cards or traveler's checks.*

Lodging

As a tourist destination, Los Cabos has traditionally been a hideaway for the wealthy, with high-class fishing resorts perched on the cliffs over the sea, many with private airstrips and marinas for their guests. Though it is becoming a more popular place in the sun for travelers of all sorts, the accommodations are mostly expensive and exclusive; look for bargains in air and hotel packages if you want to avoid stiff rates. Budget travelers may find themselves searching for a beach to camp on, as rooms in this category are rare.

Many of the hotels, particularly those in the more remote areas, offer the American Plan (AP) with three meals. Many of the remote resorts do not accept credit cards at checkout. Some will help you arrange a cash advance on your card if given a few days' notice, and if you make advance reservations in the United States you will be able to charge your stay. Otherwise, make sure you've got enough cash or traveler's checks to cover your bill. The resorts also tend to tack a 10%–20% service charge onto the bill. Most properties also raise their rates for the December–April high season. Rates here are based on high-season standards. Expect to pay 25% less during the off-season.

Highly recommended lodgings in each price category are indicated by a star ★.

Category	Cost*
Expensive	over $150
Moderate	$50–$150
Inexpensive	under $50

Prices are for a standard double room, excluding service charge and sales tax (15%).

Cabo San Lucas

Expensive **Hacienda.** If you stand at the marina and look across the water
★ you'll see the white arches of the Hacienda, the only hotel in central Cabo San Lucas with a safe swimming beach, on the Bahía Cabo San Lucas. It resembles a Spanish colonial inn, with white arches and bell towers, stone fountains, and statues of Indian gods set amid scarlet hibiscus and bougainvillea. The white rooms have red-tile floors, tile baths, and folk art hanging on the walls; the bar is a veritable museum of Indian arti-

facts. This is the most Mexican of all the in-town hotels: lush and tropical. If you are planning to pay with a credit card, present the card when you check in. The hotel does not accept unapproved cards at checkout time. *Across from the marina, tel. 684/3–0122; reservations in the U.S.: Box 48872, Los Angeles, CA 90048, tel. 2/655–7777. 112 rooms, suites, and beachfront cabanas. Facilities: beach, pool, aquatic center, restaurant, bar, shops. MC, V.*

Meliá San Lucas. Of the many new properties in Cabo, this Meliá stands out for its long, clean beach, dramatic palapa lobby looking out to Los Arcos, and tasteful architecture, with sand-colored buildings draped in vines and bougainvillea. All rooms have patios overlooking the pool and beach, couches, comfortable chairs and tables for spreading your belongings about, and in-room safes. A pedestrian shortcut runs along the hillsides overlooking the beach and into town. *Just north of town off the Los Cabos Hwy., tel. 684/3–4020; reservations in the U.S.: tel. 800/336–3542. 198 rooms. Facilities: pool, beach, water activities equipment, fishing fleet, 2 restaurants, bar. AE, MC, V.*

Solmar. From afar, the Solmar looks like a space colony, with stark white buildings set against gray cliffs leading into the sea. Up close it retains a rugged feeling: The rooms are set right into the cliffs (some even have boulders as headboards), and the beach, though one of the prettiest in town, is also one of the most dangerous. Most visitors hang out around the pool and swim-up bar, joining in with the ever-present musicians who play a blend of mariachi, salsa, and rock 'n' roll. The Solmar's sportfishing fleet is one of the best in Los Cabos. *Blvd. Marina, tel. 684/3–0022; reservations in the U.S.: Box 383, Pacific Palisades, CA 90272, tel. 2/459–9861. 66 rooms, 4 suites. Facilities: pool, beach, aquatic center, tennis, restaurant, bar, shops. AE, MC, V.*

Moderate **Giggling Marlin Inn.** This small, all-suite hotel by the waterfront is charmingly decorated with flowers, birds, and fish stenciled in bright colors on the white walls. The suites have large living rooms and bedrooms as well as full kitchens. Clients and staff are like family, hanging out together in the hot tub or at the restaurant next door, one of the most popular watering holes in Los Cabos. *Blvd. Marina and Av. Matamoros, tel. 684/3–0606; reservations in the U.S.: 13455 Ventura Blvd., Suite 207, Sherman Oaks, CA 91423, tel. 818/907–7219. 9 suites. Facilities: hot tub, restaurant, bar. MC, V.*

Mar de Cortés. This colonial-style hotel is one of the few in downtown Cabo San Lucas. The rooms are spread out in single-story buildings surrounding the pool; there's a newer two-story section at the back of the compound overlooking the pool. The mattresses are soft and lumpy in both sections, and the color scheme is a dull brown and yellow combo with no art on the walls. The gardens by the pool are beautifully tended, though, and the clientele amiable. *Calles Cárdenas and Guerrero, tel. 684/3–0032; reservations in the U.S.: Box 1827, Monterey, CA 93942, tel. 408/375–4755. 72 rooms. Facilities: pool, restaurant, bar. MC, V.*

Inexpensive **Hotel Marina.** This establishment is conveniently located across from the marina (though the view is now blocked by the massive Plaza las Glorias hotel/timeshare complex). The rooms are air-conditioned, with blue and yellow flowers painted on the walls, and bathrooms sport tile baths. Some rooms face a pretty courtyard with pools and Jacuzzi, and are quieter than those facing the street. *Blvd. Marina at Calle Guerrero, tel. 684/3–0030. 30 rooms. Facilities: pool, Jacuzzi, restaurant. MC, V.*

Between Cabo San Lucas and San José del Cabo

Expensive **Calinda Cabo Baja.** The hot tubs on the cliffs overlooking the Sea of Cortés are this hotel's most striking and delightful feature. The hotel is spread out, pueblo-style, over a shady, lush cliff top, with low, terra-cotta buildings terraced up the hillside. Blue, purple, and pink predominate in the spacious rooms, with photos of Cabo on the walls and plenty of room to spread out. The setting is particularly impressive at dusk, when the hillsides turn a rosy pink and the buildings glow in the sunlight. It's a long walk down the stairway to the beach, but the snorkeling around the rocks at the base of the cliff is worth it. *Km 4.5 on the highway, tel. 684/3–0044; reservations in the U.S.: tel. 800/228–5151. 125 rooms. Facilities: 3 pools, beach, aquatic center, sportfishing, hot tubs, tennis, restaurant, bar. MC, V.*

Hotel Cabo San Lucas. Everything is done on a grand scale at this 2,500-acre resort, from the massive stone Aztec gods at the entrance to the cavernous fieldstone and glass cocktail lounge with its 11-piece mariachi band and spectacular water view. Built in 1962, the hotel is surrounded by palms, bougainvillea, and almond trees, and the buildings seem nearly buried by the vegetation. The standard rooms have firm double beds and folk art hanging on the walls; the suites have fireplaces as well. The hotel is on Chileno Bay, a prime diving and snorkeling spot; fishing is also great. *Highway 1, no phone; reservations in the U.S.: Box 48088, Los Angeles, CA 90048, tel. 2/655–4760, 800/421–0777 or 800/282–4809 in CA. 99 rooms, suites, and villas. Facilities: beach, pool, water sports, tennis, putting green, airstrip, restaurant, bar, fishing charters. No credit cards.*

Meliá Cabo Real. Even if you're staying elsewhere, stop by here for a glimpse of the future. This Meliá is incredibly huge and opulent, spread over a hilltop with a meandering crystal blue pool, fountains, waterfalls, white canopies shading rest areas, and a private beach created by a small jetty jutting out from the rocky hillside. Maya carvings and bas-reliefs adorn the walls in the rooms, which all have landscaped terraces. Several other high-end hotel chains are planning construction near the Meliá, and there will someday be an 18-hole golf course here. *KM 19.5, Los Cabos Hwy., tel. 684/3–0754; reservations in the U.S.: tel. 800/336–3542. 299 rooms. Facilities: pool, beach, fishing fleet, dive shop, water-sports equipment, tennis courts, fitness center, 24-hour room service, 2 restaurants, 24-hour café. AE, MC, V.*

★ **Palmilla.** Just outside San José, on the best swimming beach in the area, the Palmilla is a gracious, sprawling, hacienda-style resort. Tile stairways lead up from flower-lined paths to large apartments with hand-carved furniture, French doors leading to private patios, and tile baths. Colorful serapes and *moles* (embroidered and appliqued scenes) hang on the walls. The buildings are spread out along a hillside overlooking the beach, with fountains and bougainvillea-draped statues. The patio restaurant overlooks the tropically landscaped pool and is a lovely spot for breakfast. This is a pretty, peaceful, romantic spot; its little white chapel has been used for many weddings. *On Rte. 1 about 5 mi from San José, no phone; reservations in the U.S.: 4577 Viewridge Ave., San Diego, CA 92123, tel. 800/*

854–2608 or 800/542–6082 in CA. 62 rooms, 7 suites, and 2 villas. Facilities: beach, pool, water sports, tennis, airstrip, restaurant, bar. MC, V.

San José del Cabo

Expensive **Stouffer Presidente.** By far the nicest hotel in San José, the Presidente sits at the far end of the hotel zone, next to the estuary. It resembles a pueblo set amid beachside cactus gardens. The low, terra-cotta buildings curve around an enormous blue pool, with an oasis of palms and green grass circled by sand and blooming yuccas. The ground-floor rooms have shaded patios looking out to the pool, and all rooms have cable TV, mini-bars, firm king-size beds, deep bathtubs, and couches facing the sliding glass doors. Musicians perform nightly at the outdoor restaurant, crooning romantic tunes for honeymooners dancing under the starry skies. You can stroll along the beach on the Sea of Cortés from the tropical estuary to the desert hills, but stay out of the water—the currents are dangerous. *At the end of the hotel zone, tel. 684/2–0038; reservations in the U.S.: tel. 800/472–2427. 250 rooms, including 6 suites. Facilities: beach, pool, water sports, horseback riding, fishing charters, tennis courts, 4 restuarants, bar, disco, satellite TV. MC, V.*

Moderate **Calinda Aquamarina Inn.** This beige and brown hotel/motel has reasonable rates, dependable service, and clean, comfortable rooms in low-rise buildings surrounding a spacious pool. The lobby bar is filled with gringos, many on group tours. For those who want few surprises and a feeling of security and friendliness, this is the place. *In the hotel zone, tel. 684/2–0007; reservations in the U.S.: tel. 800/228–5151. 99 rooms. Facilities: pool, beach, water sports, restaurant, bar, satellite TV. MC, V.*

Inexpensive **Hotel Colli.** This small inn in the center of town is remarkably peaceful and picturesque, with a flowering back yard and third-floor terrace. Rooms have ceiling fans and carpeting; some have balconies over the street, which isn't very noisy. *Calle Hidalgo, no phone. 12 rooms. No credit cards.*

Hotel San Jose Inn. This new, small hotel is about a 5-minute walk from town and offers simple rooms with concrete floors, showers, and pastel furnishings. The rates are the lowest in town, and the proprietress is very accommodating. *Calle Degollado s/n, tel. 684/2–1428. 11 rooms (more under construction). Facilities: snack bar. No credit cards.*

Posada Terranova. As with many small properties, the Terranova is undergoing changes, with construction beginning on 14 more rooms and a swimming pool. For now, you feel like you're staying in an old hacienda neatly outfitted with private tiled baths in the 5 colonial-style rooms. The clientele is made of mostly regulars who return year after year. Call ahead for reservations. *Calle Degollado at Zaragoza, tel. 684/2–0534. 5 rooms. Facilities: restaurant, bar. MC, V.*

Nightlife

With fishing and diving boats departing by 7 AM, there's not much nightlife in Los Cabos. People tend to turn in early and save their energy for exploring in the water. The nightlife in Cabo San Lucas took a definite up-turn when rocker Van Halen opened **Cabo Wabo** (Calle Guerrero, no phone). The latest U.S.

hits play over an excellent sound system, but the real highlight is the impromptu jam sessions with appearances by Halen's many friends in the music biz. Music, dancing, and general revelry also reign at **Squid Roe** (Av. Cárdenas), **Giggling Marlin** (Blvd. Marina), **Señor Sushi** (Blvd. Marina), **Shooterz** (Calle Guerrero), and **The One That Got Away** (Calle Guerrero). Traditionally, the best disco in town has been **El Oasis** (Av. Cárdenas), but now there is competition from **Lukas** (Av. Cárdenas at Blvd. Marina).

10 Guerrero Negro and Scammon's Lagoon

Introduction

Humans aren't the only ones to migrate below the border for warmth in the winter months. Every winter, hundreds of great gray whales swim south from the Bering Sea off the coast of Alaska to the tip of the Baja Peninsula. Just over the state line between Baja Norte and Baja Sur, at the 28th parallel, they stop to give birth at Scammon's Lagoon. Up to 6,000 whales show up each year, stopping not far from shore for the calves to be born.

If it weren't for the whales, and for the Transpeninsular Highway (Mexico Highway 1) near town, few travelers would venture to **Guerrero Negro,** 720 kilometers (450 miles) south of Tijuana. Guerrero Negro is near the Vizcaíno Desert, on the Pacific Ocean. The area is best known for its salt mines, which produce a third of the world's salt. Salt water collects in about 800 square kilometers (300 square miles) of sea-level ponds and evaporates quickly in the desert heat, leaving huge blocks of pure white salt. The waters around the island are deep enough for huge freighters to pick up the salt and deliver it to the United States, Canada, and Japan.

Guerrero Negro (Black Warrior) received its strange name from the whaling ship that ran aground near Scammon's Lagoon in 1858. The town did not exist until the 1950s, when an American entrepreneur decided to take advantage of the climate by engaging in the solar production of salt. The town's most distinctive landmark is a 120-foot-high steel eagle marking the state line and the change from Pacific to Mountain time. The town's population is 10,000, with many employed by the salt company. Each year, from January to March, the whales and the tourists arrive. The rest of the year, Guerrero Negro is just a way station, a place to stop for gas and supplies, and maybe a meal. But during the whaling season, Guerrero Negro is a popular place.

Scammon's Lagoon is 27 kilometers (17 miles) south along a rutted sand road that crosses the salt flats; the road is passable, but rough. The lagoon got its name from the American explorer Charles Melville Scammon of Maine. In the mid-1800s, he discovered the lagoon in Bahía Sebastián Vizcaíno, off the coast of Baja. The whales and calves that populated the waters were a much easier and more plentiful prey for the whalers than the leviathans swimming in the open sea. On its first expedition to the lagoon, Scammon's crew collected over 700 barrels of valuable whale oil, and the whale rush was on. Within 10 years, nearly all the whales in the lagoon had been killed, and it took almost a century for the whale population to increase to what it had been before Scammon arrived. It wasn't until the '40s that the American and Mexican governments took measures to protect the whales and banned the whalers from the lagoon.

Today even whale-watching boats are forbidden in Scammon's Lagoon, known in Mexico as Laguna Ojo de Liebre (Hare's Eye Lagoon). The area around it is now a national park, **Parque Natural de Ballena Gris** (Gray Whale Natural Park). Each year the 50-foot, 40-ton leviathans migrate 9,600 kilometers (6,000 miles) from the Bering Sea and congregate in the lagoon, where the warm, calm waters are ideal for birthing. Whale-watching from the shores of the lagoon can be disappointing without binoculars, but the sight of them spouting water high into the air,

Guerrero Negro and Scammon's Lagoon

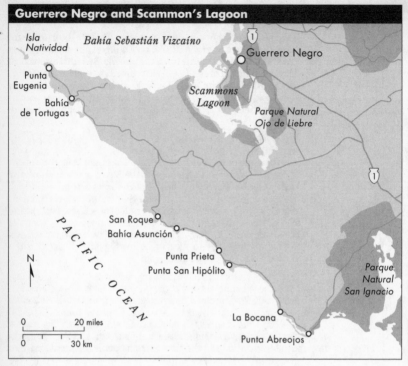

and their 12-foot-wide tails smashing into the water, is memorable.

A few kilometers south at **Laguna de San Ignacio,** fishermen will take you out in their boats to get closer to the whales. But for a better view and an easier stay in this rugged country, travel with an outfitter who will arrange your travel, accommodations, and your precious time on the water. The whales come close to the boat, rising majestically from the water, and sometimes swim close enough to be petted on their encrusted backs.

Essential Information

Arriving and Departing by Plane

The closest international airport to Guerrero Negro is in La Paz, 800 kilometers (500 miles) southeast; there is a small airstrip in town.

Arriving and Departing by Car and Bus

Guerrero Negro is just south of the Baja Norte/Baja Sur state line, 720 kilometers (450 miles) from Tijuana. There is a gas station in town, and basic auto supplies are available. **Tres Estrellas de Oro** (tel. 682/2–3063 in La Paz) runs buses to Guerrero Negro from La Paz and Tijuana.

Guided Tours

The best way to see the whales is to go with a tour company familiar with the area. **Baja Expeditions** (2625 Garnet Ave., San Diego, CA 92109, tel. 800/843–6967) has whale-watching trips by boat and kayak and is the premier Baja adventure operator in the United States. Their adventure tours span the peninsula and the Sea of Cortés. **Baja Discovery** (Box 152527, San Diego, CA 92115, tel. 619/262–0700, 800/829–BAJA) operates a whale-watching camp at Laguna San Ignacio south of Guerrero Negro, with tent camping on an island in the lagoon and boat trips among the whales.

Dining

The best restaurant is **Malarrimo,** at a trailer park near the entrance to town. Seafood is the specialty, and though the prices have climbed to the high-moderate range, the food is still worth the cost. **Mario's,** by El Morro hotel, is good for seafood and Mexican dishes.

Lodging

There are few decent hotels in Guerrero Negro, with a total of 100 rooms. Double occupancy rooms cost from about $10 to $25 per day but rise by 15–20% during whale-watching season. Credit cards are normally not accepted, though traveler's checks are. Highly recommended lodgings are indicated by a star ★.

El Morro. A small inn on a more primitive scale, El Morro has rooms with private baths and hot showers. *Blvd. Zapata, no phone.*

★ **La Pinta.** Part of a small chain of hotels in Baja, this motel has clean, spacious rooms. It is a few kilometers outside town, looking like an oasis of palms in the barren desert. *Reservations in the U.S.: tel. 800/336–5454. 26 rooms. Facilities: coffee shop.*

Las Dunas. Near the El Morro, this hotel is even more primitive, but clean. *Blvd. Zapata, no phone.*

11 Mazatlán

Introduction

Mazatlán is the Aztec word for "place of the deer," and long ago it sheltered far more deer than humans on its islands and shores. Today it is a city of some 600,000 residents and draws over 1,500,000 tourists a year. Sunning, surfing, and sailing have caught on here, and in the winter months visitors from inland Mexico, the United States, and Canada flock to Mazatlán for a break in the sun. The winter temperature, from November through April, ranges between 70° and 80°, and the summer months are not nearly as warm as in the more popular tourist areas farther south. Hotel and restaurant prices are lower than elsewhere on the coast, and the ambience is more that of a fishing town than a tourist haven.

Upscale Mazatlán is not known for its part of fancy resorts and ritzy restaurants, though at El Cid, Camino Real, and Pueblo Bonito resorts are fairly luxurious, and condos and time-share developments are popping up on the few remaining lots in the Zona Dorada, Mazatlán's beach/hotel/shopping/nightclub strip. The stretch north from El Cid resort beyond Punta Cerritos (Cerritos Point) seems destined to become a haven for the wealthy as luxury high-rise towers are built on the beach.

Hunting and fishing are what originally drew visitors to Mazatlán. At one time, jaguars, mountain lions, rabbits, and coyotes roamed the surrounding hills, and duck, quail, pheasant, and other wildfowl fed in nearby lagoons. Nowadays, hunters have to search a little harder and farther for their quarries, but there's still an abundance of game birds within a few miles of the city. Mazatlán is the base for Mexico's largest sportfishing fleet; fishermen haul in the biggest catches (in size and number) on the coast. The average annual haul is 10,000 sailfish and 5,000 marlin; a record 973-pound marlin and 203-pound sailfish were pulled from these waters. Mazatlán also has the largest shrimping fleet in Mexico. Sinaloa, one of Mexico's richest states, uses Mazatlán's port to ship its agricultural products.

The Spaniards settled in the Mazatlán region in 1531 and used the indigenous people as a labor force to create the port and village. The center of Mazatlán gradually moved north so that the original site is now 32 kilometers (20 miles) southeast of the harbor.

The port has a history of blockades. In 1847, during the Mexican War, U.S. forces marched down from the border through northeast Mexico and closed the port. In 1864, the French bombarded the city and then controlled it for several years. Mexico's own internal warring factions took over from time to time. And after the Civil War in the United States, a group of southerners tried to turn Mazatlán into a slave state.

Essential Information

Important Addresses and Numbers

Tourist Information Information on Mazatlán and city tours is available at the hotels, which do a more thorough job of promoting the area than the tourism office does. The **City Tourism Bureau** is next to the Los Sábalos Hotel. *Av. Loaiza 100, tel. 69/83-25-45. Open Mon.–Sat., hours vary.*

Consulates   **Unites States** (Circunvalación 120 Centro, tel. 69/85–22–05); **Canadian** (Hotel Playa Mazatlán, tel. 69/83–73–20).

Emergencies   **Police** (tel. 69/81–39–19), **Red Cross** (tel. 69/81–48–18), and 24-hour **Medical Clinic** (tel. 69/84–29–98).

Arriving and Departing by Plane

Airport and Airlines   Mazatlán's Rafael Buelna International Airport is serviced by several airlines. **Aeroméxico** (tel. 800/237–6639) has flights from Houston, Los Angeles, Denver, and Tucson; **Alaska Airlines** (tel. 800/426–0333) flies in from San Francisco, Seattle, and Portland; **Delta** (tel. 800/221–1212) from Los Angeles; and **Mexicana** (tel. 800/531–7921) from Denver, Los Angeles, San Francisco, San Diego, and Seattle.

Between the Airport and Hotels   The airport is a good 40 minutes from town. Shuttle services using Volkswagen vans charge about $5 for the trip to the major hotels.

Arriving and Departing by Car, Train, Bus, and Ship

By Car   Mazatlán is 1,192 kilometers (nearly 750 miles) from the border city of Nogales, Arizona via Mexico Highway 15. An overnight stop is recommended, as driving at night in Mexico is hazardous (*see* Getting Around Mazatlán, below).

By Train   Trains arrive daily from Mexicali, at the California border, and Nogales, at the Arizona border. Others come in from Guadalajara. The train depot is located south of town. Tickets may be purchased at Viajes Harsuna (Av. Camarón Sábalo 355, tel. 69/84–12–39).

By Bus   **Transportes Nortes de Sonora** travels to Mazatlán from Nogales, Arizona; other companies connect the coast with inland Mexico. The bus terminal is at Calle Río Tamazula and Highway 15 (tel. 69/81–23–35).

By Ship   Cruise ships from the Admiral, Carnival, and Princess lines, among others, include Mazatlán on their winter itineraries. A ferry service operates between La Paz, on the Baja peninsula, and Mazatlán. It leaves the main pier daily at 5 PM (tel. 69/81–58–08). *Note:* Service on the Baja Express ferry was suspended after a week, but there has always been regular ferry service.

Getting Around Mazatlán

Most tourist hotels are located in the Zona Dorada (Golden Zone), north of town. It's a long walk from downtown, about 25 kilometers (15 miles), but taxis and buses cruise the strip regularly. A fun way to get around is on the *pulmonías* (open-air jitneys, literally "pneumonias") that cost the same as taxis.

By Car   A car is not necessary in town, since public transportation is good, but you might want one for a self-guided tour of the area. Rentals usually include free mileage. A Volkswagen Beetle costs about $60 per day with insurance; a sedan with automatic transmission is about $90 per day. All the rental firms following have desks at the airport: **Avis** (Av. Camerón Sábalo 314, tel. 69/83–62–00), **Budget** (Av. Camerón Sábalo 402, tel. 69/83–20–00), **Hertz** (Av. del Mar 1111, tel. 69/83–60–60), and **National** (Av. Sábalo in the Plaza el Camarón, tel. 69/83–40–77), *Rent*

Me!, between the Quijote Inn and the Caravelle hotel, rents golf-cart-type cars (tel. 69/84–64–33).

Guided Tours

Orientation Tour agencies have offices in most hotels and along the Zona Dorada. Mazatlán's tourist areas are filled with sidewalk stands staffed by persuasive individuals offering free tours of the area along with free drinks and meals. They want to sell you more than a tour. They are actually selling time-shares and condos, and the tour/sales pitch can take up the better part of a day.

The three-hour **city tour** is a good way to get the lay of the land, particularly downtown, which can be a bit confusing. It includes Zona Dorada, the cathedral and *zócalo* (main square) downtown, the Mazatlán Arts and Crafts Center, and the waterfront.

Boat **Harbor cruises** feature live mariachi or marimba music and free refreshments and normally last about three hours. A cruise aboard the YATE *Fiesta* costs about $5. You'll see the bay, harbor, islands, and sportfishing fleet. A five-hour tour goes to Isla de la Piedra (Stone Island), with time allowed for lunch and a swim.

The **country tour**, also called the **mountain tour**, goes to **Concordia**, known for its furniture makers (a huge wood chair marks the entrance to the small town), then proceeds to **Copala**, a scenic colonial mining town. The **jungle tour** goes to **San Blas** and the **Río Tovara** (in the state of Nayarit), where boats travel upriver through mangrove jungle to a small spring- fed pond. The tour companies also offer individual guided tours and sportfishing outings.

Exploring

Numbers in the margin correspond with points of interest on the Mazatlán map.

❶ Mazatlán's **Zona Dorada** is the tourist area, and it is from here that most visitors begin exploring the city. Since Mazatlán's other highlights are spread far and wide, walking from one section of town to the other can take hours. The best way to travel is via pulmonías, so you can sunbathe and take pictures as you cruise along. If you choose to rent a car and drive, you can tour at your own pace. There are no traffic jams in Mazatlán, except near the market downtown, where parking can also be a major problem.

❷ The Zona Dorada begins on Avenida Camarón Sábalo at **Punta Camarón** (Shrimp Point), which resembles a rocky outcropping. Valentino's disco, a Moorish palace, is perched here, above the sea. Going north, Camarón Sábalo forms the eastern border of the zone, while Avenida Loaiza runs parallel to the beach. In this four-block area are most of the hotels, shops, and restaurants—this is where it's "at" in Mazatlán.

❸ A stroll through the **Mazatlán Arts and Crafts Center** gives you a good idea of the available souvenirs—onyx chess sets, straw sombreros, leather jackets, and Mickey Mouse piñatas. The

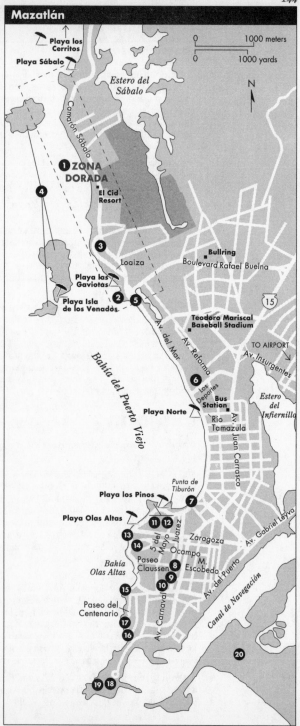

center is closed for siesta (1–4 PM), as are many of the nearby shops. *Av. Loaiza, tel. 69/82–50–55.*

Time Out You must take a break from shopping, or your head will be swimming with all you've seen. **Tequila Charlie's,** right in the Arts and Crafts Center, is a good spot for a beer or *agua mineral* (carbonated purified water) and lime. Mexico's version of Baskin-Robbins, **Helados Bing,** has good hot-fudge sundaes and ice-cream cones. It's at the corner of Camarón Sábalo and Gaviotas. Enjoy the fragrant cinnamon-flavored coffee at **Panadería Damaka** on Camarón Sábalo, a bakery with tables and chairs.

Traveling north, Avenida Loaiza merges into Camarón Sábalo at Gaviotas and continues along the coast past El Cid Resort, one of the largest tourist developments in Mexico. Along the beach side of Camarón Sábalo are some of Mazatlán's more luxurious and priciest hotels; opposite the beach are many of the better low-cost motels. Along this route there is a good view of ❹ Mazatlán's three islands—**Isla de los Pájaros** (Bird Island), **Isla de los Venados** (Deer Island), and **Isla de los Chivos** (Goat Island). Just past the Camino Real resort, Camarón Sábalo becomes Sábalo Cerritos and goes through the Estero del Sábalo, a lagoon popular with bird-watchers. The area to the north will one day feature exclusive resorts.

If you head south on Avenida Camarón Sábalo from the southernmost part of Punta Camarón, you'll notice that this 24-kilometer (15-mile) main road changes names frequently. At one point it becomes Avenida del Mar, which is where the 16-kilo❺ meter (10-mile) **malecón,** Mazatlán's version of a main highway and beachfront boardwalk, begins.

❻ Mazatlán's **Acuario** is a few blocks south, on Avenida Deportes. The aquarium is a must-see, with its tanks of sharks, sea horses, eels, lobsters, and colorful saltwater and freshwater fish. There is a museum filled with fascinating shells and fossils and a theater where naturalist films are shown. Next door, a **botanical garden** and **zoo** are shady places for a stroll (the trees and flowers are all labeled, but only in Spanish, so bring your dictionary). The small zoo's main attraction is its pair of languorous crocodiles. A fanciful bronze fountain and sculpture of two boys feeding a dolphin is at the aquarium's entrance. *Av. Deportes, (tel. 69/81–78–15). Small admission fee. Open daily 10–6.*

A bit farther down the same street is the **Teadoro Mariscal Stadium,** where Mazatlán's Pacific League team plays from October to January.

Time Out Just before you come to the road to the aquarium, you'll see **Señor Frog** (Av. del Mar, tel. 69/82–19–25), probably the most popular restaurant and bar in Mazatlán. There's a souvenir shop at the front selling T-shirts and assorted paraphernalia bearing the Señor Frog logo. The restaurant is cool, dark, cluttered, and busy.

Avenida del Mar continues south past beaches popular with the locals and travelers staying at the budget hotels across the ❼ street. The **Monumento al Pescador** (Fisherman's Monument) is Avenida del Mar's main landmark, and it is a strange sight.

An enormous, voluptuous nude woman reclines on an anchor, her hand extended toward a naked fisherman dragging his nets. It's amusing to speculate about the statue's meaning.

Calles Juárez and Cinco de Mayo intersect with Avenida del Mar and lead to Mazatlán's real downtown, where the streets are filled with people rushing about. Many travelers never see this part of Mazatlán, but it's worth a visit. Head for the blue and gold spires of the **Mazatlán Cathedral**, at Calle Juárez and Avenida Ocampo, and you'll be in the heart of the city. The cathedral, built in 1890 and made a basilica in 1935, has a gilded and ornate triple altar, with murals of angels overhead and many small altars along the sides.

A sign at the entrance requests that visitors be appropriately attired (no shorts or tank tops inside). The **zócalo** (square) just across the street, called **Plaza Revolución,** has one of the most fascinating gazebos in Mexico—what looks like a '50s diner from Kansas inside the lower level and a wrought-iron bandstand on top. The green and orange tile on the walls, ancient jukebox, and soda fountain serving shakes, burgers, and hot dogs couldn't make a more surprising sight. On the streets facing the zócalo are the City Hall, banks, post office, and telegraph office. The **Teatro Angela Peralta,** built in 1860 and beautifully restored, is at Sixto Osuna and Carnaval, about three blocks from the zócalo. It was declared a historic monument in late 1990.

Downtown is filled with crumbling colonial homes, flowering trees, and pretty little parks. There is an outdoor flower market along Zaragoza, at Nelson, and the city's main market is also on Nelson.

Back along the waterfront, Avenida del Mar becomes Paseo Claussen as it heads south, and goes by **El Fuerte Carranza**, an old Spanish fort built to defend the city against the French, and **Casa del Marino**, a shelter for sailors. Neither sight is particularly impressive but they are good places to pause for a break and to take in the bay. Playa los Piños, a popular surfing beach, is on this road. **High-Divers Park**, where young men climb to a white platform and plunge into the sea, is located nearby. It isn't as spectacular as the performance at La Quebrada in Acapulco, but at night, when the divers leap with flaming torches, it's more exciting. Some of Mazatlán's best surfing beaches are in this area.

The malecón continues past **Cerro de la Nevería** (Ice Box Hill). Wealthy landowners in Mazatlán imported ice from San Francisco in the late 1800s and stored it in underground tunnels in this hill. Before then the hill was a lookout point for Spanish soldiers spotting pirate ships. There are some impressive old mansions along this hill, and a good view of the waterfront to the Zona Dorada. The next landmark is the statue of **La Mazateca,** a bronze nymph rising from a giant wave, and across the street is a small bronze deer.

Paseo Claussen leads into Olas Altas, site of Old Mazatlán, the center for tourism in the 1940s. The historic Hotel Belmar is here; pleasant, outdoor cafés overlook the water. Olas Altas (High Waves) ends at a small traffic circle.

On a windy hill above Olas Altas is **Cerro de Vigía**, with a lookout point, weather station, and rusty cannon. The view from here is fantastic, and takes in Mazatlán from the Pacific to the harbor. It's a steep trek up and better done by taxi than on foot.

⑰ The **Centenario Pérgola**, at the top of the hill, was once used by the Spaniards as a lookout point.

Time Out **El Mirador,** on top of Cerro de Vigía, is one of the best seafood restaurants in Mazatlán. If you can't make it to this restaurant for a meal, at least stop by and sample the ceviche (seafood marinated in lime or lemon juice), which is made with fresh shrimp.

At the end of the malecón, Olas Altas becomes Paseo Centenario and continues south to the tip of the peninsula and

⑱ ⑲ **Cerro del Crestón** (Summit Hill), where **El Faro**, said to be the second-largest lighthouse in the world, with a range of 36 nautical miles, is located. It takes about 30 minutes to hike up to the lighthouse, but you'll be rewarded with a great view of the harbor and sea. The road along the many docks and military installations is called Avenida del Puerto. The sportfishing fleet is anchored at the base of Cerro del Crestón; the docks used by cruise ships and merchant vessels are located just to the north.

⑳ Launches for **Isla de la Piedra** leave from a small dock by the military base.

Time Out The *palapas* (open-air eateries) that are sometimes set up on the sportfishing docks, sell tasty fish—try the smoked marlin. The palapas near the launches to Isla de la Piedra sell juicy sugarcane sticks (which look like bamboo) good for quenching your thirst.

What to See and Do with Children

The **Acuario Mazatlán,** with its tanks of salt- and freshwater fish, sharks, and films about sea life, is a perfect child-pleaser. On Sundays in particular it is packed with families. At the large playground next door, skateboarders practice their tricks while the younger children play on the slides and swings. There's also a zoo and a botanical garden (*see* above).

Shopping

In the **Zona Dorada,** particularly along Avenidas Camarón Sábalo and Loaiza, you can buy everything from piñatas to designer clothing. The best place for browsing is the **Mazatlán Arts and Crafts Center,** designed as a place to view artisans at work and buy their wares. Now the center is filled with shops and boutiques, and the only craft you see is the fine art of bartering. The **Mercado Viejo Mazatlán** and the **Tequila Tree,** both on Avenida Loaiza, are enormous warehouse-type stores filled with souvenirs.

For sportswear, visit **Aca Joe, Benetton, Fiorucci, Ralph Lauren,** and **Bye-Bye. Sea Shell City** is a must-see; its two floors are packed with shells from around the world that have been glued and strung and molded into every imaginable shape from lamps to necklaces. Upstairs, check out the huge fountain covered with thousands of shells. **Designer's Bazaar,** a two-story shop near the Los Sábalos Hotel, has probably the best selection of fine folk art, leather wallets and belts, and hand-embroidered clothing, as well as an assortment of swimsuits. Leather shops are in the southern end of the Zona Dorada. Try on soft leather jackets dyed in the latest colors at the **Leather House** and **Rey Solomon.**

The **Mercado Central,** downtown between Calles Juárez and Serdan, is a gigantic market that sells produce, meat, fish, and handicrafts at the lowest prices in town. It takes some searching to find good-quality handicrafts, but that's part of the fun. Browse through the stalls along the street outside the market for the best crafts.

Sports

Fishing More than a dozen sportfishing fleets operate from the docks south of the lighthouse. Charters, which include a full day of fishing, lunch, bait, and tackle, can be arranged by your hotel or directly through a charter company. Prices range from $40 per person on a party boat to $230 for an entire boat. Charter companies to contact include **Bill Heimpel's Star Fleet** (tel. 69/82–26–65), **Flota Faro** (tel. 69/81–28–24), **Estrella** (tel. 69/82–38–78), **El Dorado** (tel. 69/81–62–04), and **Del Mar** (tel. 69/82–31–30).

Golf The spectacular 18-hole course at **El Cid** (tel. 69/83–33–33), designed by Robert Trent-Jones, is reserved for members of the resort, hotel guests, and their guests. There is a nine-hole course at the **Club Campestre de Mazatlán** (tel. 69/82–57–02) on the outskirts of town on Highway 15.

Hunting Several species of duck as well as white-wing doves, mourning doves, and quail abound in the Mazatlán area. The season runs from October through April. **Aviles Brothers** (Box 222, tel. 69/81–37–28) is the most experienced outfitter, arranging licenses and the rental of firearms. The cost of a six-hour hunt is about $80, including transportation, retriever, and English-speaking guide.

Tennis Many hotels have courts, some of which are open to the public. There are a few public courts not connected to the hotels. Call in advance for reservations at **El Cid Resort,** 17 courts (tel. 69/83–33–33); **Racket Club,** 6 courts (tel. 69/82–76–44); **Club Parasol,** 2 courts (tel. 69/82–76–44); and **Tequila Charlie's,** 2 courts (tel. 69/83–31–20).

Water Sports Jet skis, Hobie Cats, and Windsurfers are available for rent at most hotels, and parasailing is very popular along the Zona Dorada. Scuba diving and snorkeling are catching on, but there are really no great diving spots. The best is around Isla de los Venados. For rentals and trips contact the following operators: **Caravelle Beach Club** (Av. Camarón Sábalo, tel. 69/83–02–00), **Chico's Beach Club** (Av. Camarón Sábalo 500, tel. 69/84–06–66), **El Cid Resort Aqua Sport Center** (Av. Camarón Sábalo, tel. 69/83–33–33), and **Los Sábalos** (Av. Camarón Sábalo, tel. 69/83–53–33).

Spectator Sports

Baseball The residents of Mazatlán loyally support their team, Los Venados, a Pacific League, Triple A team. Games are held at the Teodoro Mariscal Stadium (Av. Deportes) from October through January.

Bullfights Matches are held most Sunday afternoons between December and Easter. The bullring is located on Boulevard Rafael Buelna (tel. 69/84–16–66), and tickets are available at most hotels.

Beaches

Playa Isla de la Piedra The locals head here on weekends. Families, bearing toys, rafts, and picnic lunches, get to the island on *pongas* (small boats) from the dock near the train tracks. Shacks and palapas sell drinks and fish. On Sunday there's lots of music and fun. Sixteen kilometers (10 miles) of unspoiled beaches here allow enough room for all visitors to spread out, but this won't be the case for long: Work on another tourist megadevelopment continues at a rapid pace. When completed, 900 acres of the Island will be the site of hotels, villas, two golf clubs, and both tennis and riding clubs.

Playa Isla de los Venados Boats make frequent departures from the Zona Dorada hotels for this beach on Deer Island. It's only a 10-minute ride, but the difference in ambience is striking; the beaches are pretty, uncluttered, and clean, and you can hike around the southern point of the island to small, secluded coves covered with shells.

Playa Los Cerritos The northernmost beach on the outskirts of town runs from the Camino Real to Punta Cerritos. It is the cleanest and least populated beach. The waves can be too rough for swimming but are great for surfing.

Playa Norte This strand begins at Punta Camarón (use Valentino's as a landmark) along Avenida del Mar and the malecón and runs to the Fisherman's Monument. The dark brown sand is dirty and rocky in some places, but clean in others, and is popular with those staying at hotels without beach access. Palapas sell cold drinks, tacos, and fish; be sure to try the fresh coconut milk.

Playa Olas Altas This was the first tourist beach in Mazatlán. It runs south along the malecón from the Fisherman's Monument for about 2 miles. Surfers congregate here during the summer months, when the waves are at their highest.

Playa Sábalo and Playa las Gaviotas Mazatlán's two most popular beaches are along the Zona Dorada. There are as many vendors selling blankets, pottery, lace tablecloths, and silver jewelry as there are sunbathers. Boaters, windsurfers, and parasailers line the shores. The beach is protected from heavy surf by islands (Venados, Pájaros, and Chivos).

Dining

The emphasis in Mazatlán is on casual, bountiful dining, and the prices are reasonable. Shrimp and fish are the highlights; be sure to have a seafood cocktail along the beach. Dress is casual, and restaurants do not require reservations. When you check your bill, be aware that some restaurants, particularly in the hotels, add a service charge of 10%–15% to your total, as well as 15% tax.

Highly recommended restaurants in each price category are indicated by a star ★.

Category	Cost*
Expensive	over $15
Moderate	$10–$15
Inexpensive	under $10

per person, excluding drinks, service, and sales tax (15%)

Expensive **Casa Loma.** An out-of-the-way, elegant restaurant in a converted villa, Casa Loma serves international specialties such as chateaubriand and chicken *cordon bleu*. Lunch on the patio is less formal. Have a martini made by an expert, and save room for the fine pastries. *Av. Gaviotas 104, tel. 69/83–53–98. No credit cards*.

★ **La Concha.** Certainly the prettiest waterside dining spot, La outdoor tables by the sand. Adventurous types might attempt the stingray with black butter or calamari in black ink. The more conservative can try a thick filet mignon cooked to perfection. A singer croons Las Vegas–style ballads as couples dance, and the waiters are proper and refined. La Concha is also open for breakfast. *El Cid Resort, Av. Camarón Sábalo, tel. 69/83–33–33. AE, DC, MC, V.*

Moderate **Club Munchkins.** This huge palapa across the street from the Pueblo Bonito Hotel is an American hangout. Munchkin's has a bit of everything: Patrons linger at picnic tables under a palapa while parrots squawk in cages and wide-screen TVs blare cable news or football games. The menu includes burgers, barbecued pork sandwiches, bacon and eggs, and spaghetti (all you can eat). Try the shrimp olé, sautéed with tomatoes, onions, and bell peppers, and served with tamales, beans, and tortillas; or forget the real food and have the Killer Dessert—chocolate pecan pie with ice cream, Kahlúa, Bailey's, and rum. *Av. Camarón Sábalo, tel. 69/84–10–66. AE, D, MC, V.*

Costa Azul. This restaurant, on the malecón, is housed in an old boat that looks like it's stranded on the beach, with its outside deck half-buried in the sand. The first thing you see as you descend a ladder into the boat is a large grill, where fish is expertly prepared. There's seating in an inside cabin and on an outside deck. *Av. del Mar, no phone. MC, V. Dinner only.*

★ **Doney.** This big downtown hacienda has been serving great Mexican meals since 1959. The large dining room has old photos of Mazatlán, a high brick ceiling, and embroidered tablecloths, all of which give you the feeling that you're sitting in someone's home. The Doney is named for a restaurant in Rome, though there is nothing Italian about the menu. Try the *chilaquiles* (casserole of tortillas and chili sauce), mole dishes, or fried chicken. The meringue and fruit pies are excellent. *Mariano Escobedo at Cinco de Mayo, tel. 69/81–26–51. MC, V.*

El Marinero. The best seafood house in Old Mazatlán features a dish that includes a heaping portion of frogs' legs, turtle, shrimp, oysters covered with melted cheese, and fish grilled on a hibachi at your table. The decor is dark and woodsy, with lots of brick arches and seashell-covered chandeliers. Try the shrimp *machaca*, sautéed in olive oil with tomatoes, chives, and chilis. *5 de Mayo 530, tel. 69/81–76–82. MC, V.*

★ **El Mirador.** A real find on the top of Cerro del Vigia, this unassuming restaurant has some of the freshest, most flavorful fish around. The ceviche is made with shrimp, chopped and marinated in lime juice with tomatoes, onions, cilantro, and peppers. The salsa and chips are homemade and delicious, and meals include soup, salad, and dessert. Stick with the shrimp and fish and you'll be delighted. The wind tends to whip through the open windows, which can be quite invigorating. *Atop Cerro de Vigia, no phone. MC, V.*

Señor Frog. The Carlos Anderson chain's Mazatlán restaurant is as noisy and entertaining as the others. "Banditos" carry tequila bottles and shot glasses in their bandoliers instead of ammunition, and the drinking and carousing goes on well into the night. Barbecued ribs and chicken, served with corn on the cob, and heaping portions of standard Mexican dishes are the specialty—the tortilla soup is excellent. *Av. del Mar, tel. 69/82–19–25. MC, V.*

Shrimp Bucket. In Old Mazatlán under forest-green awnings is the original Carlos 'n Charlie's. The garden patio-restaurant is much quieter than its successors; some could call it respectable. Best bets are fried shrimp served in clay buckets and barbecued ribs. Portions are plentiful. Breakfast is also served. *Olas Altas 11, tel. 69/81–63–50. MC, V.*

Tequila Charlie's. This popular, noisy outdoor café and indoor restaurant in the Arts and Crafts Center is a convenient place to take a break from shopping for some good, basic burritos. *Av. Loaiza, no phone. MC, V. Closed during siesta.*

★ **Tres Islas.** A wonderful palapa on the beach, between El Cid and the Holiday Inn, Tres Islas is a favorite with families. Try the smoked marlin, oysters *diablo*, octopus, or the seafood platter. The setting is the nicest in town, with a good view of the three islands. The waiters are friendly and helpful, and mariachi bands encourage diners to sing along. *Av. Camarón Sábalo, tel. 69/83–59–32. MC, V.*

Inexpensive **Copa de Leche.** Though the name means "cup of milk," this indoor/outdoor café in Old Mazatlán, across from the malecón, is a good place any time of day for a cup of coffee or a beer. Locals settle in at the sidewalk tables for hours of gossip, watching the tourists, and marveling at the changes Mazatlán has undergone. The food is not spectacular, so stick with the less expensive egg dishes at breakfast and tacos and burritos at other times. *Olas Altas 33, tel. 69/82–57–53. AE, MC, V.*

★ **Karnes en Su Jugo.** A small, family-run café on the malecón, with a few outdoor tables but more indoor seating, this establishment specializes in a *karnes en su jugo*, literally beef in its juice, a Mexican beef stew with chopped beef, onions, beans, and bacon. It's a filling, satisfying meal, especially when eaten with a basketful of homemade tortillas. *Av. del Mar, tel. 69/82–13–22. AE, MC, V.*

Mucho Taco. This bright blue taco stand in the heart of the Zona Dorada is open 24 hours—a blessing for those out at the discos until the wee hours. The tacos are fresh and tasty, and you can eat at the small sidewalk tables or take your feast back to your room. *Av. Camarón Sábalo, no phone. No credit cards.*

Pizza Hut. You say you're hungry, tired, and homesick? What could be more American than a pepperoni pizza from Pizza Hut, delivered to your hotel? As dependable as ever, even if the pizza tastes a little different. *Av. Camarón Sábalo, tel. 69/82–01–02. No credit cards.*

Lodging

Most of Mazatlán's hotels are in the Zona Dorada, on the beach. Less-expensive places are in Old Mazatlán, the original tourist area along the malecón—on the south side of downtown. Although these hotels are somewhat shabby, they give the feel of Mexico. Most hotels raise their rates for the November–April high season; rates are lowest in the summer, during the rainy season. Price categories are based on high-season rates—expect to pay 25% less during the off-season.

Highly recommended lodgings in each price category are indicated by a star ★.

Category	Cost*
Expensive	over $80
Moderate	$50–$80
Inexpensive	under $50

All prices are for a standard double room, excluding 15% tax.

Expensive **El Cid.** The largest resort in Mazatlán, and perhaps in Mexico,
★ El Cid has 1,000 rooms spread over 900 acres, a tower containing only suites, and a residential area off the beach with some impressive homes and villas. A private marina is under construction. The spacious hotel rooms overlook the pool and beach (one of the longest and cleanest in the area), and the hotel is popular with convention groups as well as individual travelers. The glass-enclosed arcade has nice boutiques, and the resort's **La Concha** restaurant is one of the most romantic spots on the beach. *Av. Camarón Sábalo, tel. 69/83–33–33; reservations in U.S.: 800/525–1925. 1,000 air-conditioned rooms, suites, and villas. Facilities: beach, 6 pools, 18-hole golf course, aquatic center, 17 tennis courts, 14 restaurants, shops, disco. AE, DC, MC, V.*

Los Sábalos. A white high rise in the center of the Zona Dorada, Los Sábalos has a great location; a long, clean beach; and lots of action. You feel as though you're a part of things, amid the flight attendants who lay-over here, and it's only a short walk to **Valentino's,** the best disco in town. *Av. Loaiza 100, tel. 69/83–53–33. 185 air-conditioned rooms. Facilities: beach, pool, tennis courts, health club, 1 restaurant and 2 bars, shops. AE, DC, MC, V.*

★ **Pueblo Bonito.** By far the most beautiful property in Mazatlán, this all-suite hotel and time-share resort has an enormous lobby with chandeliers, beveled glass doors, and gleaming red and white tile floors. The pink terra-cotta rooms have dome ceilings. An arched doorway leads from the tile kitchen into the elegant seating area, which is furnished with pale pink and beige couches and glass tables. Pink flamingos stroll on the manicured lawns, golden *koi* (carp) swim in small ponds, and bronzed sunbathers repose on padded white lounge chairs by the crystal-blue pool. This is as elegant as Mazatlán gets. *Av. Camarón Sábalo 2121, tel. 69/84–37–00; reservations in the U.S.: 800/262–4500. 135 air-conditioned suites with balcony. Facilities: beach, pool, restaurant, bar. AE, DC, MC, V.*

Westin Camino Real. One of the first resorts to open in Mazatlán, the Camino Real is in a secluded location, past a rocky point

on the north end of town. The hotel is in terraces on the side of a
hill overgrown with flowering shrubs and towering palms, and
it's a long hike down the stairs to the beach and tide pools by the
point. The entire hotel has been renovated recently; this is a
good spot for really getting away from it all. *Av. Camarón
Sábalo, tel. 69/83–11–11; reservations in the U.S.: 800/228–
3000. 169 air-conditioned rooms. Facilities: beach, pool, 3 tennis courts, 3 restaurants, bars, disco. AE, DC, MC, V.*

Moderate   **Aquamarina.** Across the street from the malecón and the
beach, this midwestern-looking hotel/motel has a great view of
the beach and is conveniently located between Old Mazatlán
and the Zona Dorada—though it's a bit of a walk to the shops
and restaurants. The rooms on the malecón side can get noisy at
night; those in the back don't have much of a view but are quieter. The drapes and bedspreads in the rooms are faded and
worn, and the bathrooms could use remodeling, but they are
clean, and the water is hot. *Av. del Mar 110, tel. 69/81–70–85.
100 air-conditioned rooms. Facilities: pool, restaurant, bar,
parking. MC, V.*

Hacienda. Situated near the Fisherman's Monument, the Hacienda is an older colonial-style hotel with a rooftop sun deck.
The rooms are noteworthy for their marble baths, and not particularly impressive otherwise. The malecón and beach are
across the street, and the Zona Dorada is about 10 blocks away.
*Av. del Mar and Flamingos, tel. 69/82–70–70. 95 air-con-
conditioned rooms. Facilities: restaurant, bar, parking. AE,
DC, MC, V.*

★ **Holiday Inn.** A consistently good hotel, the Holiday Inn is a
long walk from the Zona Dorada, and so there's little traffic.
Tour and convention groups fill the 200 rooms and keep the party mood going by the pool and on the beach, where parasailing
is a big hit. There's a small play area with swings and a wading
pool for children, and live, upbeat music in the lobby. The
rooms are painted soothing grays and greens, and large sliding
glass doors open to a pretty view of the islands. *Av. Camarón
Sábalo 696, tel. 69/83–22–22; reservations in the U.S.: 800/
465–4329. 200 air-conditioned rooms. Facilities: beach, pool,
restaurant, bars. AE, DC, MC, V.*

Oceano Palace. This pretty blue and white hotel is on a nice
beach of its own, away from the bustle of the Zona Dorada.
Flowers bloom in window boxes on all five stories of the hotel
and along the walkways to the beach and pool. The rooms are
clean, airy, and quiet, with ocean breezes. *Av. Camarón
Sábalo 82, tel. 69/83–06–66. 167 air-conditioned rooms. Facilities: beach, pool, restaurant, bar. AE, DC, MC, V.*

★ **Playa Mazatlán.** Palapas are set up on the patios by the rooms
in this casual hotel, which is popular with Mexican families and
laid-back singles more concerned with comfort than with style.
The bright, sunny rooms have tile headboards over the beds
and tile tables by the windows. There's a volleyball net on the
beach, and a small taco stand sells good, inexpensive snacks.
*Av. Loaiza 202, tel. 69/83–44–44. 425 air-conditioned rooms.
Facilities: beach, pool, restaurant, bar. AE, DC, MC, V.*

Riviera Mazatlán. The Riviera is located close enough to the
malecón to walk to downtown; it's right by, but not in, the shopping district. The small, undistinguished rooms look out over
the pool, which is in the center of the courtyard. The small
beach is crowded and busy with vendors, and the hotel is popular with young singles who like to party. *Av. Camarón Sábalo*

51, tel. 69/83–46–11. 242 air-conditioned rooms. Facilities:
beach, pool, restaurant, bar. AE, DC, MC, V.

Inexpensive **Belmar.** One of the first hotels in Old Mazatlán, built near the
turn of the century, the Belmar has seen better days. It must
have been charming in its heyday, with its blue and white tile
balconies facing a central courtyard. Now the place is a bit
shabby. The dark wood arches and doorways haven't seen pol-
ish in years, and the furnishings in the rooms are quite rickety,
though there are some marvelous antiques among the clutter.
The newer rooms on the waterfront side have shag carpeting
and paneled walls. The beach across the street is one of the best
for surfing, and downtown and the market are a short walk
away. *Olas Altas 166, tel. 69/85–11–11. 196 rooms. Facilities:*
beach, pool, bar, parking. AE, DC, MC, V.

Bungalows Mar Sol. This older motel has clean, cluttered rooms
fronts the parking lot, and there are lounge chairs, a small
fountain, and a palapa-covered Ping-Pong table, but no pool.
The beach is across the street, and though the motel is north of
town buses frequently stop close by. *Av. Camarón Sábalo*
1001, tel. 69/84–01–08. MC, V.

Hotel Freemen. One of the oldest hotels in Old Mazatlán, the
Freeman looks its age but is undergoing renovation. The rooms
are run-down, with cracks in the walls and leaks by the sinks,
but the location is great for those who like a beach with good
surf. A good spot for the young and hearty. *Olas Altas 79, tel.*
69/81–21–14. 76 rooms. Facilities: beach access, restaurant,
bar. AE, DC, MC, V.

Sands. This is a beachfront hotel with many of the amenities of
the larger, and more expensive resort hotels, but at a fraction
of the price. It is popular with retirees and wanderers who
want to stay put for a while. All of the rooms are air-conditioned and have color TVs with some U.S. channels, and several of the rooms have kitchenettes. *Av. del Mar 1910, tel. 69/82–*
06–00. Facilities: pool, restaurant, bar. AE, MC, V.

Nightlife

Caracol Tango Palace (tel. 69/83–33–33) at El Cid is Mazatlán's
premier night spot. **Valentino's** (tel. 69/83–62–12) draws a
glitzy crowd. Its stark white towers rise on Punta Camarón at
the beginning of the Zona Dorada. There are dance floors for
rock, easy-listening, and romantic music.

Also at the Valentino's complex is **Bora Bora,** a casual palapa
bar on the beach, alive with music and dancing from noon to 4
AM (tel. 69/83–62–12). **Sheik,** a new restaurant extravaganza,
also at the Valentino complex, needs a lot of improvement in the
food and service departments, but it shouldn't be missed. Stop
in early in the evening for a drink.

Fandango's in the Las Palmas shopping center, is also popular.
One of the Mexican Fiestas at the Playa Mazatlán, Holiday Inn,
or the Oceano Palace, is also a good entertainment bet; the Fiesta at the Plaza Maya offers a buffet and a two-hour show that
includes a performance of the Flying Indians of Papantla. Almost all hotel travel desks can provide you with information on
days and times.

12 Puerto Vallarta

Introduction

When you hear the words "Puerto Vallarta," certain images come to mind: white adobe casas with red tile roofs on palm covered hills; pack mules clomping down steep cobblestone streets; sailboats gliding by serene beaches; huts tucked among jungle vines; fishing nets floating in crystal-clear water glistening in the sun; lush, green mountains overgrown with blossoms; rivers tumbling into waterfalls; bright yellow birds hovering above.

To some extent, PV (as it is called) is all of the above, but it can no longer claim to be as peaceful as it was in 1963, when movie director John Huston filmed the Tennessee Williams play *Night of the Iguana* here. One of the film's stars, Richard Burton, was romantically involved at the time and as soon as photos of Liz and Dick in their tropical paradise hit the press, the rush to Puerto Vallarta was on. See the movie if you crave the Puerto Vallarta myth. Then get set for the reality.

Today, Puerto Vallarta's population is 300,000 within the city; another 100,000 live in the surrounding countryside. More than 1,500,000 tourists visit each year, and during high season (November–April) the city's quaint, cobblestone streets are clogged with pedestrians and vehicles. The Bahía de Banderas (Bay of Flags) attracted pirates and explorers as early as the 1500s; it was used as a stopover on long voyages, a place for the crew to relax or a choice spot for plunder and pillage. It is said that Sir Francis Drake visited once or twice. But PV languished until the mid-1850s, when Don Guadalupe Sanchez Carrillo developed the bay as a port for the silver mines by the Río Cuale. It was known then as Puerto de Peñas, and had about 1,500 inhabitants.

The quiet, harbor village became a municipality of the state of Jalisco and was renamed after Ignacio L. Vallarta, a governor of the state, in 1918. Tourists began flying into a small landing strip on what is now Playa de los Muertos in the 1950s, and in the '60s, after the first highway was built, visitors came from Guadalajara. Puerto Vallarta became a hideaway for the wealthy as well as for hardy escapists who could survive on a subsistence level. In the 27 years since the rush of publicity from *Night of the Iguana*, the idyllic village disappeared: Airports, hotels, and highways replaced palm groves and fishing shacks. With the recent opening of several new hotels in the Marina Vallarta complex, PV now has about 10,000 hotel rooms. Everywhere you go you see bulldozers and cranes and hear the constant clatter of hammers and drills. The older hotels seem to be in a continual state of renovation and modernization, and new hotels crop up in every empty space. There is little sense of escape from civilization in Puerto Vallarta these days, though every attempt is made to keep its character and image intact. Even the parking lot at the new Gigante supermarket is cobbled, and any house built in town must be painted white. But the city is perilously close to losing its charm. The infrastructure—the roads and sewers in particular—can't keep pace with the growth. Because of this, it is strongly advised that you stick to bottled water.

The timing of a visit to PV is largely a matter of personal preference. In high season the air temperature ranges from 21° to 27°C (70s and 80s F) and the water temperature is 16° to 21°C

(60s and low 70s F). The skies are generally clear, though it can get windy and gray. But not for long. When you think of the snow, sleet, and slush in Toronto, Boulder, or Boston at that time of year, you understand why hundreds of palefaces arrive each day, and why there's an ever-increasing demand for more places to stay.

The off-season brings rain, with light afternoon showers in the early summer and major rainstorms that can last for hours in the late summer and fall. You miss out on constant sunshine, but in return you get emptier beaches, warmer water (around 26°C—high 70s F), and less-crowded streets. You also get a 25%–30% reduction in room rates and the opportunity to do a little bargaining on rental cars. If you don't mind hot, humid weather and the ever-present mosquitos and other insect life, PV in the summertime has certain advantages. The rivers swell, waterfalls appear in once-dry crevices and canyons from the mountains to the sea, and the surf picks up considerably.

Even if you only visit during its busiest times, there is one way to see the paradise of old: Get out of town. The bay and town are on the edge of the Sierra Madre range, whose western tip ends at Cabo Corrientes on the southern tip of Bahía Banderas. The town has filled the curve of habitable land between the water and the mountains, but its sprawl has not reached far north or south, and within 16 kilometers (10 miles) of either side of town there are peaceful coves, rivers rushing to the sea, steep mountain roads curving and twisting through a jungle of pines and palms, and all the tranquillity you could need.

Essential Information

Important Addresses and Numbers

Tourist Information The **State Tourism Office** is one of the best in Mexico. *City Hall on Av. Juárez, by the zócalo (plaza), tel. 322/2–0242 or 322/2–0243. Open weekdays 9–8, Sat. 9–1.*

Consulates **U.S. Consul** (tel. 322/2–0069); **Canadian Consul** (tel. 322/2–53–99).

Emergencies **Police** (City Hall on Av. Juárez, tel. 322/2–0123); **Red Cross** (Río de la Plata and Río Balsas, tel. 322/2–1533); **Hospital** (Carretera Libramiento Km 1.5, tel. 322/2–4000).

Arriving and Departing by Plane

Airport and Airlines Puerto Vallarta's **Gustavo Díaz Ordáz International Airport** is 6.4 kilometers (4 miles) north of town, not far from the major resorts. The Mexican airlines have daily direct flights from Mexico City, Los Cabos, Mazatlán, and Guadalajara and connecting flights from other Mexican cities. **Mexicana** (tel. 800/531–7921) has service from Chicago, Los Angeles, San Francisco, Dallas/Fort Worth, and Denver; **Aeroméxico** (tel. 800/237–6639), from Los Angeles. Several American carriers also serve Puerto Vallarta, including **American** (tel. 800/433–7300), **Northwest** (tel. 800/225–2525), **Continental** (tel. 800/525–0280), **Alaska** (tel. 800/426–0333), and **Delta** (tel. 800/221–1212).

Between the Volkswagen vans provide economical transportation from the
Airport and Hotels airport to hotels, and all the car rental agencies have desks at
the airport.

Arriving and Departing by Car, Train, Bus, and Ship

By Car Puerto Vallarta is about 1,900 kilometers (1,200 miles) from
Nogales, Arizona, at the United States–Mexico border, 354 kilometers (220 miles) from Guadalajara, and 167 kilometers (104
miles) from Tepic. Driving to Puerto Vallarta is not difficult,
but driving in the city can be horrid. From December to April—peak tourist season—traffic clogs the narrow cobblestone
streets; during the rainy season, from July to October, the
streets flood and hills are muddy and slippery.

By Train Trains run daily from Mexicali and Guadalajara to Tepic. (From
Tepic, it is a three-hour bus ride to Puerto Vallarta.) The train
is unreliable, crowded, and slow, and best left to those with
plenty of time and patience. Tel. 321/3–4861 for the train station in Tepic.

By Bus There is no central bus station in PV. The carriers are located
on Avenida Insurgentes between the Río Cuale and Calle
Serdan: **Estrella Blanca** (Insurgentes 180, tel. 322/2–06), **Norte
de Sonora** (Madero 343, tel. 322/2–1650),**Transportes del
Pacífico** (Insurgentes 282, tel. 322/2–1015), and **Tres Estrellas
de Oro** (Insurgentes 210, tel. 322/2–1019). There are hourly
buses to and from Tepic, Guadalajara, Mexico City, Mazatlán,
and Manzanillo.

By Ship Several cruise lines, including **Carnival** (tel. 800/327–9051) and
Admiral (tel. 800/421–5866) sail to Puerto Vallarta from Los
Angeles during the winter months. **North Star Cruises** sails in
from La Paz.

The ferry from La Paz and Cabo San Lucas on the Baja Peninsula has been discontinued indefinitely. Check at the cruise
ship terminal or the tourist office for information.

Getting Around

By Bus City buses and *combis* (Volkswagen vans) serve downtown, the
northern hotel zone, and the southern beaches. Bus stops—
marked by a blue and white sign with a drawing of a bus—are
located every two or three blocks along the highway (Carretera
Aeropuerto) and in town. To take a combi to Mismaloya or other
points south, go to the Combi Terminal on Calle Piño Suárez.
Every bus headed north from town may not stop at your hotel
so be sure you ask for your stop before you get on.

By Taxi Many hotels post fares to common destinations; be sure to
agree on a fare before the cab takes off. The ride from the
northside hotels to downtown costs about $3, plus $1 to cross
the bridge.

By Car While a car or a Jeep is handy for visiting Boca de Tomatlán,
Playa Mismaloya, and other points outside the city, it is an en-
cumbrance in town, where the traffic often slows to a dead stop
and parking is scarce.

Avenida Díaz Ordáz runs one way south through town, becoming Avenida Morelos just before the Río Cuale bridge to Playa
de Los Muertos. Avenida Juárez runs one way north over the

river and through town to the hotel zone. The narrow cobblestone streets on the hills above town are difficult to negotiate by car, and though the maps don't show it, a street can end abruptly at a cliff edge, only to continue again somewhere else. Avenida Matamoros, just behind the cathedral, is the widest and longest street, and has some nice views of downtown and the bay.

The four-lane highway at the north end of town is called Carretera a Puerto Vallarta, then Carretera a Tepic after the traffic light and turnoff to the Libramiento, a bypass around the city. Street addresses often refer to this road as Carretera Aeropuerto. If you are staying on the north side and traveling to points south, the Libramiento is a good route to take. The turnoff is near the Sheraton, and the road curves around behind the city, going through a few tunnels in the hills before winding south. There is a turnoff to town once you get through the tunnels. If you're trying to get to the south side of the bridge during early evening or other busy times, this route is actually shorter than driving along Avenida Díaz Ordáz.

There are several agencies in Puerto Vallarta that rent Jeeps, open-air Volkswagen Beetles, and automatic-transmission sedans. During high season, rentals start at $70 per day, including insurance and mileage; off-season, they start at $45 per day. All the car rental agencies below have desks at the airport; some have offices along the highway, so compare prices at the airport or call from your hotel. Agencies to contact include **Avis** (Carretera Aeropuerto Km. 2.5, tel. 322/2–1412), **Budget** (Carretera Aeropuerto Km. 5, tel. 322/2–2980), **Hertz** (Av. Díaz Ordaz 538, tel. 322/2–0024), **National** (Carretera Aeropuerto Km. 1, tel. 322/2–1107), and **Quick** (Caretera Aeropuerto Km. 1.5, tel. 322/2–3505).

Guided Tours

The three-hour city tour is a good way to get the lay of the land, from Gringo Gulch and the Río Cuale to Playa Mismaloya. If you're only staying in PV a short while, this tour will give you a taste of what you'll be missing out on. If you're staying longer, it's a good way to find out what you'd like to explore more thoroughly. Almost everyone goes on at least one daytime or sunset cruise around the bay, sighting pretty, isolated coves and barren beaches from the deck of a sailboat or yacht. An excursion to Yelapa or Playa Las Animas, seaside communities that can be reached only by boat (a 20-minute trip), gives you a feeling of what life is like in a secluded tropical paradise (*see* Off the Beaten Track, in Exploring, below).

Tropical tours visit mango and banana plantations in Nayarit and include stops in Nayarit's capital, Tepic, and the small seaside town of San Blas (*see* Excursion to Tepic and San Blas, below). Other trips head south to Boca de Tomatlán, the mouth of the river that flows from the mountains into the sea. Horseback riding is available on the beach and at ranches in the mountains. On the mountain trip, three hours are spent riding, and time is taken for lunch and a swim in a stream or lake.

A special trip for those with the time and money is a one-day or overnight tour to Guadalajara by plane (a 20-minute flight over Lake Chapala). The tour includes Guadalajara's major sights, a visit to the market, and a side trip to Tlaquepaque, a small, picturesque village where some of Mexico's most talented artists work and display their pieces. The overnight tour is best—one day is simply not enough for Guadalajara.

Tours may be arranged through your hotel or one of the many tour operators, a few of whom are listed below. It's worth the few extra dollars to go with a small group in a Volkswagen van rather than in a large tour bus. Check with a large company or travel agency for information on special-interest tours. Occasionally, PV residents allow tours of their lovely homes to benefit charity.

The following agencies are well established and offer a wide range of tours: **Aventuras Turisticas Agraz** (represented at many of the major hotels and travel agencies, tel. 322/2–2969), **Big-Al Tours** (Hamburgo and Lucerna, tel. 322/2–2818), **Servi Tours** (Hidalgo 217, tel. 322/2–4988), **Servicios Turisticos Miller** (Av. Garzas 100, tel. 322/2–1321), **Viajes Anfitriones Mexicanos** (176 Calle Corona, tel. 322/2–3132), **Viajes Costa Norte** (Melgar 140, tel. 322/2–4754), **Viajes Horizonte** (Fiesta Americana Hotel, tel. 322/2–3888), and **Viajes la Jungla** (Av. Juárez 234, tel. 322/2–5638).

Exploring

Orientation

Central Puerto Vallarta has three major parts: the northern hotel and resort region, the downtown area (also called Old Town), and the Río Cuale and Playa de los Muertos. The immediate north of downtown is not very scenic. The highway could be any main drag, and there is little concern for aesthetics. This is where most of the large hotels are located, in self-contained compounds. There are lots of shopping centers, car rental agencies, supermarkets, and restaurants along the road. It's not the place for a casual stroll, as there is loud traffic and no paved walkway, so a rental car or taxi is necessary to explore this area. Most people who visit this stretch have a specific destination in mind.

You don't want to have a car in downtown and the Río Cuale area. Most of what you want to see can be covered on foot—just be sure you wear comfortable shoes for the cobblestone streets.

Numbers in the margin correspond with points of interest on the Puerto Vallarta map.

The Hotel Zone

1 The big attraction in the north is the **Marina Vallarta** area and **Nuevo Vallarta**. Located just over the Jalisco state line in the state of Nayarit by the mouth of the Río Ameca, this development will eventually be a town unto itself with a marina, hundreds of condominiums, three major hotels, shopping centers, an 18-hole golf course, and the Royal Pacific Yacht Club.

Downtown and the Río Cuale

When you start seeing cobblestone streets, you're downtown, also known as Old Town. This is a vestige of old Puerto Vallarta. **2** The **malecón** (waterside promenade) begins at Avenida Díaz

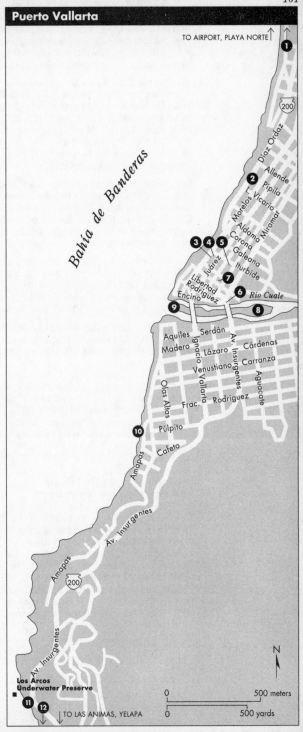

Puerto Vallarta

Ordaz and runs for about a mile. Opposite the malecón are restaurants, cafés, and shops. This is downtown's main drag, a nice place to rest on a white wrought-iron bench. There are some interesting sculptures along the walkway, including the bronze seahorse that has become Puerto Vallarta's trademark.

3 The main zócalo, **Plaza de Armas,** is located just past where Avenida Díaz Ordáz merges with Morelos at the waterfront.
4 The **City Hall** is on the north side of the plaza. This building is home to a colorful mural, painted in 1981 by Puerto Vallarta's most famous artist, Mañuel Lepe (*see* Shopping, below). The mural (above the stairs on the second floor) depicts Puerto Vallarta as a fanciful seaside fishing and farming village. The tourism office is on the first floor.

Dominating the square from a block east is the ornate crown
5 atop **La Iglesia de Nuestra Señora de Guadalupe** (Church of Our Lady of Guadalupe). The crown is a replica of the one worn by Carlota, the empress of Mexico in the late 1860s. There are signs posted at the entrances asking that you not visit the church wearing shorts or sleeveless T-shirts.

6 The **Mercado Municipal** is located at Miramar and Rodriguez, at the foot of the old bridge over the Río Cuale. The market is small enough to tour quickly. There are some good, clean lunch stands on the second floor that serve savory tacos and cool *licuados* (drinks) made with fruit juice and water.

7 The stretch above town along the river is called **Gringo Gulch,** named for the thousands of expatriates from the United States who settled here in the 1950s. Elizabeth Taylor has a home, Casa Kimberly, here.

Time Out Dining and drinking are the malecón's big attractions, from early morning till just before dawn. If you're there in the morning, have French toast and cinnamon-flavored coffee at **Las Palomas;** evening happy hours are boisterous and fun at **Carlos O'Brian's,** where a six-pack of Corona in a silver pail is the favored drink.

Exploring Río Cuale Island and Playa de los Muertos

8 **Río Cuale Island** is in the middle of the Río Cuale, which runs into the bay just past Plaza de Armas. There are steps leading under the two bridges that cross the river, then a long park and walkway that runs from Avenida Insurgentes to the waterfront. The island has an outdoor marketplace with boutiques, souvenir stands, trendy restaurants, and inexpensive cafés. This is a good place to shop for Mexican crafts at lower prices
9 than in downtown. The **Museo Arqueológico** at the western tip of the island has a small collection of pre-Columbian figures and Indian artifacts.

Time Out **Franzi Café** is a nice place for coffee and soft jazz, and **ChiliWilly's** is a good spot for a nosh and a long, cool tropical drink.

10 **Playa de los Muertos,** the beach on the south side of the Río Cuale, has long been the budget traveler's domain, though some of the more expensive restaurants and shops are here. It is the most popular and most crowded beach in Puerto Vallarta. Parasailers lift off while sunbathers recline on the sand. Beach toys for sale include everything from rubber inner tubes to Windsurfers. Vendors stroll the beach, hawking lace table-cloths, wood statues, kites, and grilled fish on a stick. Plaza Lázaro Cárdenas is a pretty spot at the north end of the beach. To the south, Playa de los Muertos ends at a rocky point called El Púlpito (The Pulpit).

Time Out Eating grilled fish on a stick at Playa de los Muertos is like hav-ing a hot dog at Coney Island: It's what you *do*. Buy it from one of the stands at the southern end of the beach, then stroll along and watch the show. For a sit-down break, get a beer and tacos or enchiladas at **El Dorado** on the north end.

Playa Mismaloya and Boca de Tomatlán

⓫ A visit to PV without a side trip to **Playa Mismaloya** (Mis-maloya Beach) is nearly unthinkable, since this is where *Night of the Iguana* was made. The -kilometer (8-mile) drive south on Highway 200 passes by spectacular homes, some of PV's oldest and quietest resorts, and a slew of condo and time-share devel-opments. Mismaloya is a pretty cove backed by rugged, rocky hills. There is a good view from here of Los Arcos, a rock forma-tion in the water. The hacienda where Elizabeth Taylor and Richard Burton stayed during the movie's filming is still stand-ing amid the palms. The beach had deteriorated to a cluster of run-down shacks and a small fishing community, but the shacks were burned down and a new condo tower is going up smack in the center of the cove.

⓬ **Boca de Tomatlán** is a small village at the mouth of the Toma-tlán River. It's a beautiful spot, where you can wade in fresh-water pools. Just before you reach the dirt road to the beach, there are several large palapas (open-air restaurants), includ-ing CheeChees, which is actually a massive restaurant, shop-ping, and swimming-pool complex that is spread over a steep hillside like a small village. Farther along the main road, through Boca, is Chico's Paradise, a large restaurant set amid giant boulders and surrounded by pools and small waterfalls.

Off the Beaten Track

Playa las Ánimas, These secluded fishing villages are accessible only by boat
Yelapa and (about a 20-minute trip). Both villages have small communities
San Sebastian of hardy isolationists; of late, Yelapa has attracted more and more foreigners who settle in for good. At Yelapa, take a half-hour hike from the beach into the jungle to see the waterfalls. Tour groups visit daily. San Sebastian, once a thriving mining town nestled in the Sierra Nevada, is a popular hiking and horseback destination.

Shopping

Shopping is a major activity of most visitors to PV. Prices are fixed in the brand-name sportswear stores, and American dol-lars and credit cards are accepted, but you are expected to bar-gain in the markets and with the beach vendors, who also freely accept American money. Most stores are open 10–1, close for siesta, then open again 4–8. If you take a tour that includes a break for shopping and lunch, be sure to shop first to avoid hitting the shops during the siesta break. The streets and stores are less crowded in the morning, but evening is the prime shopping time.

Art   Over the years, many artists have made Puerto Vallarta their home, at least temporarily, and art galleries are abundant. The late Mañuel Lepe is perhaps the most famous Puerto Vallarta artist. His primitive paintings of village scenes have inspired a host of similar works. One of Lepe's largest works, a mural, is installed on the second floor of the City Hall. His paintings can be seen and purchased at **Galería Lepe** (Lázaro Cárdenas 237).

Sergio Bustamante, the creator of life-size brass, copper, and papier-mâché animals, has expanded his repetoire to include fanciful sculptures of people. He has his own gallery, **Sergio Bustamante** (Av. Juárez 275). Bring your camera, or you'll wish you had.

Other galleries worth a visit include: **Galería Uno** (Morelos 561), **Galería Pacifico** (Av. Juárez 519), **Galería Vallarta** (Juárez 263), and **Galería Estudio Y** (Calle Encino 60).

Clothing   Most of the brand-name sportswear stores are located along the malecón and down its side streets. Many of these stores also have branches in the shopping centers or on Carretera Aeropuerto. Some of the most popular shops are **Aca Joe, Bye-Bye, Esprit, Benetton, Ocean Pacific, Ruben Torres, Polo Ralph Lauren,** and **Ferrioni.**

In shops that sell designer-label clothing such as Esprit, Guess?, and Ralph Lauren, prices are comparable to, if not higher than, those in the States. Dozens of shops that sell comfortable, locally made cotton clothing are scattered about PV.

More elegant, dressier clothes, made of soft, flowing fabrics in tropical prints, can be found at **Sucesos, Originales Yolanda,** and **Boutique Nabu.** There is a fine selection of men's resort wear at **Guillermo's.** The **Barefoot Eagle** and **Irene Pulos** have gorgeous appliquéd clothing.

Folk Art   Few other cities in Mexico have as representative a collection of the country's fine folk arts as Puerto Vallarta. Masks, pottery, lacquerware, clothing, mirrors, glass dishes, windows and lamps, carved wood animals and doors, antiques and modern art, hand-dyed woven rugs, and embroidered clothing are all available in the markets. The following boutiques are also recommended: **Viva** (Madero 272), **Olinala** (Madero 268), **Studio Zoo** (Vallarta and Madero), **Arte Antiguo** (by Hotel Pelícanos), **Galería de Arte Huichol** (Corona 164), and **St. Valentin** (Morelos 574).

Jewelry   There is a good selection of Mexican silver in Puerto Vallarta, but watch out for fake silver made with alloys. Real silver carries the 925 silver stamp required by the government. It is best to visit a reputable jeweler, such as **Taxco,** on the malecón; **Joyería la Azteca,** which has two stores on the malecón and others in the shopping centers; **Platería Plata Forma** (Juárez 207); and **Tane** (Hotel Camino Real).

Markets   The **Mercado Municipal** (Miramar and Libertad), in the busiest part of town, is a typical market. Flowers, piñatas, produce, and plastics are all crowded together in indoor and outdoor stands that cover a full city block. The strip of shops along Río Cuale Island is an outdoor market of a sort, with souvenir stands and exclusive boutiques interspersed with restaurants and cafés. Bargaining at the stalls in the market and on the island is expected.

Shopping Centers The highway on the north side of town is lined with small arcades as well as large shopping centers with innumerable handicrafts and sportswear shops. The **Plaza Malecón,** at the beginning of Avenida Díaz Ordáz, has more than two dozen shops and boutiques. **Plaza Marina,** by the airport, has a large department store and an ever-growing number of specialty shops. An enormous **Gigante,** in a new center across from the Fiesta Americana Hotel, is a K-Mart and supermarket in one. **Villa Vallarta,** by the Plaza las Glorias hotel, has a super-store called **Commercial Mexicana,** a huge handicrafts store, **La Fiesta,** dozens of smaller shops, ice-cream parlors, and a good Italian restaurant.

Sports

Swimming, sailing, windsurfing, and parasailing are popular sports at the beachfront hotels. The hotels have stands on the beach that rent equipment and boats, and you need not be a guest to use these services.

Fishing Sportfishing is good off Puerto Vallarta most of the year, particularly for billfish, roosterfish, dorado, yellowtail, and bonita. The marlin season begins in November. The Fishermen's Association, which has a shack on the north end of the malecón, offers a variety of options for fishing trips; most hotels can arrange your reservations. Large group boats cost about $40 per person for a day's fishing; the smaller cruisers may be chartered for $150 a day and higher, depending on the size of the boat and the length of the trip. Charters include a skipper, license, bait, and tackle; some also include lunch.

Golf **Los Flamingos Country Club** (tel. 322/8–0034) has an 18-hole golf course (called a *buceria*). Reservations should be made a day in advance through your hotel. The country club is about 12 kilometers (8 miles) north of the airport, and transportation is provided with your reservations. A new course is being built near the marina just south of the airport.

Tennis Most of the larger hotels have tennis courts. Nonmembers may also play at the **John Newcombe Tennis Club** (tel. 322/2–4850), **Los Tules** (tel. 322/2–2010), **Los Flamingos Country Club** (tel. 322/8–0034).

Water Sports The snorkeling and diving off the coast of PV aren't very good. Those activities are best at Los Arcos (about 8 kilometers 5 miles south by boat), a natural underwater preserve on the way to Playa Mismaloya. Punta Mita, about 80 kilometers (50 miles) north of Puerto Vallarta, has some good diving spots, as does Quimixto Bay, 32 kilometers (20 miles) south and accessible only by boat. Experienced divers prefer Las Tres Marietas, a group of three islands about 80 kilometers (50 miles) northwest of PV.

Some of the hotels rent snorkeling and diving equipment and offer short courses on diving at their pools. For dive trips and rentals, contact: **Chico's Dive Shop** (Av. Díaz Ordáz 772, tel.

322/2–1895) and **Paradise Divers** (Olas Altas 443, tel. 322/2–4004).

Beaches

Beaches in Mexico are federal property and not owned by the hotels; some hotels try to keep their beaches exclusive by roping off an area around the hotel's lounge chairs.

Playa de los Muertos
The Dead Men's Beach is the site of a long-ago battle between pirates and Indians. The town's boosters keep trying to change the name to Playa del Sol (Beach of the Sun), but have not been successful. The budget travelers hang out here, and vendors selling kites, blankets, and jewelry seem as abundant as the sunbathers. This beach is crowded all the time, but there's always room for one more bronzed body in a bikini. It's a good place for parasailing, since you get a great bird's-eye view of the town. Open-air restaurants line the beach, which ends at the rocky point called El Púlpito.

Playa Norte
Also known as **Playa de Oro,** this is the northernmost beach, stretching from the marina and cruise-ship terminal to downtown. The beach changes a bit with the character of each hotel it fronts; it is particularly pleasant by the Fiesta Americana and the Krystal.

Dining

Puerto Vallarta has so many good restaurants that you could eat every meal in a different place during your stay and still say, "Oh, no, I missed that one!" If you'd like a change of pace from the malecón and Río Cuale, hire a taxi and head out of the city. There are some great little hideaways with terrific views in the hills overlooking town. PV is truly an enchanting sight just before dusk, when the sun glows on the red-tile roofs. Because PV has so many fine restaurants it is impossible to review them all here. Hotel restaurants are listed only if they are exceptional.

Dining prices are comparable to those in the United States, and there are few real bargains. Many fine restaurants are owned by young Americans, and trends in American cooking are reflected in this cuisine.

Dress is casual, even at the most glamorous spots, though shorts are frowned upon at dinner. Reservations are not usually required, and many places don't accept them. It is noted in the description below only if reservations are suggested.

Highly recommended restaurants in each price category are indicated by a star ★.

Category	Cost*
Expensive	over $25
Moderate	$10–$25
Inexpensive	under $10

*per person, excluding drinks, service, and sales tax (15%)

Expensive **Casablanca.** Tiger and leopard skins are stretched on the walls, and papier-mâché animal heads hang from pillars in the middle of the room. This open-air malecón bar gets crowded and noisy in the evening; the glassed-in restaurant upstairs is more sedate for dining on steaks, seafood, and Mexican specialties. *Av. Díaz Ordáz 570, tel. 322/2–1723. Reservations advised. AE, MC, V.*

★ **Chez Elena.** Wind around behind the cathedral and you'll eventually come to the Cuatro Vientos Hotel, home to this restaurant, which has a good view of downtown and the bay. Nowhere else will you find an Indonesian brochette with peanut sauce, authentic dark-chocolate chicken mole and the original café mulato, a blend of coffee, liqueurs, and ice cream. All elements combine for an enjoyable evening, from sunset on into the night. *Av. Matamoros 520, tel. 322/2–0161. AE, DC, MC, V. Dinner only.*

El Set. Located just south of town at Las Conchas Chinas Hotel, El Set is perched above the cliffs with a view of spectacular private homes and condos. Rustic wood steps and railings lead to three dining areas, each on a different level. The grilled lobster is filling, but save room for the sweet caramel crepes. Get here in time for sunset, and stay for the splendid show of city lights. *Highway 200 Km. 2.5, tel. 322/2–0302. Reservations advised. AE, MC, V. Dinner only.*

Kamakura. Authentic Japanese meals are featured in this pleas-ant restaurant on the Krystal Vallarta Hotel's lavish grounds. *Krystal Vallarta Hotel, tel. 322/2–1459. AE, DC, MC, V. Dinner only.*

La Jolla de Mismaloya. This pretty condo complex overlooking Playa Mismaloya is a wonderful spot for sunset watching. The beach looks like a movie set from here (though the high rise going up on the beach is an eyesore), and *Night of the Iguana* is screened nightly. The cheeseburger served at lunch is great, and the seafood platter makes a filling and pleasurable dinner. *Playa Mismaloya on Hwy. 200, tel. 322/2–1374. AE, DC, MC, V.*

★ **Le Bistro.** By far the classiest restaurant along Río Cuale, Le Bistro is owned by two Californians, and it looks it. It has a gleaming black and white tile bar, gray and white striped tablecloths, and handsome waiters. The food is excellent. Try the brochette Brubeck (grilled giant shrimp and generous hunks of tenderloin) or classic steak Diane. The shrimp Gabardin is dipped in ale and a Teotihuacán batter, then deep-fried and served with a *cordon bleu* sauce. The pecan pie is a must, as is the Russian Quaalude, made with coffee, Frangelico, vodka, and cream. *Río Cuale Island, tel. 322/2–0283. Reservations advised. AE, MC, V. Dinner only. Closed Mon. evening and Sun.*

Panorama. This is a hard place to find (take a taxi) but it's worth the search. High atop the Hotel Siesta, Panorama lives up to its name with a 180-degree view of downtown and the harbor. There is a rooftop patio and a top-floor dining room with lace cloths on the tables. The shrimp soaked in tequila are unusual; better yet, have the shrimp Panorama with onions and green peppers. Adventuresome types might want to visit the nightclub downstairs to watch the transvestite show. *Hotel Siesta, Dominguez and Miramar, tel. 322/2–1818. Reservations advised. MC, V. Dinner only.*

Señor Chico's. On the Alta Vista hill overlooking all of Puerto Vallarta, Señor Chico's is a magnificent spot from sunset on— claim a table at the edge of the patio and settle in. The Caesar salad is good, as is any seafood choice, but it's the view that really makes the place. *Púlpito 377, tel. 322/2–3570. MC, V. Dinner only.*

Moderate   **Brazz.** A big, airy place decorated with brightly colored piñatas, Brazz, a branch of the Guadalajara chain, is known for its generous steaks and chops and good Mexican dishes. Mariachi music plays continuously. *Morelos at Galleana, tel. 322/2–0324. AE, DC, MC, V.*

Carlos O'Brian's. A long line forms outside this noisy, popular restaurant/bar where clutter and chaos reign. The restaurant—part of the Carlos Anderson chain—specializes in barbecued ribs, chicken, tacos, and tequila. The food is good and plentiful, but not worth the wait. *Av. Díaz Ordáz 786, tel. 322/2–1444. AE, MC, V.*

CheeChees. If ever a place was designed for the tourist biz, CheeChees—on the edge of Boca de Tomatlán, where the river meets the sea—is it. It helps to be in good shape—several flights of stairs lead down a cliff to a large restaurant and outdoor buffet, as well as a big pool and sunbathing area. Tour buses and boats stop here regularly, and there are short boat trips to the small settlement by the mouth of the river. *About 16 km (10 mi) south of Boca de Tomatlán on Hwy. 200, tel. 322/2–0920. MC, V. Lunch only.*

★ **Chico's Paradise.** This *is* a paradise: A river rushing down the mountain over massive boulders; guests sunbathe on a rock by the waterfall or sip mighty margaritas under a palapa perched above the river. If you're hungry, have the drunken shrimp—it's marinated with wine and mushrooms, then grilled with onions, peppers, and bacon. The chips, salsa, and homemade tortillas are great. *About 8 km (5 mi) south of Boca de Tomatlán on Hwy. 200, tel. 322/2–0747. AE, DC, MC, V.*

ChiliWilly's. Once the prime spot under the bridge along the Río Cuale, Chili's has lost some of its charm, but it's one of the cheapest places on the river for an afternoon drink in the shade, while listening to old Beatles tunes. *Río Cuale Island, no phone. MC, V.*

★ **El Dorado.** A must for at least one lunch, this Playa de los Muertos palapa is a popular hangout for American expatriates. The eclectic menu includes spaghetti, burgers, and crepes, but stick with specialties like Dorado-style fish, broiled with a thick layer of melted cheese. The waiters, who've been around a long time (the restaurant's been open since 1960), seem to know all the customers by name. *Amapas and Púlpito, tel. 322/2–1511. AE, DC, MC, V.*

Franzi Café. Close to the mouth of the Río Cuale, near the beach, Franzi is set amid huge trees, so watch out for the birds. Breakfast is good, and it's a great spot for coffee and dessert—cheesecake, perhaps. The Sunday brunch is fun, and there's a library with comfortable couches. It's a good place to wait while your companions shop. During the day, the talented pianist will play any request, from a lullaby to a polka. There's live jazz at night. *Río Cuale Island, no phone. MC, V.*

★ **Las Palomas.** Breakfast at this malecón café is a daily ritual for many, and a place for the reunion of PV regulars upon their return to town. Have *jugo de lima* (a drink similar to lemonade but made with the region's tart limes). The dark coffee, spiced with cinnamon, is a tasty eye-opener. Homesick? Have hot oatmeal with cinnamon and sugar; otherwise, stick with the *huevos con chorizo* (eggs with spicy sausage). For dinner, try the sweet and sour pork. Insist on (and wait for) a window table. *Av. Díaz Ordáz at Aldama, tel. 322/2–3675. AE, MC, V. ID required for traveler's checks.*

★ **Le Gourmet.** The small Posada Río Cuale Hotel has one of the best restaurants in town, offering a great Caesar salad, shrimp *à l'orange*, and a large selection of flambéed entrées and desserts. The pepper steak, sautéed at your table, is a good choice, and the piano music is a pleasant change from mariachis. This is a friendly spot for good open-air dining on the Playa de los Muertos side of the river. *Serdan 284, tel. 322/2–0914. AE, MC, V. Dinner only.*

Moby Dick. Some say this is the best seafood house in town, and from the size of the crowds packing the dining area this must be true. This is one of the less-expensive places for lobster and shrimp. *31 de Octubre 128, tel. 322/2–0655. MC. V.*

Prego. The aroma of flaky pizza crust coming from this Italian café set in the middle of the Villa Vallarta shopping center stimulates the taste buds. The outdoor tables are set around a bright green gazebo; indoors, posters of Italy and red and white floor tiles give a Continental feeling. The espresso is exceptionally good, and the pizzas are highly unusual—when's the last time you had pizza topped with bacon and eggs? This is a good place to stop for a bite after some strenuous shopping in the nearby boutiques. *Plaza Villa Vallarta, Carretera Aeropuerto, tel. 322/2–6744. AE, MC, V.*

Inexpensive **Andale.** This Playa de los Muertos hangout is a good spot for an
★ afternoon beer with the locals. The downstairs bar gets rowdy, in a friendly way; the upstairs restaurant is a peaceful change, with its candle lanterns and glass tables. Good fettuccine with scallops, great garlic bread, and an unusual chicken *mestizo* with white wine, pineapple juice, and jalapeño peppers are suggested. *Paseo de Velasco 425, tel. 322/2–1054. AE, MC, V.*

Bonita Chicken. Here you can get one of the cheapest meals around. For less than $5 you get two pieces of chicken, salad, and potatoes—a great, filling meal. *Carranza and Vallarta, tel. 322/2–6757. No credit cards.*

California. For those who prefer U.S.-type decor, California is the place, with its vinyl booths, mock stained-glass windows, and Formica tables. The American-style breakfast, including hash browns and toast, is inexpensive and good, as are the tacos and enchiladas. *Villa Vallarta, tel. (322/2–6757). MC, V.*

El Ostion Feliz. Vines trail from the trellises and balconies on this red-tile house, flowers bloom at the doorway, and the smell of grilled fish sparks the appetite. Like its sister restaurant in Guadalajara, El Ostion Feliz serves a terrific bouillabaisse and a heaping seafood platter. *Libertad 177, tel. 322/2–2508. MC, V.*

Fresh Company. This is a good taco and burger spot in the Villa Vallarta shopping area; it only has a few small tables but serves great *chilaquiles* (tortillas cooked in a tomato sauce and served with cream and grated cheese). *Villa Vallarta, tel. 322/2–6697. No credit cards.*

★ **La Fuente del Puente.** Located just across from the market, above the riverbank, this outdoor café is popular with budget travelers and American residents. The bright pink and blue neon along the ceiling is an unusual touch for PV. The prices are low, the food good, and the crowd amiable. *Av. Miramar at the old bridge, tel. 322/2–1141. MC, V. Closed Sun.*

Miramar. Located in the small fishing village 20 kilometers (12 miles) north of Vallarta, La Cruz de Huanacaxtle is the kind of place where entire families settle in for hours for beer, sangría, and platters of fresh fish. *La Cruz de Huanacaxtle, no phone. No credit cards.*

Tucán. As charming and popular as the hotel where it is located, and a great spot for a filling and economically priced meal. *Posada de Roger, Basilio Badillo 237, tel. 322/2-0836. MC, V.*

Tutifruti. Sample great fresh-squeezed juices at this small stand in the downtown shopping area. Choose from mango, papaya, melon, and pineapple. Filling *tortas* (sandwiches) cost less than $2. *Morelos at Corona, tel. 322/2-1068. No credit cards. Closed Sun.*

Lodging

Most of PV's deluxe resorts are located to the north; south of downtown and the Río Cuale, in the Playa de los Muertos and Olas Altas areas, the rates are lower, but the streets are even more crowded than in downtown. Some of the nicest older hotels are a few kilometers south of town, set among palatial private homes on cliffs overlooking the bay. In the winter, budget rooms run $30 to $50, and the large resorts start at $150 per night. Rates go down from April to November by 25%–30%. Reservations are a must at Christmas, New Year's, and Easter.

Highly recommended lodgings in each price category are indicated by a star ★.

Category	Cost*
Very Expensive	over $135
Expensive	$70–$135
Moderate	$50–$70
Inexpensive	under $50

All prices are for a standard double room, excluding 15% tax.

Very Expensive **Camino Real.** One of PV's first luxury resorts and still revered by locals and guests, Camino Real is undergoing major renovation to update its image. Its orange and brown rooms are standard fare, but the long, clean, secluded beach is one of the nicest around, and the location takes you away from the bustle of the Zona Dorada. Small palapas offer shade on the beach, and fragrant white flowers grow along the banks of the river that flows through the property. The services and facilities are predictable; if you just want a comfortable room, a good beach, and a dependable restaurant, this is the place. *Carretera a Barra de Navidad, tel. 322/3-0123; reservations in the U.S.: 800/228-3000. 330 rooms (80 in a new tower). Facilities: beach, 2 pools, 2 tennis courts, playground, restaurant, bar, disco, shops. AE, DC, MC, V.*

★ **Fiesta Americana.** A seven-story palapa covers the lobby and a large round bar, giving some idea of the lavishness to come. The dramatically designed terra-cotta building rises above a deep-blue pool that flows under bridges, palm oases, and palapa restaurants set on platforms over the water. The rooms, recently remodeled, have a blue, pink, and lavender color scheme. Each has a balcony, white marble floors, and tile bath with a powerful shower. The beach bustles with activity—parasailing, windsurfing, boat tours, snorkeling, and, of course, sunbathing. The food is excellent, especially the breakfast buffet by the pool. Of all the full-service resorts, this hotel has the most tropical and luxurious feel. *Carretera Aeropuerto, tel. 322/2–2010 or 800/FIESTA–1. 282 rooms. Facilities: beach, pool, tennis court, 4 restaurants, 3 bars, disco, Mexican fiestas with fireworks, shops, beauty salon, travel agency. AE, DC, MC, V.*

Garza Blanca. Condos have been built next to this long-favored hideaway, but it's still a lovely, exclusive resort. Many of the bright, white hillside villas and chalets have private pools. The beachfront suites (round cottages) are more comfortable than glamorous, though they run $220 per night (villas with pools start at $275). The restaurant is popular for breakfast and lunch and overlooks the cloverleaf-shape pool and a clean, quiet beach. *Carretera a Barra de Navidad, tel. 322/2–1023. 95 rooms (16 on the beach). Facilities: pool, beach, tennis court, restaurant, bar. AE, MC, V.*

★ **Hyatt Coral.** This stunning new hotel south of town is one of the prettiest on the coast. The pale pink palace is surrounded by lush landscaping; rushing waterfalls and a crashing surf mask the noise from the nearby highway. The lobby is filled with lavish floral arrangements and high-quality folk art and paintings. The rooms, all suites, have pale pink spreads and drapes, glass-top tables and wall-length sliding glass doors, white lounge chairs on the terrace, and white tile floors. The master suites have private whirlpools. This is as picturesque a hotel as you'll find in PV, with loving attention to details such as the beveled glass in the restaurant doors and the many shades of blue tile in the pool. *Carretera a Barra de Navidad, tel. 322/2–5191; reservations in the U.S.: 800/233–1234. 120 suites. Facilities: beach, pool, water sports, tennis court, health club, 2 restaurants, 2 bars, shops, beauty salon. AE, DC, MC, V.*

Sheraton Buganvilias. The largest hotel near town, the Sheraton can seem miles long, and visitors sometimes walk 11 miles, as does the bougainvillea, which is everywhere. The large, blue tile lobby faces the beach and pool; on the lower level, long hallways filled with shops connect the towers. Framed textiles and niches with statues break up the boredom in the upper-level hallways. The rooms are nice enough, with bright blue carpeting; big, firm beds; and plenty of closet space. If you are traveling alone, you might find this hotel a bit overwhelming. *Carretera Aeropuerto 999, tel. 322/3–0404. Reservations number in U.S.: 800/325–3535. 501 rooms, 169 suites. Facilities: beach, pool, water sports, 5 tennis courts, 3 restaurants, tour desk, shops, beauty salon, travel agency. AE, DC, MC, V.*

Villas Quinta Real. Reminiscent of a Palm Springs estate, this pale pink mansion with white columns is simply but elegantly decorated throughout. Fresh flowers and plants, antiques, and original works of art grace the rooms and corridors of this spaciously designed property. Built in 1990, the Villas Quinta Real includes 50 suites and 25 villas, which command views of the sea, or the golf course at the new Marina Vallarta complex. Though not directly on the beach, this hotel's amenities are many, and a private health club is in the works. *Marina Vallarta, Pelícanos 311, 48300, tel. 322/1–0800 or 800/345–3457. 50 suites and 25 1–3-bedroom villas. Facilities: golf* *course, outdoor pool, cable TV, 24-hour room service. AE, MC, V.*

Expensive   **Holiday Inn.** The accommodations are standard here, but the hotel has been newly renovated. Some rooms are decorated in tan and orange and have splashy floral drapes; others are in cool pastels. The twin towers attract an amiable crowd of families and singles who play on the beach and by the pool to the constant music of mariachis and marimbas. The restaurants are good, the disco action goes on into the early morning, and the emphasis is on fun. *Carretera Aeropuerto, tel. 322/2–1700 or 800/HOLIDAY. 229 rooms and 236 suites. Facilities: pool, beach, tennis courts, 3 restaurants, shops, disco. AE, DC, MC, V.*

Krystal Vallarta. A full-service resort compound the size of a small town, the Krystal has 48 villas, each with a private pool, plus two larger pools for the guests in the 500 rooms. You can easily get lost here—it seems more like a suburban housing development than a hotel. There are eight restaurants, including Tango, which serves Argentine *churrasco* (barbecue), and Kamakura, which features Japanese food. Not all rooms are by the ocean, but the secluded beach can accommodate all sunseekers. The disco is one of the most popular around, and the Mexican fiesta is one of the best. *Carretera Aeropuerto, tel. 322/2–1459; reservations in the U.S.: 800/231–9860. 500 rooms. 48 villas with pools. Facilities: beach, pools, tennis courts, 7 restaurants, bars, shops, disco, travel agency. AE, DC, MC, V.*

La Jolla Mismaloya. Prettier than most condos, this large complex on a cliff looking out toward Playa Mismaloya is a good place to stay put and enjoy the setting. The suites have cool marble floors, bamboo furniture, kitchen and dining areas, and large bedrooms and baths all decorated in browns and pale pastels. *Playa Mismaloya, Carretera a Barra de Navidad, tel. 322/2–1374 or 800/322–2344. 450 1- and 2-bedroom suites. Facilities: beach, pool, whirlpool, tennis courts, restaurant, bar, disco, shops. AE, DC, MC, V.*

Plaza Vallarta. A heavenly resort for tennis buffs and athletic types, this Mediterranean-style complex houses the John Newcombe Tennis Club, which has 8 courts and offers daily tennis clinics. The resort is a village unto itself, with a shopping plaza, several restaurants and bars, a large swimming pool, and a pleasant beach. *Carretera Aeropuerto, tel. 322/2–2224; reservations in the U.S.: 800/FIESTA–1. 438 rooms with bath. Facilities: 8 tennis courts, beach, pool, restaurants, bars, shopping center. AE, DC, MC, V.*

Moderate   **Buenaventura.** This hotel is ideally situated on the edge of
★ downtown within walking distance (10 blocks or so) of the Río Cuale; in the opposite direction, it's five blocks to the shops, hotels, and restaurants on the airport highway. From the street it looks rather austere, but just inside the door is an enormous five-story open lobby and bar. The bright, cheerful rooms in yellows and whites have beamed ceilings and pale wood furnishings. The hotel's location is so convenient that taxis and rental cars are unnecessary. However, the beaches are better farther north. *Av. Mexico 1301, tel. 322/2–3737; reservations in the U.S.: 800/223–6764. 206 rooms and 4 suites. Facilities: beach, pool, restaurant, bar. AE, DC, MC, V.*

★ **Casa del Puente.** Molly Stokes, a longtime resident of Puerto Vallarta, runs a bed-and-breakfast without the breakfast, but with use of the full kitchen, on the edge of the Río Cuale, with apartments for rent by the night or however long you want. Like old city apartments, these have huge rooms, windows overlooking the river, comfortable kitchens, and lots of antiques. There are two-bedroom, one-bedroom, and studios with maid service. The location—Stokes calls it "Number One Gringo Gulch"—can't be beat. Reservations are advised as the casa is often filled. *Rodriguez and Libertad, tel. 322/2–0749. No credit cards. No small children.*

Club del Sol. The water slide curving through the trees around the satellite TV dish in the courtyard of this hotel tells you this is a good place to stay if you enjoy the sound of children playing. It's a family place—there's a bar for the grown-ups next to the slide, and all the rooms have kitchenettes. The drapes and furnishings are pretty worn, the vines on the building are overgrown, and there's no elevator (don't stay on the fifth floor), but the hotel has character and a friendly staff. The beach is a block away. *Carretera Aeropuerto Km 2, tel. 322/2–2188. 106 rooms, some with kitchenettes. Facilities: pool, children's pool, snack bar. AE, MC, V.*

★ **Conchas Chinas.** This hotel is a short distance south of town, but it's one of the most comfortable places to stay, and there is frequent bus service just out the door. The three-story building is on the beach, and all 31 rooms and 8 suites face the water. The rooms have dark beams, orange bedspreads, heavy wood furniture, and small kitchenettes. Some rooms have whirlpool bathtubs. Near the small restaurant on the rocky beach, sea creatures hide under rocks in the tide pools. **El Set,** one of PV's best restaurants, is next door. *Carretera Barra de Navidad Km 2.5, tel. 322/2–0156; reservations in the U.S.: 800/424–4441. 31 rooms and 8 suites with kitchenette and bath. Facilities: beach, pool, 2 restaurants. MC, V.*

★ **Las Palmas.** The palapa entrance at this hotel is worth seeing—four bamboo bridges are suspended from the ceiling and parrots screech under the palms. The rooms, all with an ocean view, have balconies and green and yellow floral bedspreads and drapes. The accommodations are first-rate for this price category. The setting is dark and woodsy, and far enough from the road to be peacefully isolated. *Carretera Aeropuerto Km 2.5, tel. 322/2–0650; reservations in the U.S.: 800/421–0767. 153 rooms. Facilities: pool, water sports, restaurant, bar. AE, DC, MC, V.*

Mar Elena. These suites on the north side of town a block from the beach are a good bargain if you want a kitchen–living room setup. The building is rather plain, but the kitchens and baths are beautifully tiled, and the bedrooms have woven rugs on the floors and flowers stenciled on the walls. The pool is on the roof, and there's a good view of downtown. *Carretera Aeropuerto Km 2, tel. 322/2–4425. 30 suites with bath. Facilities: pool, restaurant. MC, V.*

★ **Molino de Agua.** A real find on the Río Cuale, the hotel's bungalows are spread out along the riverbank amid lush trees and flowers, and the small hotel-room building faces the beach. Stone paths wind under willows, past caged parrots and monkeys, leading to cottages that have wood shuttered windows, yellow tile baths, and red brick walls. A bubbling whirlpool sits half hidden under a willow by the pool, where guests rest and read on bamboo lounge chairs. The only drawback: There's an abundance of mosquitos, so wear strong bug repellent in the evening. *Vallarta 130, tel. 322/2–1907. 62 rooms. Facilities: beach, 2 pools, whirlpool, restaurant. MC, V.*

Oro Verde. This five-story, motel-like hotel above El Dorado restaurant on Playa de los Muertos is a good spot for those who want to play on the most popular beach in town and be close to the action. Flowers and birds are stenciled on the bright white halls, the baths are tiled in blue and white, and though it's nice to look out at the beach, the rooms facing the hillside are quieter. *Gomez 111, tel. 322/2–3050 and 800/458–6888. 160 rooms with bath. Facilities: beach, pool, restaurant, bar. MC, V.*

Pelícanos. One of the less expensive hotels along the northern strip, Pelícanos is not right on the beach, but it's much quieter than hotels that are. The three-story building has dark hallways but the rooms are bright and airy, done in blue and white. *Carretera Aeropuerto Km 2.5, tel. 322/2–2107. 186 rooms. Facilities: pool, beach access, restaurant, coffee shop, tour desk. AE, MC, V.*

Inexpensive **Fontana del Mar.** Across the street from Los Arcos and about two blocks from the beach, the Fontana is a pretty blue and white hotel with a small courtyard and fountain in the colonial style. The pool is on the roof, and guests have use of the oceanside pool and beach at Los Arcos. The air-conditioned rooms are simple and spacious. This is a good choice if you want to save some money by not staying right on the beach. *Dieguez and Olas Altas, tel. 322/2–0712. 42 rooms, some with kitchenettes. Facilities: beach access, pool, restaurant, bar. AE, DC, MC, V.*

Los Arcos. By far the most popular hotel on the beach by the Río Cuale, Los Arcos has a pretty central courtyard and pool and lots of activity on the beach. Guests rave about the helpful staff, and though the hotel is always busy, it maintains a friendly air. A glass elevator goes from poolside to the rooms, which have bright orange furnishings and small balconies. *Olas Altas 380, tel. 322/2–0583. 140 rooms with bath. Facilities: beach, pool, restaurant, bar. AE, DC, MC, V.*

★ **Los Cuatro Vientos.** The most charming small hotel in PV, Cuatro Vientos (Four Winds) is located on a steep hill behind town, tucked among the red tile–roofed cottages. Its 16 rooms are often booked a year in advance by guests who return again and again. The simple rooms have arched brick ceilings, colorful flowers stenciled on the walls, and folk art knick-knacks and tin mirrors. The *llamado de amorado* (flame of love) vines twining along the balconies produce fragrant orange blossoms in spring. The restaurant, **Chez Elena,** is among PV's best, and a pleasant rooftop bar is open in high season. The price includes an ample continental breakfast. *Matamoros 520, tel. 322/2–0161. 16 rooms. Facilities: restaurant, bar. AE, MC, V.*

★ **Posada Río Cuale.** This small, friendly inn on the south side of the Río Cuale has one of the best gourmet restaurants in town (aptly named **El Gourmet**) and a nice sense of serenity. There's classical music at the pool, where guests read and sleep peacefully, just blocks away from the frenetic action at the beach. The beds are big and cozy, fresh flowers bloom on the nightstands, and with only 25 rooms, it rarely gets noisy. *Serdan 242, tel. 322/2–0450. 25 rooms. Facilities: pool, restaurant, bar. AE, MC, V.*

Nightlife

Puerto Vallarta is a party town, where the discos open at 10 PM and stay open until 3 or 4 AM. A minimum $5 cover charge is common in the popular discos, many of which are at the hotels. The Krystal has **Christine; Friday Lopez** is at the Fiesta Americana; and **Yesterday's** (Pulpito 127) has live and disco music for dancing under the stars. **El Panorama,** at the Hotel La Siesta, is a real nightclub, with a floor show and live music for dancing. Jazz can be heard at **Le Bistro** and **Franzi Café** on Río Cuale Island.

Mexican fiestas are popular at the hotels and can be lavish affairs with plentiful buffet dinners, folk dances, and fireworks. Most hotels have a fiesta just one night a week, but not on the same days, so there is one going on somewhere nearly every night. Fiestas usually cost about $25 per person. Reservations may be made with the hotels or through travel agencies. Some of the more spectacular shows are at the La Iguana Tourist Center, Fiesta Americana, the Krystal, the Camino Real, Las Palmas, and the Sheraton.

Excursion to Tepic and San Blas

Tepic, located about 40 kilometers (25 miles) inland from the coast, is the capital of the state of Nayarit. It is a scenic three-hour bus trip north from Puerto Vallarta along the coast on Highway 200, a distance of about 167 kilometers (104 miles).

The town was founded in 1532 by the Spanish conqueror Nuño de Guzman, who named it Villa del Espíritu Santo de la Mayor España. Later, the name became Santiago de Galicia de Compostela, which somehow was shortened to Tepic.

Tepic is best known for its sugar refineries, which cast a distinctive aroma of burning sugar into the air. Though it is the capital and has a population of more than 200,000, there is little to attract tourists, but it is a necessary transfer point to and from the coast for those traveling by train.

The most noted site in town is **La Iglesia de Santa Cruz,** built centuries ago when someone noticed that the grass on the site was growing in the shape of a cross. Fray Junípero Serra spent a year here, and there is a monument to him in the church. The church's two Gothic spires have been restored and tower over the flowers and trees in the Plaza Principal.

The **Museo Regional de Nayarit** is in the former palace of the Counts of Miravalle and has a collection of Mesoamerican pottery and jewelry. On weekends, the Huichol and Cora Indians come down from their villages in the mountains around Tepic to sell their crafts, including bead necklaces, God's Eyes woven of colored wool, and scarves. *Av. México 91. Closed Mon.*

San Blas would be a tropical paradise if not for the infernal gnats that swarm around the beach and riverbeds and nip at your skin—bug repellent is an absolute necessity. The drive west to San Blas from Tepic via Highway 15 is spectacular. Within 37 kilometers (23 miles), you drop 1,000 feet through the jungle to sea level. At the entrance to town, the bridge over the Estero San Cristóbal marks the mouth of the **Río La Tovara.** Small tour boats leave from here for a trip up the river, through the jungle. Huge turtles sun on the riverbank under the mangrove trees, and bright yellow birds fly out from the thick foliage. After about a half-hour ride, you reach a large freshwater pool fed by mountain springs, where you can swim in the clear cool water. Jaguars are said to drink from this pool at night. The town of San Blas is a pleasant little village where the locals congregate at the small central plaza. Two churches in comparable states of disrepair fill one side of the plaza. **El Templo de San Blas,** practically a ruin, has a life-size statue of Jesus wearing the crown of thorns, his face dripping with blood. **La Apostólica Romana de San Blas,** the cathedral, has been under construction for more than 30 years, and its roof is not yet complete. The small market sells chicken-defeathering machines.

The beaches are about five blocks from the plaza, past the military base. The sand flies along these beaches form thick, anklehigh clouds in the evening, so don't bother with sunset strolls along the sand. During the day, though, the beaches are great—nearly empty and with good surf. Shacks on the sand sell fresh grilled fish.

The ruins of an old Spanish fort sit at **Cerro de San Basilio,** a high hill overlooking town. **Las Ruinas la Contaduría,** as the site is known, marks the place where 70 Spanish families founded San Blas in 1768. **La Iglesia de Nuestra Senora del Rosario,** a colonial church with an overgrown cemetery, sits on the side of the hill. Henry Wadsworth Longfellow wrote the poem "The Bells of San Blas" about this church.

Dining

Neither Tepic nor San Blas can boast of culinary hot spots. In fact, the best places to eat in San Blas are the *palapas* (open-air eateries) that serve grilled fresh fish with homemade tortillas and rice. Dress is casual, and none of the restaurants listed here accept reservations.

Highly recommended restaurants are indicated by a star ★.

Category	Cost*
Expensive	over $10
Moderate	$8–$10
Inexpensive	under $8

per person, excluding drinks, service, and sales tax (15%)

San Blas
★ **El Delfin.** This classy hotel dining room is the best place in town for seafood, Mexican specialties, and a variety of international dishes. *Hotel Las Brisas, Cuauhtémoc 106, tel. 321/5–0112. MC, V. Dinner only. Expensive.*
La Familia. A lovely place owned by a former mayor of San Blas, whose paintings of tropical scenes hang on the walls. La Familia is known for its great seafood cocktails and shrimp. *Batellon 18, tel. 321/5–0298. No credit cards. Dinner only. Moderate.*

Tepic **Roberto's.** A family-run restaurant known for its well-prepared international dishes and exceptionally good service. *Paseo de la Loma and Insurgentes, tel. 321/3–3005. AE, MC, V. Expensive.*

★ **Mariscos del Farallón.** An informal spot with the best seafood in town, but better for fish than lobster or shrimp. *Insurgentes 276, tel. 321/3–1124. MC, V. Closed Mon. Moderate.*

Lodging

Rooms in Tepic are generally inexpensive. In San Blas they run a little higher, but the rates are nothing compared to the resort areas.

Highly recommended lodgings are indicated by a star ★.

Category	Cost*
Expensive	over $45
Moderate	$25–$45
Inexpensive	under $25

*All prices are for a standard double room, excluding 15% tax.

San Blas **Las Brisas.** The nicest hotel in town is near the beach and has fan-cooled rooms in a three-story building draped with bougainvillea. *Cuauhtémoc 106, tel. 321/5–0112. 42 rooms. Facilities: pool, restaurant, parking. MC, V. Expensive.*

Los Flamingos. A pretty, colonial hotel in an old hacienda, this establishment has a junglelike garden and a tile patio. *Poniente 105, no phone. 25 rooms. Facilities: restaurant, parking. MC, V. Moderate.*

El Bucanero. This is a crumbling mansion with a stuffed crocodile in the lobby and a somewhat overgrown courtyard; all rooms have ceiling fans. *Poniente 75, tel. 321/5–0101. 33 rooms. Facilities: pool, restaurant, bar. MC, V. Inexpensive.*

Posada del Rey. A motel by the sea, Posada del Rey has only 14 *321/5–0123. 14 rooms. Facilities: pool. MC, V. Inexpensive.*

Tepic **Fray Junípero Serra.** This hotel is centrally located on the main square and features colonial-style, air-conditioned rooms. *Lerdo 23, tel. 321/2–2525. 85 rooms. Facilities: restaurant, bar, disco. MC, V. Moderate.*

Altamirano. A small, comfortable place, Altamirano is just off the main plaza. *Minas 19 Pte., tel. 321/2–7131. 30 rooms. Facilities: cafeteria, parking. No credit cards. Inexpensive.*

★ **Corita.** Located on the main road east, this hotel has pretty gardens and small clean rooms. *Insurgentes 310, tel. 321/2–0477. 35 rooms. Facilities: restaurant, bar, parking. MC, V. Inexpensive.*

13 Manzanillo

Introduction

Tourism is booming in Manzanillo, although the city maintains its reputation as a sleeper. Yes, there is construction here, but not on every corner. And, yes, there are fine hotels and restaurants, including Las Hadas, the most opulent resort on the coast. But Manzanillo's best attraction is its natural beauty. Its twin *bahías* (bays), Manzanillo and Santiago, with their crystal blue water and beaches backed by mountains, have drawn outsiders since Hernán Cortés conquered Mexico.

Manzanillo (part of the state of Colima), a city of 90,000 people, is bunched between the mountains and the sea. Railroad tracks crisscross the town, running right down to the docks, as the city is Mexico's main Pacific port and railhead. The downtown area is cluttered and jumbly. Except for the lively *zócalo* (plaza), there is little of interest to see, though the harbor has a certain fascination. Freighters are usually tied up at the docks along with a few small ships of the Mexican navy. Fishing boats may be chartered here and yachts depart on bay cruises.

Fishing is one of Manzanillo's big draws—the city is the unofficial sailfishing capital of the world. But the Sea of Cortés is also full of marlin, yellowtail, shark, red snapper, dorado, and other tropical varieties.

Manzanillo is located more than halfway south on Mexico's Pacific Coast between the United States and Guatemala. Guadalajara is 350 kilometers (217 miles) and a five-hour drive to the northeast; Puerto Vallarta is 280 kilometers (173 miles) and four hours by car to the northwest; and Acapulco is 660 kilometers (409 miles) and about a nine-hour trip to the southeast.

Manzanillo lies in the Tropic of Cancer and has a temperate climate. The ocean breezes keep temperatures moderate, though this can be deceiving for sunbathers, who may think that as long as they are cool they are not getting burned. Be forewarned—the sun's rays are more direct than in the northern latitudes, and you can easily get too much of a good thing. The rainy season runs from June to October, starting with light afternoon showers in early summer. By September, the showers have become downpours, and the air is muggy and humid.

The countryside to the north of Manzanillo is rugged and lush. Rivers rush down from the mountains and mangos grow under the pines. Highway 200 runs past small towns and banana and coconut plantations that stretch like Kansas cornfields. Dirt roads branch off to luxury resorts. Rocky cliffs jut out from the shore, forming isolated, picturesque bays. When it rains, rivers and lagoons swell and waterfalls and ponds form. Herons and pink flamingos flock to the fertile waters, and white butterflies mask the flowers in the chamomile fields. (Manzanillo is Spanish for chamomile.)

On the south side of the Santiago Peninsula, which divides Santiago and Manzanillo bays, is the resort Las Hadas (The Fairies) which, when viewed from the water or a high point, seems like a mirage with its white domes that radiate in the midday heat. Bolivian tin magnate Anteñor Patiño conceived of Las Hadas in the 1960s, when Manzanillo, known as a port, was easier to reach by sea than land. It was a primitive place, a spot for the hardy who didn't mind creating their own tropical paradise. In 1974, when Señor Patiño's palace was completed, the international social set began to visit Manzanillo and the city received worldwide media attention. Even so, Manzanillo remained essentially a port city with only a few tourist attractions.

In the last decade, other resorts have been built in Manzanillo, and the city has become popular as a resort where vacationers can simply relax. Siesta hours are common in shops and at some hotel desks. On Sunday most businesses and restaurants are shut, and everyone heads for the beach.

Essential Information

Important Addresses and Numbers

Street addresses are not often used in Manzanillo; instead, locations are designated by neighborhood—the Las Brisas area, Santiago Peninsula (also known as the Las Hadas Road), and so on. Maps with actual street names are rare (or inaccurate).

Tourist Information It is difficult to get reliable information on Manzanillo in the city. The **State Tourism Office** (Juárez 244, tel. 333/2–0181) is supposed to be open Monday–Saturday 9–3, but call first to be sure. More accurate information is available from tour operators and hotels.

Emergencies **Police** (tel. 333/2–0181); **Hospital** (tel. 333/2–0029).

Arriving and Departing by Plane

Airport and Airlines Manzanillo's **Aeropuerto Internacional Playa de Oro** is 32 kilometers (20 miles) north of town, on the way to Barra de Navidad. **Aeroméxico** (tel. 800/237–6639) and **Mexicana** (tel. 800/53–7921) fly in from several U.S. and Mexican cities. **Mexicana** serves Manzanillo from Puerto Vallarta.

Between the Airport and Hotels Volkswagen vans transport passengers from the airport to the major resorts; these shuttle services are less expensive than taxis.

Arriving and Departing by Car, Train, and Bus

By Car The trip south from the Arizona border to Manzanillo is about 2,420 kilometers (1,500 miles); from Guadalajara, it is 320 kilometers (200 miles); from Puerto Vallarta, 242 kilometers (150 miles). Highway 200 runs south along the coast from Tepic, in the state of Nayarit, to Manzanillo. This road is gradually being upgraded to a four-lane highway between Puerto Vallarta and Manzan-illo, and hazardous conditions and unexpected, drastic detours are common.

By Train Trains run to Manzanillo from Guadalajara—an adventure for some, but for most it is a tedious trip, lasting a minimum of eight hours and ending at the ship and freight yards outside town.

By Bus **Tres Estrellas de Oro** (tel. 333/2–0135) travels to Manzanillo from Nogales, Arizona, at the U.S.–Mexico border; from Mexico City and Guadalajara; and from the coastal towns. Many of the area's resorts are located a few kilometers from the bus stop on the highway.

Getting Around

By Car   A car is almost essential for exploring the area on your own.
The highway from Santiago to Manzanillo is commonly called
Carretera Santiago–Manzanillo, Manzanillo–Aeropuerto,
Salahua–Santiago, or any number of things depending on the
closest landmark. It's called the Santiago–Manzanillo Road
throughout this chapter to lessen confusion. Highway 200 runs
north along the coast past Manzanillo and Santiago bays to
Barra de Navidad and Melaque; Highway 110 goes east to
Colima.

Avenida Morelos, the main drag in town, runs from Manzanillo
Bay past the port and shipyards to the plaza. If you plan to explore downtown, park along the waterfront across from the plaza and walk—all the shops and hotels are within a few blocks.
Avis (tel. 333/3–0194), **Budget** (tel. 333/3–1445), and **National**
(tel. 333/3–0611) have offices in the airport, and most big hotels
have at least one company represented. **Hertz** doesn't have an
airport office but does have offices at the Las Hadas and Sierra
hotels. Rates vary depending on where you rent your car, but
rentals are generally costly ($60–$100 per day, including insurance). Most offer 200 kilometers (124 miles) free, which should
be enough for one day.

Guided Tours

The best way to see Manzanillo is with a tour guide. What is
known as the tropical tour includes a scenic drive through coconut and banana fields, and shopping, swimming, and dining in
Barra de Navidad. The colonial tour goes to Colima, the picturesque capital of the state; the shopping tour takes you to Puerto Vallarta. Operators are quite willing to arrange special-
interest or individual tours as well as sportfishing trips, sunset
cruises, and horseback riding. Most agencies have offices along
the highway that border Santiago and Manzanillo bays, and
most hotels offer at least one agency's services.

Bahías Gemelas Agencia de Viajes offers horseback riding and
fishing in addition to the standard selection. *Las Hadas Plaza
Albina, tel. 333/3–0204. Manzanillo–Santiago Rd. Km. 10,
tel. 333/3–1000.*

Recorridos Turísticos Manzanillo is a long-standing company
that offers tours of all kinds. *Plaza Santiago and the Plaza Las
Glorias Hotel, tel. 333/3–0434 or 333/3–0435.*

Viajes Anfitriones Mexicanos features shopping trips to Puerto
Vallarta and one-day or overnight excursions to Guadalajara.
*Club Maeva Hotel, tel. 333/3–1940, and Plaza Galería, local
10, Km. 10 Costera Miguel de la Madrid.*

Viajes Hectur's local guides have a good grasp of Manzanillo's
history and culture, and give no-hype, informative, small-
group and individual tours of the city and region. *Manzanillo–
Santiago Rd. Km. 11 in Plaza La Fuente, tel. 333/3–1890.*

Viajes Lizarraga offers tours of the area and Guadalajara. *Plaza Santiago #E-4, tel. 333/3–0434.*

Exploring

A vacation in Manzanillo is not spent shopping and sightseeing. You stay put, relax on the beach, and maybe take a few hours' break from the sun and sand to survey the local scene casually.

The **Santiago** area is tourist oriented, with clusters of shops and restaurants by the beach. The next area to the east, **Salahua,** today comprises a settlement with homes, a baseball field, and restaurants, but this area will eventually become a malecón, a park and waterside promenade that will link the hotels on the east side of the road with the shore. (Highway 200 is being rerouted behind the hills and hotels, so it's guaranteed to be a lengthy project.) The **Las Brisas** section is farther south, past the traffic circle. Some of the more reasonably priced hotels are located here.

Downtown is jam-packed. At the beginning of the harbor, Highway 200 jogs around downtown and intersects with Highway 110 to Colima. Avenida Morelos leads east, past the shipyards and into town. Just before you reach the port, stop at **Laguna de San Pedrito,** where graceful white herons and vivid pink flamingos assemble at sunset.

Jardín Alvaro Obregón, the main zócalo (plaza) is a small square by the waterfront. Souvenir shops, pharmacies, and clothing stores are jammed together across from the plaza and along the side streets, but residential neighborhoods are just a few blocks away. The plaza's a nice spot to sit and watch the local scene, and is nice and lively in the evening, but there aren't any great restaurants or bars in the area, and the quality of goods for sale is better elsewhere. A strange phenomenon occurs every evening around 5:30 or so, when swallows that have congregated on the power lines around town come together in a brown cloud and fill the plaza. Residents have to shut their windows at sunset to keep the birds out.

Las Hadas resort, which opened in 1974 after many years of planning and construction, is a dizzying spectacle of wealth. This luxurious fantasyland was conceived by Don Antenor Patiño, who created Las Hadas on what was then an undeveloped Santiago Peninsula, still dense with jungle. Dazzling white Moorish-style domes and spires rise amid the palms; cobblestone paths wind past private villas bathed in blooming bougainvillea; Arabian tents of white gauze billow in the breeze on the beach. The movie *10* was filmed here—and the most luxurious villa bears Bo Derek's name. Most tourists visit the 200-room hotel at least for lunch—there are a number of fine restaurants to choose among.

What to See and Do with Children

Manzanillo's best bet for children is the giant waterslide at the entrance to Club Maeva. *Santiago–Manzanillo Rd. at Playa Miramar, tel. 333/3–0595. Admission fee. Open Tues.–Sun. 10–7.*

Off the Beaten Track

The trip north on Highway 200 to the little seaside town of **Barra de Navidad** offers a chance to take in the region's lush

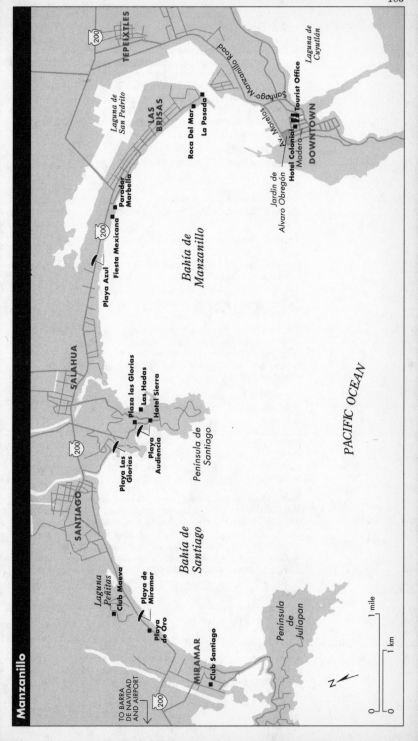

Manzanillo

200 TEPEIXTLES

Santiago-Manzanillo Road

Laguna de San Pedrito

LAS BRISAS

Roca Del Mar
La Posada

200 Parador Marbella

Fiesta Mexicana

Playa Azul

Laguna de Cuyutlán

AV. Morelos

Jardín de Alvaro Obregón

Hotel Colonia
Madera

Tourist Office
DOWNTOWN

Bahía de Manzanillo

SALAHUA

Plaza las Glorias
Las Hadas
Hotel Sierra

200

Playa Las Glorias

Playa Audiencia

Península de Santiago

PACIFIC OCEAN

SANTIAGO

Laguna Peñitas

Club Maeva

Playa de Miramar

Playa de Oro

Bahía de Santiago

MIRAMAR

Club Santiago

Península de Juliapan

TO BARRA DE NAVIDAD AND AIRPORT

200

N

1 mile
1 km

countryside, including coconut and banana plantations. Barra de Navidad, 67 kilometers (41 miles) northwest of Manzanillo, is a typical seaside village—small and compact—that's popular with budget travelers and weekenders from Guadalajara. The beach here may at first seem like those in Manzanillo, but this is a local beach, and if you're tired of the hotel scene this is the place to experience small-town life. There are *ponga* (boat) trips to **Isla Navidad,** a tiny island just offshore, where unbroken seashells are abundant. A relatively new resort, Cabo Blanco, is just west of town in Pueblo Nuevo, an area targeted for development.

When the tide is low, it's possible to walk along the beach to **San Patricio Melaque** (or you can drive), a distance of about 6 kilometers (3.7 miles). San Patricio Melaque is even smaller than Barra de Navidad. On one side of the road are the hotels and beach, and on the other side are burned-out fields and wandering pigs. This is another view of small-town life—leisurely and poor.

Farther north on Highway 200 (about an hour's drive), you come to **Tenacatita,** another small village, but with a large resort (Los Angeles Loco). A bit farther on is **Tecuane,** which also has a resort, then Costa de Careyes, home to a Club Med.

Shopping

Manzanillo has its share of sportswear boutiques, a sprinkling of fine-crafts galleries, and a substantial allotment of stores selling velvet sombreros and the like. The hotel shops have the best selections of folk art and clothing. Most of the shops are closed from 1 to 4 PM; many are also closed on Sunday.

Plaza Santiago has a good Mexican handicrafts store called **Boutique Grivel.** The new **Plaza La Fuente,** by La Bamba restaurant, houses a variety of fine folk-art and furniture boutiques. **Galería de Arte,** at Plaza Albino (Puerto las Hadas) has painting and sculptures by contemporary Mexican artists including Sergio Bustamante and Pal Kepenyes. **Tane,** probably Mexico's most prestigious silver shop for tableware, art objects, and jewelry, is also at Las Hadas.

Ruben Torres, set off by itself at Km. 16 on the Santiago–Manzanillo Road, sells the best sportswear. **Galería Jaramar,** at the Las Hadas arcade, specializes in handwoven fabrics and fine-quality jewelry and creative designs for women. For an unusual browsing experience, visit the Bodega de Mariscos fish market at Km. 4. Downtown, the selection of souvenirs and clothing becomes more typically Mexican. Some of the best spots for crafts and clothing are **El Dorado** and **Maria de Guadalajara.**

Sports

Fishing The sailfishing season runs from mid-October to March, and there are tournaments in November and February. Blue marlin, dorado, and other tropical varieties are abundant. Sportfishing charters are available at the major hotels and tour agencies.

Golf La Mantarraya (tel. 333/3–0000), the 18-hole golf course at Las Hadas designed by Roy Dye, has been rated among the world's 100 best courses by *Golf Digest*. The Salahua River runs through the course—upping the challenge considerably during the rainy season, and the setting amid coconut palms and tropical flowers is surely one of the most scenic. Club Santiago (tel. 333/3–04), has a nine-hole course designed by Larry Hughes.

Tennis Most of the resort hotels have tennis courts.

Water Sports The rocky points off Manzanillo's peninsulas and coves make for good scuba diving and snorkeling.

Beaches

Manzanillo's twin bays make for beautiful long beaches. The sand here is a mingling of black, white, and brown, with the southernmost beaches the blackest. Tourists who stick to the shores beside their hotels are missing something: In Manzanillo, people go to the beach every day of the week, and Sundays are downright festive, with half the town gathered to play on shore. Windsurfing is quite popular, and people roar about on jet skis. Vendors sell kites and small Styrofoam planes, blankets, and jewelry. Most beaches post warning flags if swimming conditions are dangerous or if jellyfish have been sighted.

Playa Miramar, at the north end of Santiago Bay, is popular for windsurfing and boogie-boarding.

Playa Audencia, in a small cove on the north side of Santiago Peninsula between two rock outcroppings, is a good spot for snorkeling. It gets very crowded on Sunday, which can be fun if you like to people-watch, while on weekdays it is nearly deserted. On the beach at **Las Hadas,** on the south side of the peninsula, sunbathers wear the latest beach styles. There is a charge for use of the changing and lounging areas.

Playa Azul, also called **Playa Santiago,** is a long strip of sand and surf that runs from Santiago along Manzanillo Bay to Las Brisas. The surf gets rough along the northern end; swimming is better toward Las Brisas. Outside of town, 49 kilometers (30.3 miles) southeast, is **Playa Cuyutlán,** a black sand beach on the open sea. Legend has it the great Green Wave (Ola Verde) rises some 30 feet each spring during the full moon. Phosphorescent marine organisms give the water its greenish glow. In reality, the surf does get high in spring, but not quite as big as the original Ola Verde, which took the tiny town of Cuyutlán by surprise in 1959. The surf can be rough here, and there are strong undertows.

Dining

Manzanillo is not exactly a gastronomical paradise, but there are a few outstanding places where the views of the jungle and water make up for the lack of culinary excitement. As more and more shops appear along the Santiago–Manzanillo Road, so do restaurants geared to tourists.

One enjoyable way to fill up without spending much is to stop at a neighborhood restaurant or bar that serves *botanas* (snacks or appetizers) included with afternoon drinks. For the price of a *cerveza* (beer) you'll get tacos, soup, ceviche, or some other treat. It's fun to sit among the crowd on a Saturday afternoon and take in the local scene. The best spots are along the road by the port and in the center of town. If you're a woman traveling alone, pick a café where families are gathered. Dress is usually casual but not sloppy (no bathing suits or bare feet), even in the more expensive restaurants. Reservations are almost never necessary, but we have indicated those places that do accept them. Be aware that some restaurants, particularly in the hotels, add a 10%–15% service charge to your tab, as well as 15% tax.

Highly recommended restaurants in each price category are indicated by a star ★.

Category	Cost*
Expensive	over $20
Moderate	$10–$20
Inexpensive	under $10

per person excluding drinks, service, and sales tax (15%)

Manzanillo

Expensive **El Vaquero.** The setting is reminiscent of a saloon, and the emphasis is on beef—marinated, seasoned, or grilled to order, American-style. *Crucero Las Brisas, tel. 333/3–1654. No reservations. Dress: casual. MC, V.*

★ **Legazpi.** Manzanillo's gourmet restaurant is at Las Hadas, naturally, and it is beautiful. Legazpi overlooks the pool and beach to the west and a hillside of white villas to the south. The service is white-gloved perfection, but friendly rather than pretentious, and the food is decidedly elegant. The menu features caviar and smoked salmon, consommés and bisques, seafood and steaks with French sauces, and wonderful pastries. Dress is casual here, but women usually wear dresses, and men wear jackets and ties. *Las Hadas, tel. 333/3–0000. Reservations accepted. Dress: chic resortwear. AE, DC, MC, V. Dinner only. Closed Wed. and Fri.*

★ **L'Récif.** Situated in a fantastic setting high atop a cliff far from town, L'Récif is a breathtaking spot any time of day—but it's particularly nice at sunset. The restaurant is unusual in that it also has a swimming pool—you can have lunch and spend the afternoon sunning and swimming, then stay for dinner. The menu includes pâté with Armagnac, quail with muscat, pepper steak with cognac, and mango mousse. Try the Conde Cream, a fragrant black bean soup with sour cream, tortillas, and green chilis. Live music adds to the sense that you're peacefully ensconced far above it all. The Sunday brunch (served only during the winter season) is a must. *Off the Santiago–Manzanillo Rd., at the sign for Vida del Mar, tel. 333/3–0604. Reservations accepted. Dress: casual for daytime; chic resortwear for night. AE, MC, V.*

Moderate **Carlos 'n Charlie's.** Yet another in the Carlos Anderson chain of fun places, where the food is well-prepared and abundant, the decor is a clutter of memorabilia and graffiti, and the accent is on having a good time. If you stick with the tacos and pastas, you can eat pretty cheaply, as long as you resist the temptation for yet another tequila shooter. *Santiago–Manzanillo Rd.*

near Las Brisas, tel. 333/3–1150. No reservations. Dress: casual. AE, MC, V. Dinner only. Closed Sun.

El Patio Restaurant and Bar. The Colonial, Manzanillo's one true Mexican hotel, was a grande dame in her time, but is now a bit seedy and worn. It's still popular with the downtown business crowd, who lunch for hours on lobster, fresh fish, and octopus. *Av. México 100, tel. 333/2–1080. MC, V.*

★ **El Terral.** Las Hadas's Mexican restaurant, with an outdoor patio, sits atop a point overlooking the ocean. It is a gracious place: When you enter you are handed a souvenir—a small clay cup of tequila. The menu focuses on regional cooking, including several varieties of *pozole* (stew), a traditional meal of the region. Pozole is made from beef, pork, or seafood, thickened with corn, and garnished with onions and cilantro. All dishes are prepared expertly and authentically. *Las Hadas, tel. 333/3–0000. AE, MC, V. Dinner only. Closed Wed.*

★ **La Bamba.** This patio and indoor restaurant on the highway is considered by locals to be the best place for good Mexican food, congenial company, and soft music. *Santiago–Manzanillo Rd., tel. 333/3–1930. Reservations accepted. Dress: casual. AE, MC, V. Dinner only.*

La Plazuela. A good view of the golf course and the bay over the red tile roofs of Plaza Las Glorias makes this a pleasant spot for a sunset meal. The food is okay, but not spectacular. There is the usual selection of seafood and meat dishes. *Plaza Las Glorias, tel. 333/3–0550. AE, MC, V.*

★ **Los Delifines.** Probably the best seafood restaurant in Manzanillo, this more casual Las Hadas restaurant is on the beach at Las Hadas. A generous plate of ceviche with bolillos and chips come with your meal. If you try the grilled *huachinango* or red snapper, you'll get a whole fish, head intact, served with salsa and **mojo de ajo** (oil with toasted bits of garlic). *Las Hadas, tel. 333/3–0000. AE, MC, V. Lunch only.*

Manolo's. This is a longtime favorite for great, reasonably priced seafood and steaks. The Mexican dishes are good, too. *Santiago–Manzanillo Rd., tel. 333/3–0475. Reservations accepted. Dress: casual. MC, V. Dinner only. Closed Sun.*

Margaritas. This is the place for lobster, served a half-dozen ways, but best *a la parilla* (grilled with lime and butter). *Santiago–Manzanillo Rd., tel. 333/3–1414. AE, MC, V.*

Oasis. Club Santiago's popular and newly remodeled restaurant is located right on the beach, and you can watch the hotel's aerobics class as you exercise your stomach with good American and Mexican breakfasts. At lunch and dinner there is mariachi music, and vendors with better-than-average wares parade along the sand, so you can accumulate souvenirs and calories simultaneously. *Club Santiago, tel. 333/3–0937. AE, MC, V.*

★ **Osteria Bugatti.** The most popular dinner spot near downtown, Bugatti's has a loyal following of locals and tourists who crave Italian-style seafood and oysters Rockefeller. *Santiago–Manzanillo Rd. near Las Brisas, tel. 333/3–2999. Reservations accepted. Dress: casual. MC, V. Dinner only. Closed Sun.*

★ **Willy's.** Some people dine at Willy's every night of their stay in Manzanillo. The food is that good, and the owner, Jean Francois, is that personable and gracious. The restaurant is located on a side street in the Las Brisas area, away from the highway. The French chef prepares delicious onion soup, unusual seafood pasta, a sublime bordelaise sauce, and decadent desserts. A guitarist strolls through the beachfront palapa's informal setting of shared tables and chairs under a bamboo roof. *Crucero Las Brisas, no phone. No reservations. AE, MC, V. Dinner only.*

Inexpensive **El Último Tren.** This is the best spot to watch the port workers and their families celebrate the weekend. Throughout the afternoon, you are served a hot, spicy soup with tiny shrimp, a heaping plateful of ceviche, fried corn tortillas, and flavorful chicken tacos. A band plays mariachi music with tropical flair on the main stage, while smaller mariachi groups wander amid the many tables. *Calle Morelos, opposite the harbor, no phone. No credit cards.*

★ **Juanito's.** This American hangout is owned by an American who married a local girl and settled in Manzanillo. The restaurant's motto—"eat well and pay little"—is true. The burgers and fries are great with a little hot sauce and lime. American breakfasts are offered, and dinner entrées include barbecued ribs and fried chicken. You can count on running into Americans, especially during football season, when the games are shown on TV. *Santiago–Manzanillo Rd., tel. 333/3–1388. No reservations. Dress: casual. No credit cards.*

★ **La Posada.** Having breakfast at this passionate-pink hotel-by-the-sea is essential to the Manzanillo experience. Delicious pancakes, French toast, and bacon and eggs are made to order—just stroll into the kitchen and tell the cook what you want. Meals are served in *la sala*, a large living room facing the ocean. Because of the congenial, casual atmosphere, guests often get to know each other and become good friends. Sandwiches and drinks are served in the afternoon, but breakfast is your best bet. *La Posada, Las Brisas, tel. 333/2–2404. No reservations. Dress: casual. MC, V.*

100% Natural. Even Manzanillo has a health food restaurant, a pleasant little palapa that looks like a tropical greenhouse. The fresh juices are cool and tasty. Breakfast and lunch include ample fruit and vegetable salads, quesadillas, granola, and yogurt. *Santiago–Manzanillo Rd., no phone. No reservations. Dress: casual. No credit cards.*

Barra de Navidad

Barra is a casual town, and most restaurants are inexpensive and simple and offer tacos, fish, or standard, Mexican dishes.

Moderate **El Acuario.** This casually elegant restaurant is in the Cabo Blanco Hotel outside town. At night, with candlelight, it's a romantic spot; during the day, there's a view of the hotel grounds and pool. It's the place to splurge in Barra. *Hotel Cabo Blanco, tel. 333/7–0182.*

★ **Pancho's.** Popular with locals, folks who come from Guadalajara for a visit, and return travelers, this palapa on the beach is packed with fishing nets, seashells, caged parrots, and beer-drinking merrymakers. It's the fresh fish that pulls them in and keeps them coming back. *Av. Legaspi 53, tel. 333/7–0176. MC, V.*

Tropical. This popular hotel's restaurant offers good American breakfasts by the sea. In the afternoon, it's a local ritual to sit on the beach and sip Coco Locos, made with coconut juice, tequila, rum, and grenadine. *Av. Legaspi 150, tel. 333/7–0020. MC, V.*

San Patricio Melaque

Here the palapas serving seafood and cerveza all afternoon and evening are clustered together on the long beach stretching through town. The selection is basic and, for the most part, good.

Moderate **Kosonoy.** One of the better beachfront palapas, popular for dinner. *Punta Melaque, no phone. No credit cards.*

Pirámide. This palapa restaurant at the Club Nautico Hotel is a good shady spot on the beach for a mid-afternoon break. Hot dogs and hamburgers are offered in addition to the standards. *Madero 1, tel. 333/7–0239. MC, V.*

Lodging

In Manzanillo, Las Hadas sets the standard for resorts. Though other hotels try to copy Las Hadas's services and prices, none come close to its opulent $1,000 per night villas. A hotel you might once have booked for $10 a night now costs $50 or more, so budget travelers are limited to staying in downtown's few remaining hotels, Barra de Navidad, or Melaque.

As with the rest of the Pacific Coast, Manzanillo is undergoing a building boom. The largest of the new hotels will be a high-rise Inter-Continental, located at Playa Audiencia on the Santiago Peninsula. Smaller places, including condos and town houses, are cropping up along the highway.

The resorts are spread out along the Santiago–Manzanillo Road, with the more expensive places clustered around Las Hadas on the Santiago Peninsula. It's advisable to have reservations in advance. If you try cruising the strip in a cab, you could chalk up a large fare. If you're traveling by bus you may want to stay in a place right on the highway or downtown, as many of the resorts are a fair hike from the road.

Most hotels raise their rates for the April–November high season; rates are lowest during the rainy season, from June to October. Rates here are based on high-season standards—expect to pay 25% less during the off-season.

Highly recommended lodgings in each price category are indicated by a star ★.

Category	Cost*
Very Expensive	over $125
Expensive	$70–$125
Moderate	$50–$70
Inexpensive	under $50

*All prices are for double room, excluding 15% tax.

Very Expensive **★** **Las Hadas.** Though Don Antenor is long gone, Las Hadas is still enchanting and Manzanillo's premiere resort. The attention to detail—from the plush, down pillows on the beds to the bathroom bidets—makes for a pleasurable feeling of luxury. A member of the Leading Hotels of the World, Las Hadas is the kind of place where you check in and stay put—there's absolutely no reason to leave. Each room has a private balcony over-

looking the pool and sea, and fresh flowers are standard.
Lounge chairs and cabanas are arranged around a waterfall
and the pool, and a swaying rope bridge leads to the bar. On the
beach, guests sit in the shade under Arabian-style tents, sunbathe, or sip tropical drinks garnished with flowers and fruit in
the bar tent. Private yachts from just about everywhere anchor
in the marina. For active types there's an excellent golf course,
10 tennis courts, deep-sea fishing trips, sunset cruises, pad-
dleboats and windsurfing, snorkeling and diving, and dancing
in the disco. Some of Manzanillo's finest shops are on the Las
Hadas grounds in the Plaza de Doña Albina. Weekly Mexican
fiestas take place here, and excellent guitarists entertain each
night under the stars. Brides arrive still wearing their veils
(honeymoons are big here), and movie stars mingle with guests
who've saved for years for a taste of the high life. This is where
you go when you think you've seen it all. *Santiago Peninsula,
off the Santiago–Manzanillo Rd., tel. 333/3–0000; reservations in the U.S. 800/228–3000. 220 rooms and 41 suites. Facilities: beach, pool, marina, 10 tennis courts, golf course, 4
restaurants, 5 bars, disco, theme parties, shops, beauty parlor,
massage, travel agency. AE, DC, MC, V.*

Expensive   **Club Maeva.** Families love this huge all-inclusive resort, with
its towering water slide, children's pools, playgrounds, thea-
ter, tennis courts, and disco. There's something for everyone
(except those trying to get away from it all). The blue and white
buildings are spread out on a high hillside. The beach is across
the highway from the hotel. Lots of activities for children and
adults keep this place hopping. *Santiago–Manzanillo Rd. at
Playa Miramar, tel. 333/3–0595. 514 rooms. Facilities: beach
access, 2 pools, Super Maeva Splash, 12 tennis courts, several
restaurants, disco. MC, V.*

★   **Fiesta Mexicana.** This bright, white 5-story building looks
somewhat imposing and austere. Inside, though, it combines
the best of classic colonial Mexican hotels with the latest creature comforts. A large swimming pool in a lovely central courtyard is surrounded by blooming hibiscus and towering palms.
The rooms have pretty, wood-frame windows and comfortable
bentwood lounges. Be sure your room faces the water, as it can
be noisy on the highway side. *Santiago–Manzanillo Rd. in
Playa Azul, tel. 333/3–1100. 200 rooms. Facilities: beach, pool,
water aerobics classes, restaurant, bar, disco, piano bar,
shops, tour desk. AE, DC, MC, V.*

Roca Del Mar. This condominium complex on the beach beside
La Posada in Las Brisas consists of 39 enormous apartments,
each with a full kitchen and living room, two bedrooms, two
baths, private balconies, and lots of English-language books.
Rates are about $100 per night, but one apartment can easily
accommodate four people. *Las Brisas, tel. 333/2–0805. 39
units. Facilities: beach, pool, restaurant, bar, tour desk. AE,
MC, V.*

Sierra. Manzanillo's newest hotel is a somewhat overbearing
20-story giant with white stucco walls and a red-tiled roof.
Most of the 351 rooms and suites have private balconies and a
view of the bay; a large free-form pool, four tennis courts, and
several bars and restaurants round out the property. Light
wood and pastel colors decorate the rooms in a pleasant but un-
inspired fashion. *Avenida de la Audiencia, tel. 333/3–2000. 351
rooms and suites. Facilities: beach, pool, 4 tennis courts, restaurants, bars. AE, DC, MC, V. Expensive.*

Moderate **Buganvillas.** This is a friendly hotel in the Playa Azul/Las Brisas area on a nice, unpopulated stretch of beach. The rooms are spacious and there is English-language TV reception. The drapes, orange with huge black circles, have got to go. *Santiago–Manzanillo Rd. in Playa Azul, tel. 333/3–2504. 37 rooms and 20 condominiums. Facilities: beach, 2 pools, restaurant. AE, MC, V.*

Club Santiago Tenisol. This condominium complex of villas, apartments, and studios is in a neighborhood setting with a lovely view of Santiago Peninsula and Manzanillo. The beach is one of the most popular, and there's a golf course and restaurant. *Playa Santiago, tel. 333/3–04; reservations in the U.S.: 800/525–1987. 60 rooms. Facilities: 2 mi of beach, 6 tennis courts, 9-hole golf course, restaurant, bar. AE, MC, V.*

★ **La Posada.** What Las Hadas is to luxury travelers, La Posada is to those on a more modest budget. The last hotel on the Las Brisas strip, the "passionate-pink" Posada has been a hangout for Americans since the 1950s. The mood is informal and friendly, and guests get to know each other. The familial ambience is fastened by the *sala*, a large, comfortable living room with a communal coffee pot and library. Drinks are served on the honor system—you keep track of your bottle caps and settle your tab at the end of your stay. Rooms are comfortable and simple. Large wood keys unlock the doors, though it's so laid back here some people don't even bother to lock up. Tipping is discouraged; the proprietor suggests that you just leave 10% of your total bill in the tip box by the coffee urn. *Las Brisas, tel. 333/3–1899. 24 rooms. Facilities: beach, pool, restaurant, bar. AE, MC, V.*

★ **Plaza las Glorias.** Situated in the center of Santiago Peninsula, Las Glorias is in a lovely setting with a view of the rivers and lakes of the Las Hadas golf course and the bit of remaining undeveloped jungle on the peninsula. The terra-cotta villas and small hotel buildings change color as the day's light shifts, going from gold in early morning to deep amber at sunset. Rooms are spacious and comfortable, with plush, white upholstered couches and chairs, firm mattresses, and glass and wood dining sets. It's a bit of a hike from the rooms at the top of the complex to the pool and golf course, and there is no direct beach access. *Av. Tesoro off the Las Hadas Rd., tel. 333/3–0440; reservations in the U.S.: 800/635–8483. 150 rooms. Facilities: use of Las Hadas beach and golf course, pool, 7 tennis courts, restaurant, bar. AE, MC, V.*

Inexpensive **Hotel Colonial.** This was once the grandest hotel in Manzanillo, where formally dressed waiters served the town's elite in the cavernous marble-floored lobby. The Colonial has gone downhill, but it's still a good place to stay if you want to be in town, and it's away from the noise of the plaza. *Av. México 100, tel. 333/2–1080. 38 rooms. Facilities: restaurant, bar. MC, V.*

Parador Marbella. One of the few moderately priced places on the beach, Marbella looks pretty run-down from the highway. It's more appealing from the ocean side, and the best rooms are here, on the second story. The furnishings are plain and mismatched: there are pastel-pink sheets, brown and rust bedspreads, and red and yellow plastic flowers on the nightstand. But this is about as good as it gets in the moderate range. *Santiago–Manzanillo Rd., tel. 333/3–1103. 60 rooms. Facilities: pool, restaurant, bar. MC, V.*

Playa de Oro. A newer hotel, Playa de Oro has grown in the past year to include a hillside colony of white buildings with red-tile roofs across the highway from Playa Santiago. It's not right on the water, but the enormous pool makes up for that. *Santiago–Manzanillo Rd., tel. 333/3–2540; reservations in the U.S.: 800/ 458–5677. 260 rooms and 40 villas. Facilities: beach access, 2 pools, 2 tennis courts, 2 restaurants, coffee shop, 2 bars, disco, tour desk. MC, V.*

Barra de Navidad

Inexpensive **Bogavante.** The nicest place in town. It's so clean, you'd think
★ you were in a school for hotel workers. The room furnishings are newer than most and comfortable. *Av. Legaspi, tel. 333/7–0384. 22 rooms. Facilities: beach. MC, V.*

Cabo Blanco. By far the swankiest hotel in the area, Coco Blanco is on the Barra de Navidad lagoon, a few kilometers from the beach. This self-contained resort is situated in undeveloped jungle outside town. The individual units are spread out on the grassy property, and there's a large pool beside the green lagoon. Shuttles to the beach leave every half hour. *Off Hwy. 15 east of Barra de Navidad, tel. 333/7–0168. 125 rooms. Facilities: beach shuttle, pool, children's pool, marina, tennis courts, playground, restaurant, bar. AE, DC, MC, V.*

Motel El Marquez. A new spot a few blocks outside town, this is a classic motel, with a big parking lot out front. There is a pool, but no lounge chairs, and the rooms are basic and clean. *Calle Filipinas near the entrance to town, tel. 333/7–0304. 18 rooms. Facilities: pool, parking lot. MC, V.*

Tropical. This is by far the most popular hotel in town, and it books up well in advance during high season, but it hasn't lived up to its reputation of late. The bar is a hangout in the afternoon, and being on the main drag, it gets as noisy as Barra can get, which isn't all that bad unless a group of surfing or fishing buddies decides to close down the town. *Av. Legazpi 96, tel. 333/7–0020. 57 rooms with bath. Facilities: beach, wading pool, restaurant, bar. AE, MC, V.*

Costa de Careyes

Very Expensive **Club Mediterranee Playa Blanca.** A Club Med property, this resort has all the amenities. The club is located on a secluded bay about one hour north of Manzanillo on Highway 200. Membership is required. *Costa De Careyes, tel. 333/2–0005 or 800/258–2633. 300 rooms. Facilities: beach, pool, marina, tennis courts, 2 restaurants, disco. AE, MC, V.*

Costa Careyes. On the same bay as Club Med, Costa Careyes is a serene white villa surrounded by coconut palms on a private beach. The adobe rooms are decorated with fine-quality folk art and tropical colors, and hot-pink bougainvillea is abundant throughout the lush grounds. *Costa de Careyes, tel. 333/7–0010. About 90 rooms, villas, and condos. Facilities: beach, airstrip, pool, tennis courts, shops, tour desk. AE, DC, MC, V.*

Melaque

Expensive **Coco Club Hotel Melaque.** This block-long high rise is an all-inclusive resort: activities, meals, drinks, taxis, and tips are included in the rates. The rooms facing the beach are the best ones—they have ceiling fans, private balconies, and are appointed in a simple blue and white color scheme. The beach scene is an active one, but the pool area is more restful—that is, until hordes of people settle in at the bar for their share of unlimited free drinks. *On the main road; tel. 333/7–0001. 150 rooms. Facilities: beach, pool, tennis court, volleyball, Ping-Pong, Spanish and dance classes, tour desk. MC, V.*

Moderate **Hotel de Legazpi.** This hotel at the far end of town, surrounded by empty lots with wandering pigs, is an inexpensive place to settle in for a rest after a long tour. There are no distractions except the lobby TV and daily happy hour in the room of General Lee, a local character. The large rooms have safe-deposit boxes in the closets but no curtains on the showers. It's a popular spot with RV travelers and fishermen. *Av. de las Palmas, tel. 333/7–0397. 24 rooms, some with kitchenettes. MC, V.*

Tecuane

Moderate **El Tecuan.** This solitary, rustic resort is set midway between Puerto Vallarta and Manzanillo on a hillside overlooking the ocean. The air-conditioned rooms are beautifully designed: The ceiling beams are made of *quayabillo* wood, and tropical paintings adorn the walls. Surf-fishing, horseback riding, tennis, and swimming are the major activities, and there is plenty of pristine beach to roam in peace. *Hwy. 200, tel. 333/7–0132. 40 rooms. Facilities: pool, restaurant, bar. MC, V.*

Tenacatita

Expensive **Los Angeles Loco.** This all-inclusive resort is located 56 kilometers (35 miles) north of Manzanillo on Tenacatita Bay. Activities, meals, drinks, taxes, and tips are included in the rates. A Fiesta-Americana property, Los Angeles Loco has all the makings for a wild time (the name means "Crazy Angels"), or it can be a chance to get away from it all (if this is your intent, request a room on the outskirts of the compound). Busloads of tourists arrive almost daily. Most guests stay a week or so and are content to play on the beach, sun by the pool, and take advantage of all the included meals and drinks. Like summer camp, there are all sorts of planned and impromptu activities—volleyball, softball, aerobics, horseback riding, Ping-Pong, and so on. *Tenacatita Bay, about 8 km (5 mi) down a side road off Hwy. 200, tel. 333/7–0221. 217 rooms. Facilities: beach, pool, water and land sports, tennis courts. AE, MC, V.*

Nightlife

During the high season, there is nightlife at two discos on the Santiago–Manzanillo Road—**Pip's** and **Enjoy**—and at **Cartouche** at Las Hadas. The piano bar at **Bugatti's** (tel. 333/2–15) is also a good spot for a nightcap.

Spanish Vocabulary

Note: *Mexican Spanish differs from Castillian Spanish.*

Words and Phrases

	English	*Spanish*	*Pronunciation*
Basics	Yes/no	Sí/no	see/no
	Please	Por favor	pore fah-**vore**
	May I?	¿Me permite?	may pair-**mee**-tay
	Thank you (very much)	(Muchas) gracias	(**moo**-chas) **grah**-see-as
	You're welcome	De nada	day **nah**-dah
	Excuse me	Con permiso	con pair-**mee**-so
	Pardon me/what did you say?	¿Perdón?/Mande?	pair-**doan**/**mahn**-dey
	Could you tell me?	¿Podría decirme?	po-**dree**-ah deh-**seer**-meh
	I'm sorry	Lo siento	lo see-**en**-toe
	Good morning!	¡Buenos días!	**bway**-nohs **dee**-ahs
	Good afternoon!	¡Buenas tardes!	**bway**-nahs **tar**-dess
	Good evening!	¡Buenas noches!	**bway**-nahs **no**-chess
	Goodbye!	¡Adiós!/¡Hasta luego!	ah-dee-**ohss**/**ah**-stah-**lwe**-go
	Mr./Mrs.	Señor/Señora	sen-**yor**/sen-**yore**-ah
	Miss	Señorita	sen-yo-**ree**-tah
	Pleased to meet you	Mucho gusto	**moo**-cho **goose**-to
	How are you?	¿Cómo está usted?	**ko**-mo es-**tah** oo-**sted**
	Very well, thank you.	Muy bien, gracias.	**moo**-ee bee-**en**, **grah**-see-as
	And you?	¿Y usted?	ee oos-**ted**?
	Hello (on the telephone)	Bueno	**bwen**-oh
Numbers	1	un, uno	oon, **oo**-no
	2	dos	dos
	3	tres	trace
	4	cuatro	**kwah**-tro
	5	cinco	**sink**-oh
	6	seis	sace
	7	siete	see-**et**-ey
	8	ocho	**o**-cho
	9	nueve	new-**ev**-ay
	10	diez	dee-**es**
	11	once	**own**-sey
	12	doce	**doe**-sey
	13	trece	**tray**-sey
	14	catorce	kah-**tor**-sey
	15	quince	**keen**-sey
	16	dieciséis	dee-**es**-ee-**sace**
	17	diecisiete	dee-**es**-ee-see-**et**-ay
	18	dieciocho	dee-**es**-ee-**o**-cho

| | 19 | diecinueve | **dee-es**-ee-new-**ev-ay** |
| | 20 | veinte | **vain**-tay |

Colors	black	negro	**neh**-grow
	blue	azul	ah-**sool**
	brown	café	kah-**feh**
	green	verde	**vair**-day
	pink	rosa	**ro**-sah
	purple	morado	mo-**rah**-doe
	orange	naranja	na-**rahn**-hah
	red	rojo	**roe**-hoe
	white	blanco	**blahn**-koh
	yellow	amarillo	ah-mah-**ree**-yoh

Days of the Week	Sunday	domingo	doe-**meen**-goh
	Monday	lunes	**loo**-ness
	Tuesday	martes	**mahr**-tess
	Wednesday	miércoles	me-**air**-koh-less
	Thursday	jueves	**who**-ev-ess
	Friday	viernes	vee-**air**-ness
	Saturday	sábado	**sah**-bah-doe

Months	January	enero	eh-**neh**-ro
	February	febrero	feh-**brair**-oh
	March	marzo	**mahr**-so
	April	abril	ah-**breel**
	May	mayo	**my**-oh
	June	junio	**hoo**-nee-oh
	July	julio	**who**-lee-yoh
	August	agosto	ah-**ghost**-toe
	September	septiembre	sep-tee-**em**-breh
	October	octubre	oak-**too**-breh
	November	noviembre	no-vee-**em**-breh
	December	diciembre	dee-see-**em**-breh

Useful phrases	Do you speak English?	¿Habla usted inglés?	**ah**-blah oos-**ted** in-**glehs**?
	I don't speak Spanish	No hablo español	no **ah**-blow es-pahn-**yol**
	I don't understand (you)	No entiendo	no en-tee-**en**-doe
	I understand (you)	Entiendo	en-tee-**en**-doe
	I don't know	No sé	no **say**
	I am American/ British	Soy americano(a)/ inglés(a)	soy ah-meh-ree-**kah**-no(ah)/ in-**glace**(ah)
	What's your name?	¿Cómo se llama usted?	**koh**-mo say **yah**-mah oos-**ted**?
	My name is . . .	Me llamo . . .	may **yah**-moh
	What time is it?	¿Qué hora es?	keh **o**-rah es?
	It is one, two, three . . . o'clock.	Es la una; son las dos, tres	es la **oo**-nah/sone lahs dose, trace
	Yes, please/No, thank you	Sí, por favor/No, gracias	**see** pore fah-**vor**/no **grah**-see-us

How?	¿Cómo?	**koh**-mo?
When?	¿Cuándo?	**kwahn**-doe?
This/Next week	Esta semana/ la semana que entra	**es**-tah seh-**mah**-nah/lah say-**mah**-nah keh en-trah
This/Next month	Este mes/el próximo mes	**es**-tay mehs/el **proke**-see-mo mehs
This/Next year	Este año/el año que viene	**es**-tay **ahn**-yo/el **ahn**-yo keh vee-**yen**-ay
Yesterday/today/ tomorrow	Ayer/hoy/mañana	ah-**yair**/oy/mahn-**yah**-nah
This morning/ afternoon	Esta mañana/tarde	**es**-tah mahn-**yah**-nah/ **tar**-day
Tonight	Esta noche	**es**-tah **no**-cheh
What?	¿Qué?	keh?
What is it?	¿Qué es esto?	keh es **es**-toe
Why?	¿Por qué?	pore **keh**
Who?	¿Quién?	kee-**yen**
Where is . . .?	¿Dónde está . . .?	**dohn**-day es-**tah**
the train station?	la estación del tren?	la es-tah-see-**on** del **train**
the subway station?	la estación del Metro?	la es-ta-see-**on** del **meh**-tro
the bus stop?	la parada del autobús?	la pah-**rah**-dah del oh-toe-**boos**
the post office?	la oficina de correos?	la oh-fee-**see**-nah day koh-**reh**-os
the bank?	el banco?	el **bahn**-koh
the . . . hotel?	el hotel . . .?	el oh-**tel**
the store?	la tienda . . .?	la tee-en-dah
the cashier?	la caja?	la **kah**-hah
the . . . museum?	el museo . . .?	el moo-**seh**-oh
the hospital?	el hospital?	el ohss-pea-**tal**
the elevator?	el ascensor?	el ah-**sen**-sore
the bathroom?	el baño?	el **bahn**-yoh
Here/there	Aquí/allá	ah-**key**/ah-**yah**
Open/closed	Abierto/cerrado	ah-be-**er**-toe/ ser-**ah**-doe
Left/right	Izquierda/derecha	iss-key-**er**-dah/ dare-**eh**-chah
Straight ahead	Derecho	der-**eh**-choh
Is it near/far?	¿Está cerca/lejos?	es-**tah** **sair**-kah/ **leh**-hoss
I'd like . . .	Quisiera . . .	kee-see-**air**-ah
a room	un cuarto/una habitación	oon **kwahr**-toe/ **oo**-nah ah-bee-tah-see-**on**
the key	la llave	lah **yah**-vay
a newspaper	un periódico	oon pear-ee-**oh**-dee-koh
a stamp	un timbre de correo	oon **team**-bray day koh-**reh**-oh

I'd like to buy . . .	Quisiera comprar . . .	kee-see-**air**-ah kohm-**prahr**
cigarettes	cigarrillo	ce-gar-**reel**-oh
matches	cerillos	ser-**ee**-ohs
a dictionary	un diccionario	oon deek-see-oh-**nah**-ree-oh
soap	jabón	hah-**bone**
a map	un mapa	oon **mah**-pah
a magazine	una revista	**oon**-ah reh-**veess**-tah
paper	papel	pah-**pel**
envelopes	sobres	so-**brace**
a postcard	una tarjeta postal	**oon**-ah tar-**het**-ah post-**ahl**
How much is it?	¿Cuánto cuesta?	**kwahn**-toe **kwes**-tah
It's expensive/ cheap	Está caro/barato	es-**tah kah**-roh/ bah-**rah**-toe
A little/a lot	Un poquito/ mucho . . .	oon poh-**kee**-toe/ **moo**-choh
More/less	Más/menos	mahss/**men**-ohss
Enough/too much/too little	Suficiente/de- masiado/muy poco	soo-fee-see-**en**-tay/ day-mah-see-**ah**- doe/**moo**-ee **poh**-koh
Telephone	Teléfono	tel-**ef**-oh-no
Telegram	Telegrama	teh-leh-**grah**-mah
I am ill/sick	Estoy enfermo(a)	es-**toy** en-**fair**-moh(ah)
Please call a doctor	Por favor llame un médico	pore fa-**vor ya**-may oon **med**-ee-koh
Help!	¡Auxilio! ¡Ayuda!	owk-**see**-lee-oh/ ah-**yoo**-dah
Fire!	¡Encendio!	en-**sen**-dee-oo
Caution!/Look out!	¡Cuidado!	kwee-**dah**-doh

On the Road

Highway	Carretera	car-ray-**ter**-ah
Causeway, paved highway	Calzada	cal-**za**-dah
Route	Ruta	**roo**-tah
Road	Camino	cah-**mee**-no
Street	Calle	**cah**-yeh
Avenue	Avenida	ah-ven-**ee**-dah
Broad, tree-lined boulevard	Paseo	pah-**seh**-oh
Waterfront promenade	Malecón	mal-lay-**cone**
Wharf	Embarcadero	em-bar-cah-**day**-ro

In Town

Church	Templo/Iglesia	**tem**-plo/e-**gles**-se-ah
Cathedral	Catedral	cah-tay-**dral**
Neighborhood	Barrio	**bar**-re-o
Foreign Exchange Shop	Casa de Cambio	**cas**-sah day **cam**-be-o
City Hall	Palacio Municipal	pah-**lah**-see-o moo-**ni**-see-pal
Main Square	Zócalo	**zo**-cal-o
Traffic Circle	Glorieta	glor-e-**ay**-tah
Market	Mercado (Spanish)/ Tianguis (Indian)	mer-**cah**-doe/ tee-**an**-geese
Inn	Posada	pos-**sah**-dah
Group taxi	Colectivo	co-lec-**tee**-vo
Group taxi along fixed route	Pesero	pi-**seh**-ro

Items of Clothing

Embroidered white smock	Huipil	whee-**peel**
Pleated man's shirt worn outside the pants	Guayabera	gwah-ya-**beh**-ra
Leather sandals	Huarache	wah-**ra**-chays
Shawl	Rebozo	ray-**bozh**-o
Pancho or blanket	Serape	seh-**ra**-peh

Dining Out

A bottle of . . .	Una botella de . . .	**oo**-nah bo-**tay**-yah deh
A cup of . . .	Una taza de . . .	**oo**-nah **tah**-sah deh
A glass of . . .	Un vaso de . . .	oon **vah**-so deh
Ashtray	Un cenicero	oon sen-ee-**seh**-roh
Bill/check	La cuenta	lah **kwen**-tah
Bread	El pan	el pahn
Breakfast	El desayuno	el day-sigh-**oon**-oh
Butter	La mantequilla	lah mahn-tay-**key**-yah
Cheers!	¡Salud!	sah-**lood**
Cocktail	Un aperitivo	oon ah-pair-ee-**tee**-voh
Dinner	La cena	lah **seh**-nah
Dish	Un plato	oon **plah**-toe

Dish of the day	El platillo de hoy	el plah-**tee**-yo day oy
Enjoy!	¡Buen provecho!	bwen pro-**veh**-cho
Fixed-price menu	La comida corrida	lah koh-**me**-dah co-**ree**-dah
Fork	El tenedor	el ten-eh-**door**
Is the tip included?	¿Está incluida la propina?	es-**tah** in-clue-**ee**-dah lah pro-**pea**-nah
Knife	El cuchillo	el koo-**chee**-yo
Lunch	La comida	lah koh-**me**-dah
Menu	La carta	lah **cart**-ah
Napkin	La servilleta	lah sair-vee-**yet**-uh
Pepper	La pimienta	lah pea-me-**en**-tah
Please give me	Por favor déme	pore fah-**vor** **day**-may
Salt	La sal	lah sahl
Spoon	Una cuchara	**oo**-nah koo-**chah**-rah
Sugar	El azúcar	el ah-**sue**-car
Waiter!/Waitress!	¡Por favor Señor/Señorita!	pore fah-**vor** sen-**yor**/sen-yor-**ee**-tah

Menu Guide

English	Spanish
Full service restaurant	Restaurante
Coffee shop	Cafetería
Small café serving local dishes, often found in marketplaces	Fonda
Snack bar or stand, usually for stand-up eating	Taquería
Fixed-price menu	Comida corrida
Special of the day	Menú del día
Drink included	Bebida incluida
Local specialties	Platillos típicos
Made to order	Al gusto
Extra charge	Extra
In season	De la estación

Breakfast

Toast	Pan tostado
Bread	Pan
Corn tortillas	Tortillas de maíz
Jam	Mermelada
Honey/syrup	Miel
Soft-boiled egg	Huevo tibio
Bacon and eggs	Huevos con tocino
Ham and eggs	Huevos con jamón
Eggs with chili tomato sauce over tortillas	Huevos rancheros
Fried eggs	Huevos estrellados
Scrambled eggs	Huevos revueltos
Eggs scrambled with vegetables	Huevos mexicanos
Eggs scrambled with tortilla strips, cheese and chili sauce	Chilaquiles
Hard rolls	Bolillos
Sweet rolls or bread	Pan dulce
Whole-wheat bread	Pan de trigo
Yogurt	Yogurt/búlgaro

Soups

Soup of the day	Sopa del día
Vegetable soup	Sopa de verduras
Chicken soup	Sopa de pollo
Broth, consommé—beef or chicken	Caldo
Light soup with beef and vegetables—beef broth	Caldo de res
Onion soup	Sopa de cebolla
Garlic soup	Sopa de ajo
Lentil soup	Sopa de lentejas
Cold vegetable soup	Gazpacho
Tortilla soup	Sopa de tortilla, sopa azteca
Spicy chicken-vegetable soup	Caldo tlalpeño
Piquant pork-hominy soup	Pozole

Vegetables

Olives	Aceitunas
Avocado	Aguacate
Garlic	Ajo
Artichokes	Alcachofas
Celery	Apio
Eggplant	Berenjena
Beet	Betabel
Zucchini	Calabacita
Winter squash, pumpkin	Calabaza
Chayote squash, vine pear	Chayote
Peas	Chícharos
Chilies	Chiles

Mild–medium: ancho, pasilla, poblano, verde, güero
Hot (picante): jalapeño, chipotle, pequín, mulato, serrano, habanero

Cabbage	Col
Cauliflower	Coliflor
Green beans	Ejotes
Corn on the cob	Elote
Asparagus	Espárragos
Spinach	Espinaca
Squash flower	Flor de calabaza
Red beans	Frijoles colorados
Pinto beans in seasoned sauce	Frijoles de olla
Black beans	Frijoles negros
Refried beans	Frijoles refritos
Mushrooms	Hongos
Lettuce	Lechuga
Corn	Maíz
Turnip	Nabo
Cucumber	Pepino
Sweet pepper	Pimiento dulce
Green pepper	Pimiento verde
Radish	Rábano
Tomato	Tomate
Carrot	Zanahoria

Dairy Products

Cream	Crema
Sour cream	Crema agria
Milk	Leche
Butter	Mantequilla
Cheese	Queso

Potatoes, Rice, and Noodles

Rice	Arroz
White rice	Arroz blanco
Yellow rice	Arroz a la mexicana
Pilaf	Sopa seca
Spaghetti	Espagueti
baked with cheese	al horno
Noodles	Fideos
Macaroni	Macarrón(es)
Pasta, noodles	Pastas
Potatoes	Papas

mashed	puré de papas
french fries	papas fritas en aceite

Fish and Seafood

Abalone	Abulón
Tuna	Atún
Cod	Bacalao
Squid	Calamares
in their own ink	en su tinta
Shrimp	Camarones
Crab	Cangrejo
Red Snapper	Huachinango
Crab	Jaiba
Lobster	Langosta
Prawns, crayfish	Langostinos
Octopus	Pulpo
Small saltwater fish	Mojarras
Haddock	Róbalo
Pompano	Pámpano
Sardines	Sardinas
Salmon	Salmón
Shark	Tiburón
Sea turtle	Tortuga
Trout	Trucha

Meat

Meatballs	Albóndigas
Steak	Bistec/biftec de lomo
Goat	Cabrito
Lamb, mutton	Carnero
Beef	Carne de res
Beef stew with vegetables	Carne guisada con verduras
Fried pork	Carnitas
Cutlet	Chuleta
Ribs	Costillas
Steak strips	Fajitas
Fillet steak	Filete
Liver	Hígado
Loin strip steak	Filete de lomo
Shoulder	Hombro
Pork loin	Lomo
Dried, shredded beef	Machaca
Breaded veal	Milanesa de ternera
Leg	Pierna
Pork	Puerco
Sausages	Salchichas
Veal	Ternera

Game and Poultry

Rabbit	Conejo
Chicken, hen	Gallina
Turkey	Guajolote
Wild hare	Liebre
Duck	Pato
Turkey	Pavo
Chicken breast	Pechugas de pollo

| Chicken | Pollo |
| Venison | Venado |

Typical Dishes

Chicken with rice	Arroz con pollo
Steamed meat wrapped in leaves	Barbacoa
Slow-steamed goat or lamb with mild chili flavor	Birria
Broiled beef with vegetables	Carne asada
Fried pork	Carnitas
Sweet peppers stuffed with beef filling in cream and nut sauce	Chiles en nogada
Stuffed mild green chilies fried in batter	Chiles rellenos
Tortillas with filling and served in a sauce	Enchiladas
chicken	de pollo
cheese	de queso
chicken-filled with cream sauce	Suizas
Red mole sauce with meat, fowl, and fruit	Manchamanteles
Rice with seafood, meat, and vegetables	Paella
Spicy ground beef mixture with raisins	Picadillo
Chicken steamed in citrus juices	Pollo píbil
Hash	Salpicón
Filled cornmeal wrapped in corn leaf	Tamal
Pork with smoky tomato sauce, potatoes, and avocado	Tinga

Sauces and Preparations

Red chili marinade	Adobo
Avocado sauce/dip	Guacamole
Spicy sauce of chili, chocolate, sesame, and almonds	Mole
Green tomato and nut sauce	Mole verde
Spicy sesame-seed sauce	Pipián
Béchamel sauce	Salsa bechamela
Uncooked or slightly cooked tomato, onion, chili sauce	Salsa cruda/mexicana
Red chili tomato sauce	Salsa de chile rojo
Tartar sauce	Salsa tártara
Green tomato, chili, coriander sauce	Salsa verde

Fruits and Nuts

Almond	Almendra
Hazelnut	Avellana
Chestnut	Castaña
Peanut	Cacahuate
Apricot	Chabacano
Cherimoya, vanilla-flavored fruit	Chirimoya
Plum	Ciruela
Prune	Ciruela pasa
Coconut	Coco

Date	Dátile
Peach	Durazno
Strawberry	Fresa
Dried Fruit	Frutas seca
Pomegranate	Granada
Passion fruit	Granadilla
Soursop	Guanábana
Guava	Guayaba
Fig	Higo
Lime	Limón
Large tropical fruit, related to mango	Mamey
Tangerine	Mandarina
Mango	Mango
Cantaloupe	Melón
Honeydew melon	Melón verde
Orange	Naranja
Walnut	Nueces
Raisin	Pasas
Papaya	Papaya
Pear	Pera
Green apple	Perón
Pineapple	Piña
Pine nut	Piñón
Watermelon	Sandía
Tamarind	Tamarindo
Grapefruit	Toronja

Nonalcoholic Beverages

Coffee	Café
black	*negro*
American	*americano*
with cream	*con crema*
with milk	*con leche*
decaffeinated	*descafeínado*
cappuccino	*capuchino*
espresso	*exprés/solo*
Chocolate corn gruel	Champurrada
Mexican hot chocolate	Chocolate
Lemonade	Limonada preparada
Mineral water	Agua mineral
carbonated	*con gas*
noncarbonated	*sin gas*
Fruit ade	Agua de . . .
Hibiscus flower drink	*jamaíca*
Bottled soft drink	Refresco
Fruit-flavored corn gruel	Atole
Cold drink flavored with seeds, coconut, fruit or oatmeal	Horchata
. . . juice	Jugo de . . .
Milk	Leche
Malted milk	Leche malteada
Pureed fruit drink	Licuado
Tea	Té
Herb tea	Té de hierbas
Chamomile tea	Té de manzanilla

Alcoholic Drinks

. . . straight	Copa de . . .
On the rocks	En las rocas
With water	Con agua
Rum and Coke	Cuba libre
Tequila with Triple Sec and lime juice	Margarita
Red wine with fruit	Sangría
Beer	Cerveza
light/dark	*clara/oscura*
Champagne	Champaña
Sugarcane brandy	Chicha
Hard cider	Sidra
Cognac, brandy	Coñac
Strong Mexican brandy (firewater)	Aguardiente
Liqueur	Licor
Agave liquor	Tequila
Agave liquor with a worm in the bottle	Mezcal
Fermented agave drink	Pulque
Alcoholic eggnog liqueur	Rompope
Rum	Ron
Whiskey	Wisky

Index

Personal Itinerary

Departure *Date*

Time

Transportation

Arrival *Date*   *Time*

Departure *Date*   *Time*

Transportation

Accommodations

Arrival *Date*   *Time*

Departure *Date*   *Time*

Transportation

Accommodations

Arrival *Date*   *Time*

Departure *Date*   *Time*

Transportation

Accommodations

Personal Itinerary

Arrival	*Date*	*Time*
Departure	*Date*	*Time*
Transportation		
Accommodations		

Arrival	*Date*	*Time*
Departure	*Date*	*Time*
Transportation		
Accommodations		

Arrival	*Date*	*Time*
Departure	*Date*	*Time*
Transportation		
Accommodations		

Arrival	*Date*	*Time*
Departure	*Date*	*Time*
Transportation		
Accommodations		

Personal Itinerary

Arrival *Date*   *Time*

Departure *Date*   *Time*

Transportation

Accommodations

Arrival *Date*   *Time*

Departure *Date*   *Time*

Transportation

Accommodations

Arrival *Date*   *Time*

Departure *Date*   *Time*

Transportation

Accommodations

Arrival *Date*   *Time*

Departure *Date*   *Time*

Transportation

Accommodations

Addresses

Name	Name
Address	Address
Telephone	Telephone
Name	Name
Address	Address
Telephone	Telephone
Name	Name
Address	Address
Telephone	Telephone
Name	Name
Address	Address
Telephone	Telephone
Name	Name
Address	Address
Telephone	Telephone
Name	Name
Address	Address
Telephone	Telephone
Name	Name
Address	Address
Telephone	Telephone
Name	Name
Address	Address
Telephone	Telephone

Fodor's Travel Guides

U.S. Guides

Alaska
Arizona
Boston
California
Cape Cod, Martha's
  Vineyard, Nantucket
The Carolinas & the
  Georgia Coast
The Chesapeake
  Region
Chicago
Colorado
Disney World & the
  Orlando Area
Florida
Hawaii

Las Vegas, Reno,
  Tahoe
Los Angeles
Maine, Vermont,
  New Hampshire
Maui
Miami & the
  Keys
National Parks
  of the West
New England
New Mexico
New Orleans
New York City
New York City
  (Pocket Guide)

Pacific North Coast
Philadelphia & the
  Pennsylvania
  Dutch Country
Puerto Rico
  (Pocket Guide)
The Rockies
San Diego
San Francisco
San Francisco
  (Pocket Guide)
The South
Santa Fe, Taos,
  Albuquerque
Seattle &
  Vancouver

Texas
USA
The U. S. & British
  Virgin Islands
The Upper Great
  Lakes Region
Vacations in
  New York State
Vacations on the
  Jersey Shore
Virginia & Maryland
Waikiki
Washington, D.C.
Washington, D.C.
  (Pocket Guide)

Foreign Guides

Acapulco
Amsterdam
Australia
Austria
The Bahamas
The Bahamas
  (Pocket Guide)
Baja & Mexico's Pacific
  Coast Resorts
Barbados
Barcelona, Madrid,
  Seville
Belgium &
  Luxembourg
Berlin
Bermuda
Brazil
Budapest
Budget Europe
Canada
Canada's Atlantic
  Provinces

Cancun, Cozumel,
  Yucatan Peninsula
Caribbean
Central America
China
Czechoslovakia
Eastern Europe
Egypt
Europe
Europe's Great Cities
France
Germany
Great Britain
Greece
The Himalayan
  Countries
Holland
Hong Kong
India
Ireland
Israel
Italy

Italy 's Great Cities
Jamaica
Japan
Kenya, Tanzania,
  Seychelles
Korea
London
London
  (Pocket Guide)
London Companion
Mexico
Mexico City
Montreal &
  Quebec City
Morocco
New Zealand
Norway
Nova Scotia,
  New Brunswick,
  Prince Edward
  Island
Paris

Paris (Pocket Guide)
Portugal
Rome
Scandinavia
Scandinavian Cities
Scotland
Singapore
South America
South Pacific
Southeast Asia
Soviet Union
Spain
Sweden
Switzerland
Sydney
Thailand
Tokyo
Toronto
Turkey
Vienna & the Danube
  Valley
Yugoslavia

Wall Street Journal Guides to Business Travel

Europe

International Cities

Pacific Rim

USA & Canada

Special-Interest Guides

Bed & Breakfast and
  Country Inn Guides:
  Mid-Atlantic Region
New England
The South
The West

Cruises and Ports
  of Call
Healthy Escapes
Fodor's Flashmaps
  New York

Fodor's Flashmaps
  Washington, D.C.
Shopping in Europe
Skiing in the USA &
  Canada

Smart Shopper's
  Guide to London
Sunday in New York
Touring Europe
Touring USA